IMAGES
of America

MARSHFIELD

On the Cover: A number of Marshfield's men are pictured gathering on the town square in the early 1900s. (Courtesy of the Webster County Historical Museum.)

IMAGES
of America

MARSHFIELD

Kaitlyn McConnell for the
Webster County Historical Society

ARCADIA
PUBLISHING

ISBN 978-0-7385-8303-7

Published by Arcadia Publishing
Charleston, South Carolina

Printed in the United States of America

Library of Congress Control Number: 2010937733

For all general information, please contact Arcadia Publishing:
Telephone 843-853-2070
Fax 843-853-0044
E-mail sales@arcadiapublishing.com
For customer service and orders:
Toll-Free 1-888-313-2665

Visit us on the Internet at www.arcadiapublishing.com

This book is dedicated to the people of Marshfield,
both past and present.

Contents

ACKNOWLEDGMENTS

It has been over 150 years since Marshfield was established. In that time, things have changed. Instead of horses and buggies traversing the town's streets, now it is a wide variety of cars, trucks, and SUVs. There is no Style Shop, movie showings at the Ritz, or lazy Saturday evenings spent on the Marshfield Square. Andrews Café has been gone for nearly 30 years.

These things may be in the past; but they are not far back there. Squint a little, turn the page just so, and see if you can't envision the pictures in this book come to life. Because in the whole scheme of things, the scenes and stories in these photographs really didn't happen all that long ago. It is not far-off history; they are things that have happened right in our backyards, both figuratively and literally.

Yet there are other things that are just the same as they were years ago. Qualities that make Marshfield the wonderful place it is to live and grow up exist everywhere. Everything in life has shortcomings, so I'm not saying Marshfield is perfect. But I hope you will agree that there is a whole lot of good that makes up the difference.

That is why this book exists—for the people, places, and events that have made, and continue to make, Marshfield the town that it is today.

Please realize that this book is by no means a complete account of Marshfield's history; there are many other people, businesses, and events that undoubtedly played roles in the area's history. Also, though I have striven for accuracy with everything written on the following pages, it is a fact that historical records often contradict themselves. Despite every effort on my part, it is likely there may be dates and details that are not presented just as you remember them to be.

I should also give a wholehearted thanks to everyone who has worked so hard to preserve Marshfield and Webster County's history so well, especially members of the Webster County Historical Society. There is no way this book would have been possible without the hard work of many others before me.

So kick off the shoes, read, and step back in time with a few images of Marshfield's past. I hope you will enjoy reading it as much as I enjoyed writing it.

INTRODUCTION

Marshfield has been in existence since the mid-1800s. Officially established in 1856, some of the town's first settlers were members of the Flanigan family, immigrants from North Carolina. The family was traveling and looking for a new place to call home. The 1850s Ozarks caught their attention; not for bustling towns or great cultural scene, but for the good water supply provided by a single spring, now known as Shackleford. The Flanigans wrote and told of the peaceful setting they had found to settle in and encouraged others to join them. By 1880, Marshfield had grown into a thriving village of nearly 1,000 citizens.

However, most of that growth came to naught just years later when, in 1880, the town received a devastating blow. On April 18, Marshfield was hit by a day of massive devastation. Nearly the entire town was wiped out in a cyclone that also killed 10 percent of the town's population. In just 60 seconds, 75 percent of the town was destroyed, and 105 souls had been wounded. The town in ruins, it could have been easy to give up and move elsewhere. But the settlers decided to persevere, and most of the town was rebuilt shortly thereafter.

There was, however, a faint silver lining to the tornado's destruction—nationwide fame. After the high-powered winds whipped through town, several mineral springs were discovered nearby. After a man claimed that washing with the water from the springs healed his eyes, Marshfield quickly became a health resort, attracting people from across the nation to take advantage of the water's healing powers.

Additionally, Marshfield became well known because of John Williams "Blind" Boone, a pianist who composed "The Marshfield Cyclone," which re-created the emotions connected with the tornado. It was played at the end of all of Boone's performances until 1927, when it closed Boone's final performance and was lost to history.

Marshfield's next claim to fame occurred in 1889, with the birth of Edwin P. Hubble. After leaving Marshfield as a young boy, Hubble explored numerous career endeavors before he began his study of astronomy at Yerkes Observatory in Wisconsin. Hubble's life contributed a great deal to the knowledge about the universe as well as producing several written works. In commemoration of his lifetime of discovery, Hubble became the namesake of the Hubble Telescope, which provided many glimpses of places far into space.

In 1911, Marshfield received a $5,000 grant from Andrew Carnegie for the construction of a town library. At the time, the town was the smallest community on record to receive such a grant. The building housed the town library until 1995, when pressing maintenance and Americans with Disabilities Act concerns forced a new building to be constructed for the library. The building, however, maintained historical notoriety. Several years later, it became home to the Webster County Historical Museum.

There was a routine in Marshfield: work hard during the week and go to church on Sunday. Faith was, and is, a component of Marshfield life that has remained important since the town began. Faith served more than just as an inspiration; it also served as a social outlet through

Sunday School classes, quilting circles, ladies' aid societies, and other opportunities to have fun while extending the good word of the church.

Business and industry are what made the town grow. Marshfield became a railroad stop in 1886, connecting the small community with the rest of the world. Local businesses, as well as individuals, took advantage of the benefit of having a railroad nearby. Rural tomato-canning factories shipped their wares from the depot, as did other businesses such as Sugar Creek Creamery, whose butter went nationwide via the depot.

Another element of Marshfield's progress was obvious through the introduction of Route 66 in the early 1920s. Local businesses such as the Skyline Café, Williams Station, and Red Top Court served adventurers as they traveled through Marshfield on the "Mother Road." One of the biggest highlights occurred in 1928, when the Bunion Derby brought runners through town on a 3,422-mile footrace from Los Angeles to New York City.

There is no doubt about it, Marshfield has been characterized with a hard work ethic from the very beginning. The town's residents, however, also knew when to relax and have fun, like on Saturdays on the Marshfield Square. After stocking up on food as well as the local gossip, one might catch a show at the Ritz or stay a while on the Square and listen to the band concert that evening. The Fourth of July was another excuse to relax and have a good time. Consistent celebrations are on the books as far back at 1901, and the town is known as home to the longest-running Fourth of July celebration west of the Mississippi River. In 1991, Marshfield was recognized for its Fourth festivities when Pres. George H. Bush and his wife, Barbara, visited the community because of its famed celebration.

Other major celebrations were held in 1955, 1976, and 2005, when Webster County was celebrating the county's centennial and sesquicentennial as well as the country's bicentennial. In addition to the typical Independence Day merriment, county residents went all out with period dress, beard, and queen contests, window displays, and a trip back to the county's founding in 1855.

Marshfield has industry, churches, education, and history to define it on the books for generations to come. There is more, however, that makes Marshfield really stand out—the people who have worked to make the town what is has become today. Now over 150 years old, Marshfield continually declares why it is one of the best communities in Missouri to call home: a place that upholds its history, its heritage, and its values that make it "Top of the Ozarks."

One

Early Days to Today

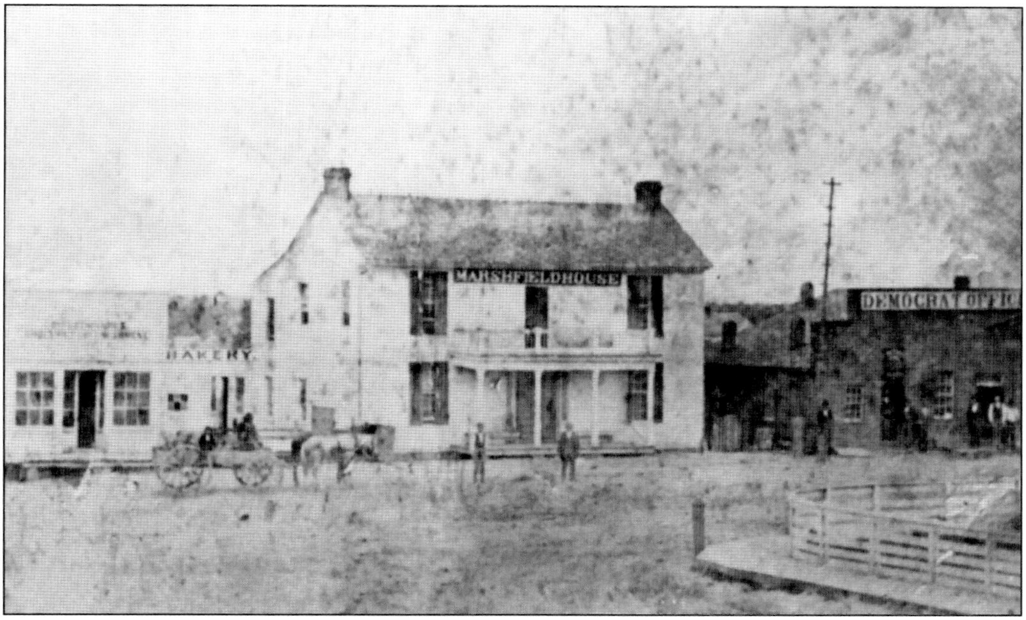

The northeast side of the Marshfield Square is pictured here in 1868. On the left side of the block is a bakery and confectionery. Next to it is the Marshfield House, and on the right is the *Democrat*, a newspaper that operated in Marshfield for several years beginning in 1870. (Courtesy of Randy Clair.)

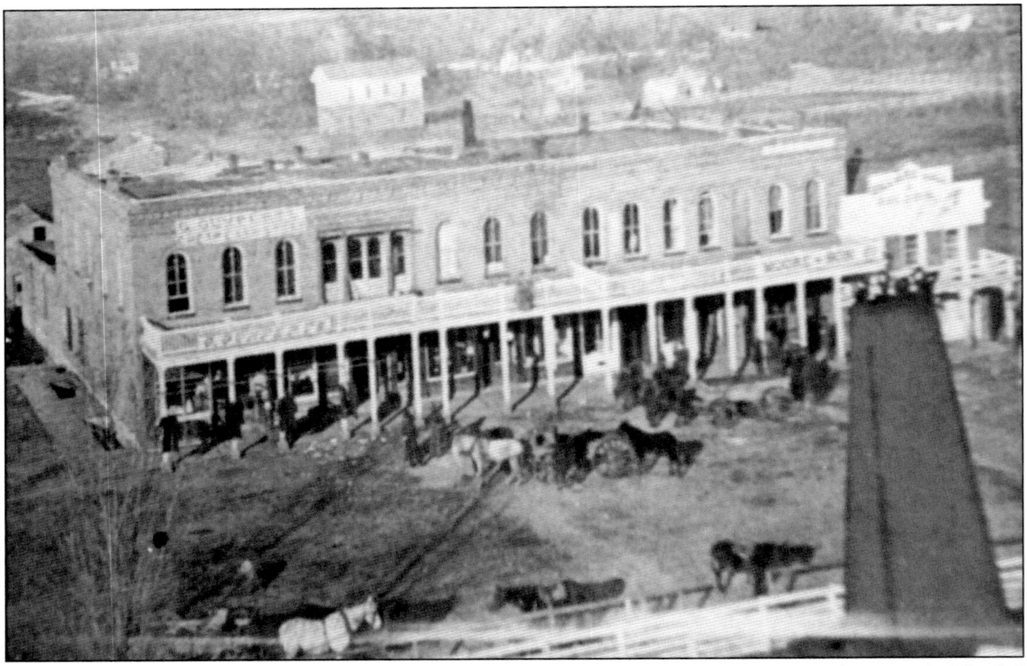

Pictured in 1872, the Brooks brothers owned what was commonly known as the "Brick Block." At one time, a portion of the square's northeast side contained a saloon and billiards hall. The buildings housed various businesses over the years, including the C.W. Brooks Mercantile in the early 1900s. Much of the Brick Block was destroyed by fire in 1921. (Courtesy of Randy Clair.)

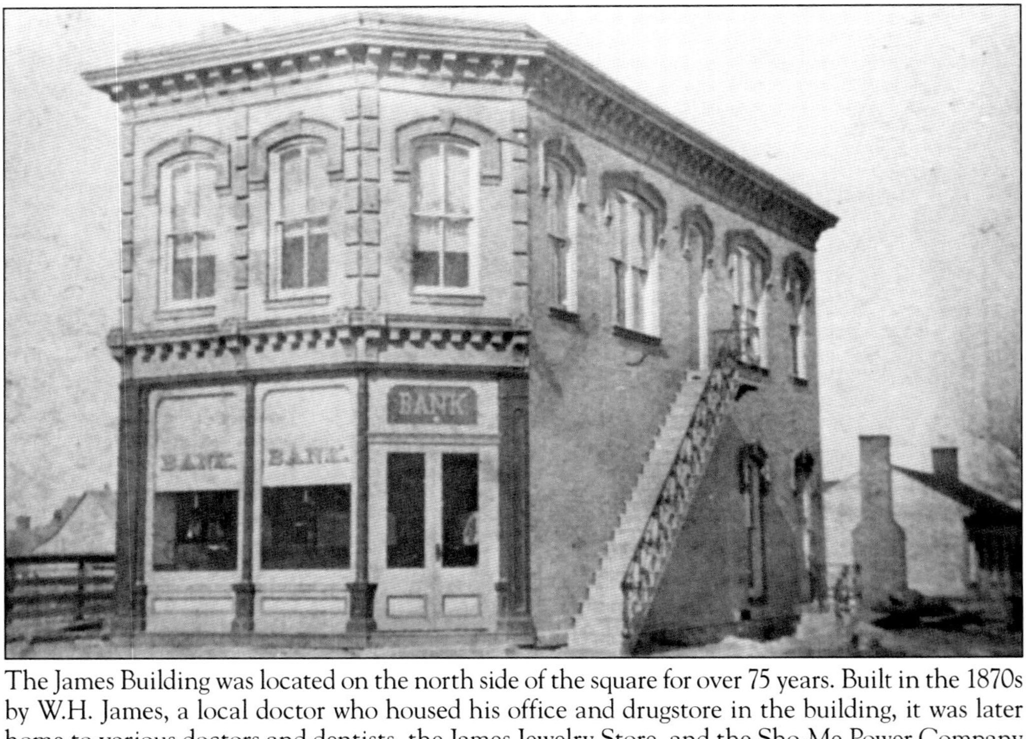

The James Building was located on the north side of the square for over 75 years. Built in the 1870s by W.H. James, a local doctor who housed his office and drugstore in the building, it was later home to various doctors and dentists, the James Jewelry Store, and the Sho-Me Power Company before it was torn down in 1959. (Courtesy of Randy Clair.)

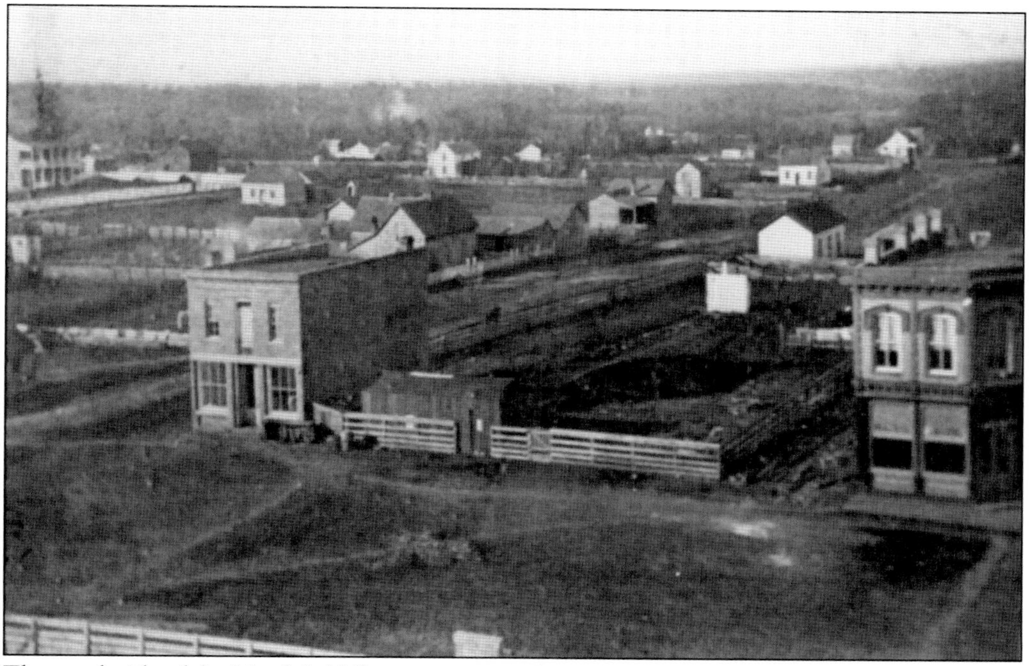

The north side of the Marshfield Square is pictured in 1872. R.W. Fyan owned the house pictured in the far left corner, and the building on the left corner of the street is one of the oldest standing in Marshfield. On the right is the James Building, which was torn down in 1959. (Courtesy of Randy Clair.)

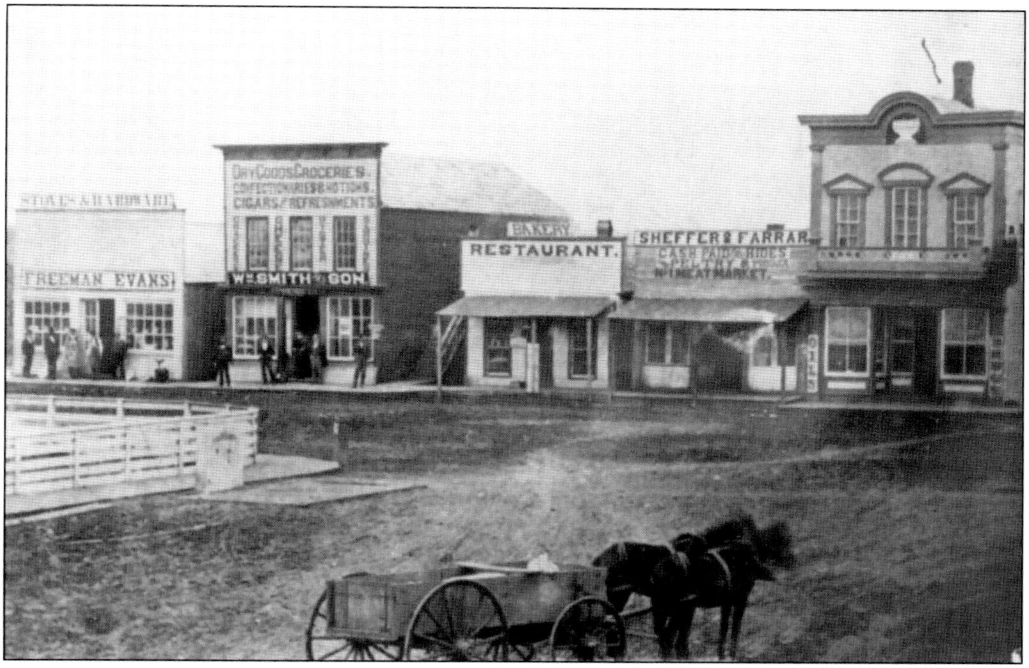

This 1895 view of the south side of the square shows the Fairbanks scale (near the fence), which was used as a weighing station for wagons. Businesses of the time included the Freeman Evans store, the William Smith & Son dry goods store, a bakery and restaurant, and Sheffer & Farrar, a selling and purchasing point for hides as well as a meat market. (Courtesy of Randy Clair.)

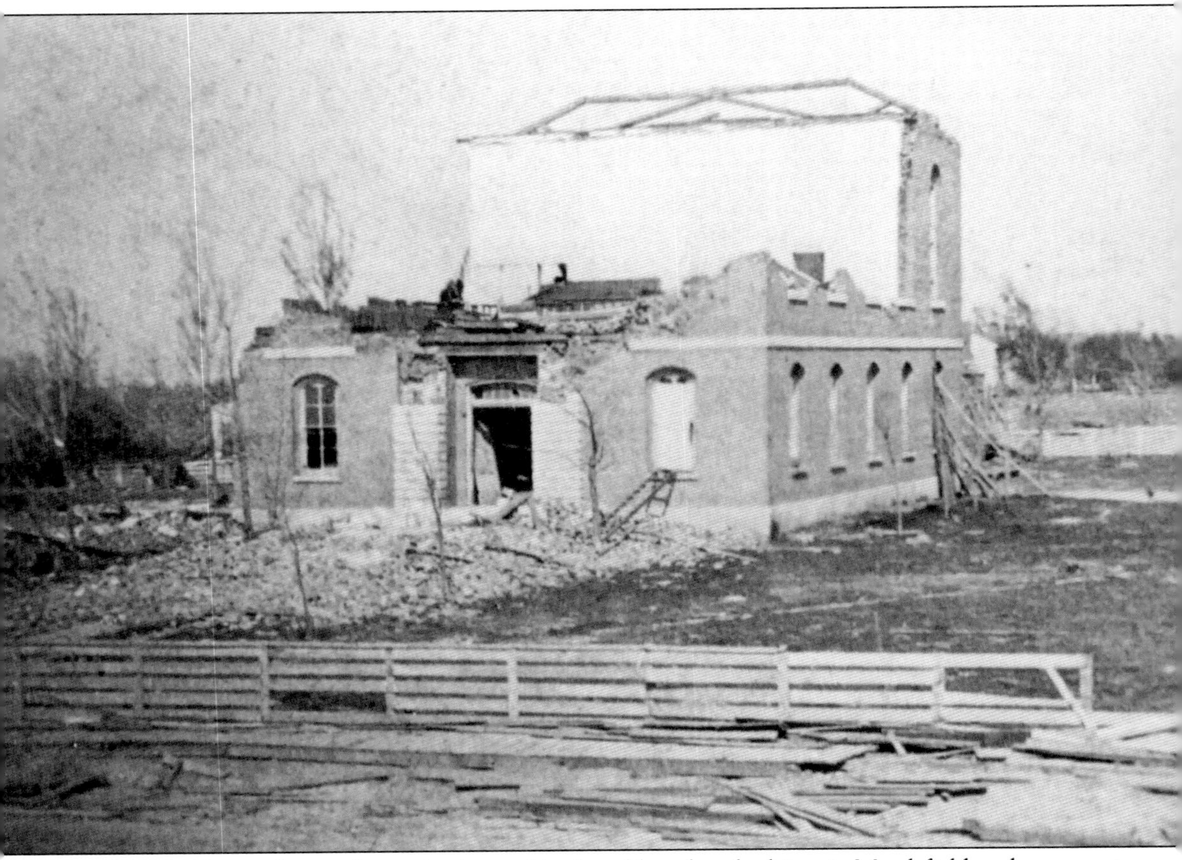

Webster County's courthouse is pictured in shambles after the historic Marshfield cyclone swept through town on April 18, 1880. Accounts of the day describe it beginning as any other peaceful Ozarks spring day did. It was a Sunday morning, with many people leaving church, when the afternoon began to change. The wind began to blow, the atmosphere became dreary and cold, and currents of clouds began circling overhead. A journal stated that soon after hail "the size of goose eggs" began to fall and something later described as a "train of fire" filled the sky. People ran in all directions to escape the twister, which spared little in its path. One minute later, the cyclone was gone and so was nearly 75 percent of the town's buildings and 10 percent of the town's population. (Courtesy of Randy Clair.)

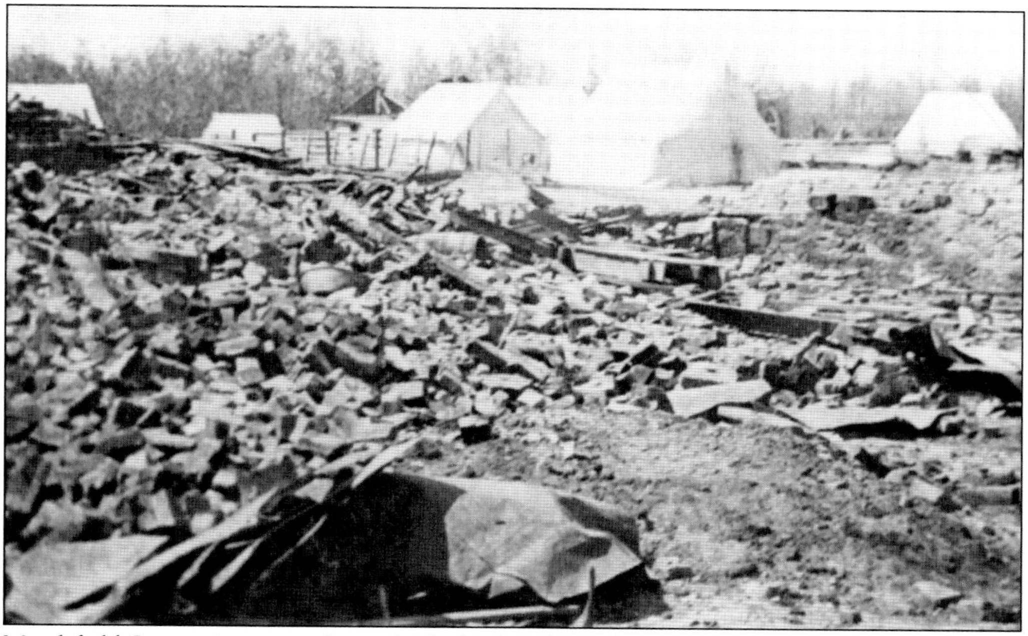

Marshfield Square is pictured as it looked after the cyclone of 1880. The white tents in the background were furnished by the US Army to serve as temporary housing for displaced families. Help began arriving from Springfield, Niangua, and Lebanon the next day, and the town was eventually rebuilt with state aid and private donations from across the country. (Courtesy of Randy Clair.)

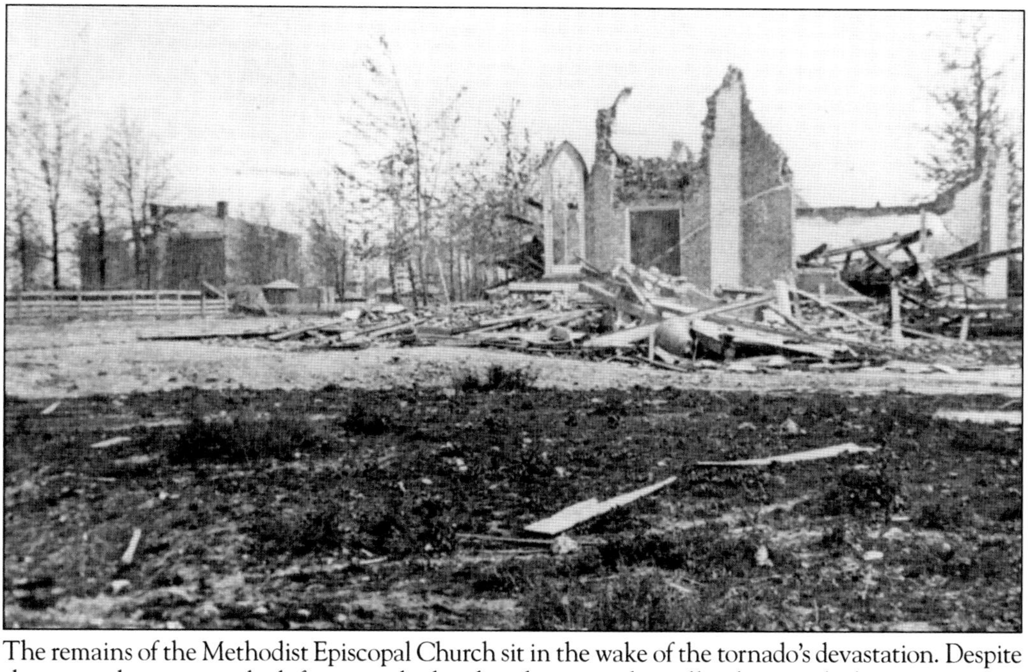

The remains of the Methodist Episcopal Church sit in the wake of the tornado's devastation. Despite the storm, however, a clock from inside the church survived—still ticking with the correct time. The church was rebuilt and renamed the Condo Church, after the church's minister, Reverend Condo, who died in the storm. In the background is the school, which was used as a hospital for the injured. (Courtesy of Randy Clair.)

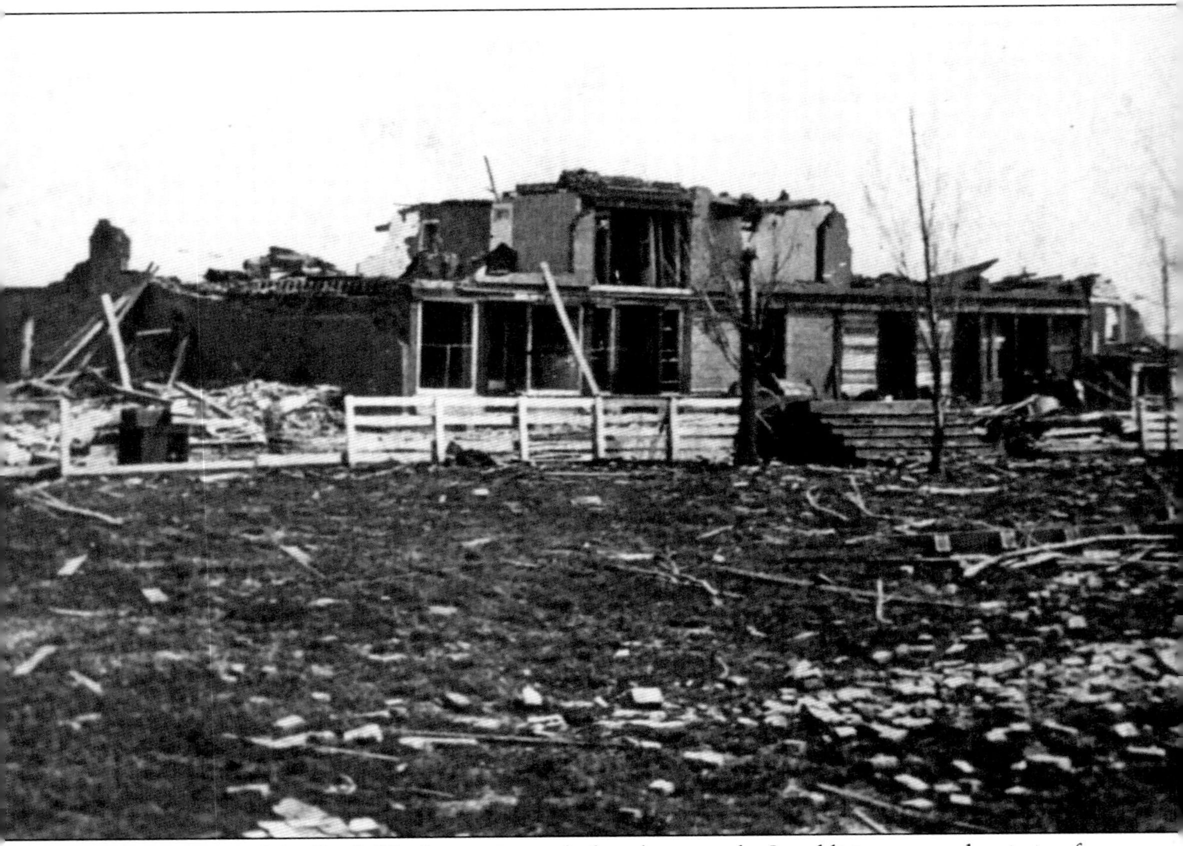

The remains of the Brick Block are pictured after the tornado. In addition to much missing from the buildings due to the tornado's devastating winds, another element out of place is the set of stairs in front of the wooden fence. They were from the courthouse and were blown up against the fence during the storm. (Courtesy of Randy Clair.)

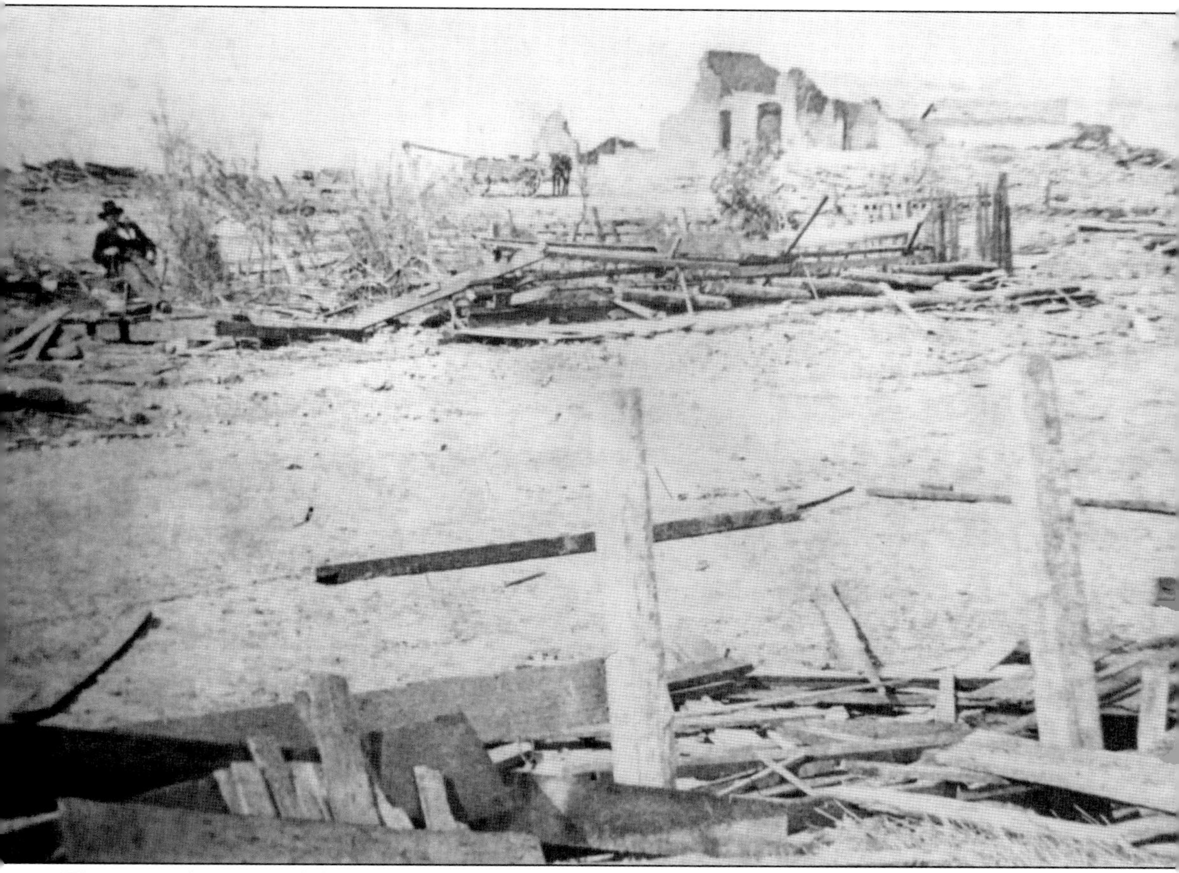

This is another view of the town square taken after the tornado whipped through town on April 18, 1880. Sitting at left is R.W. Fyan, from whose property this photograph was taken. Nearly everything on the square was completely destroyed by the cyclone that just lasted for little over 60 seconds. (Courtesy of Randy Clair.)

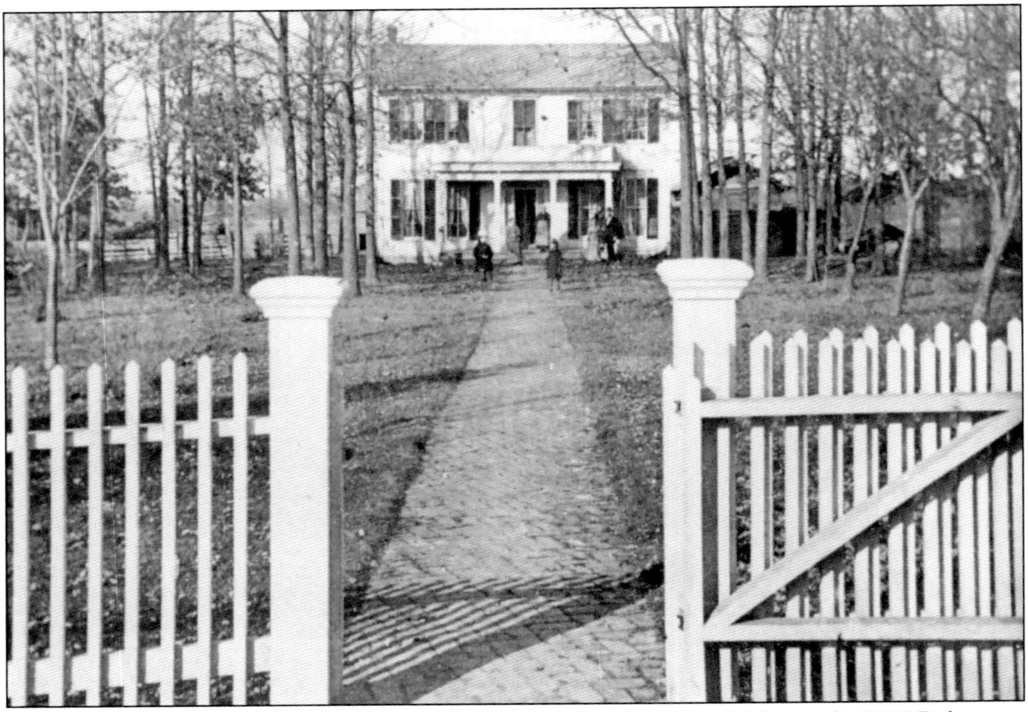

The E.W. Barnes residence in 1872 is shown before and after the Marshfield tornado. D.W. Robertson would later own the property; however, the house was completely destroyed in the Marshfield cyclone on April 18, 1880. The storm's origin was in the Camp Bliss Springs area in northeast Barry County and entered Webster County following the James River. Just prior to the storm hitting, many citizens did not know that anything out of the ordinary was about to happen. Just minutes after the tornado whipped through town, all that remained of the two-story Barnes house were a few felled trees that could not take the high winds of the storm. (Both courtesy of Randy Clair.)

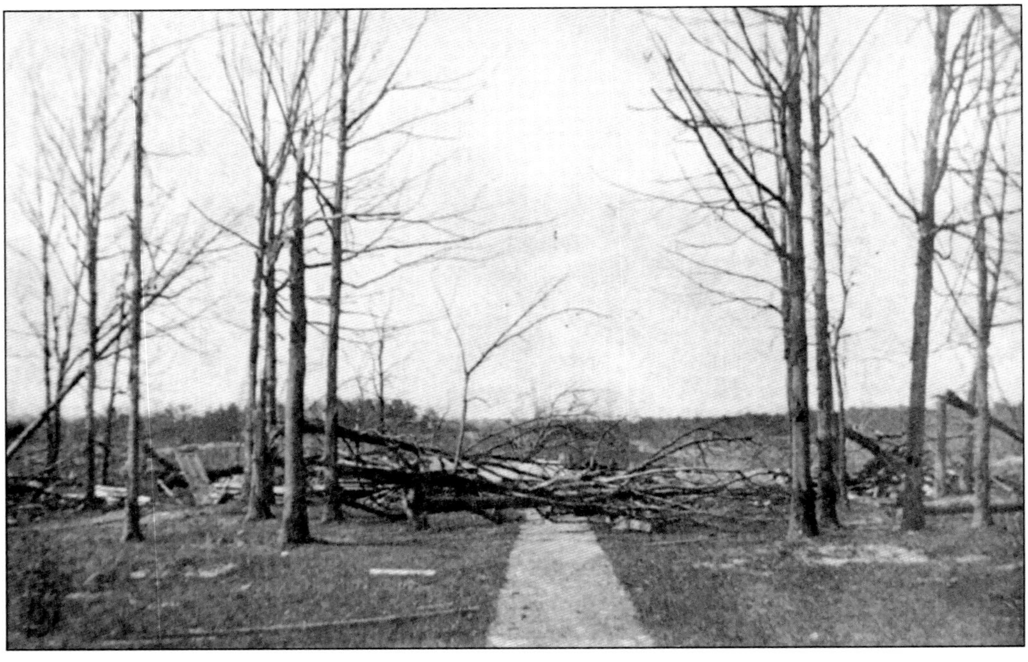

Sheriff and Mrs. W.A. Marlin are pictured during his time as Webster County sheriff. Marlin only served a one-year term from 1885 to 1886; at the time, short-term lengths were fairly common. Prior to Marlin's term, only two sheriffs, Isaac Johnson and Jordan Johnson, served longer than three years at a time. (Courtesy of the Webster County Historical Museum.)

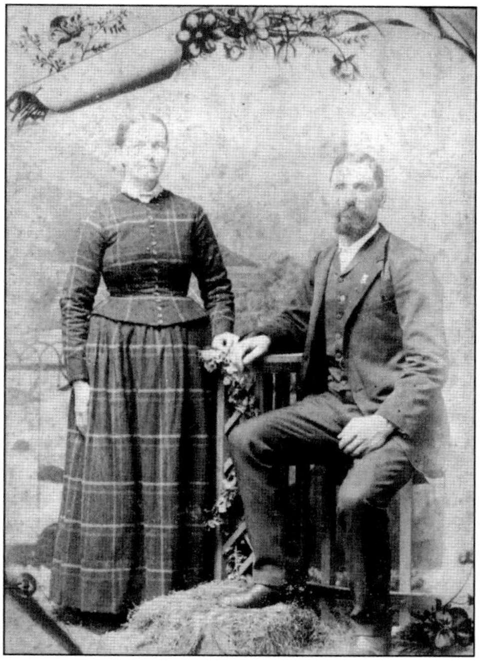

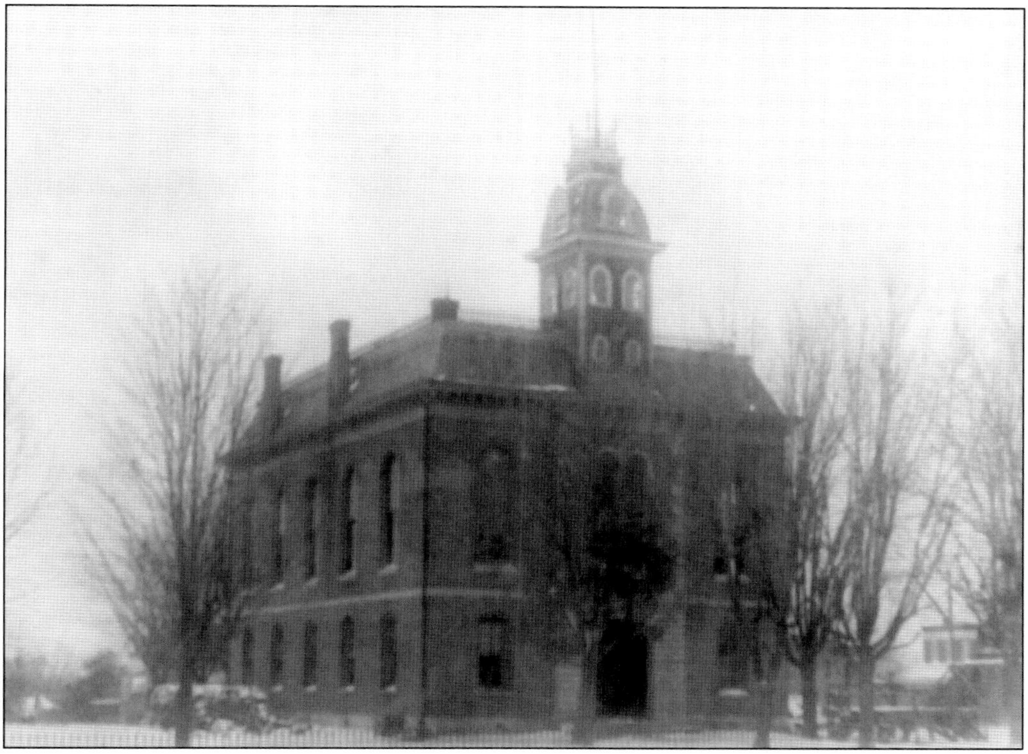

The Webster County Courthouse is pictured in either 1907 or 1908. A bit of mystery surrounds the photograph, as a look to the right reveals a gallows, which may have been erected for a hanging. However, Webster County only had one legal hanging throughout the county's existence, and it took place outside of Marshfield's city limits; it is unknown why the gallows in the photograph existed. (Courtesy of Randy Clair.)

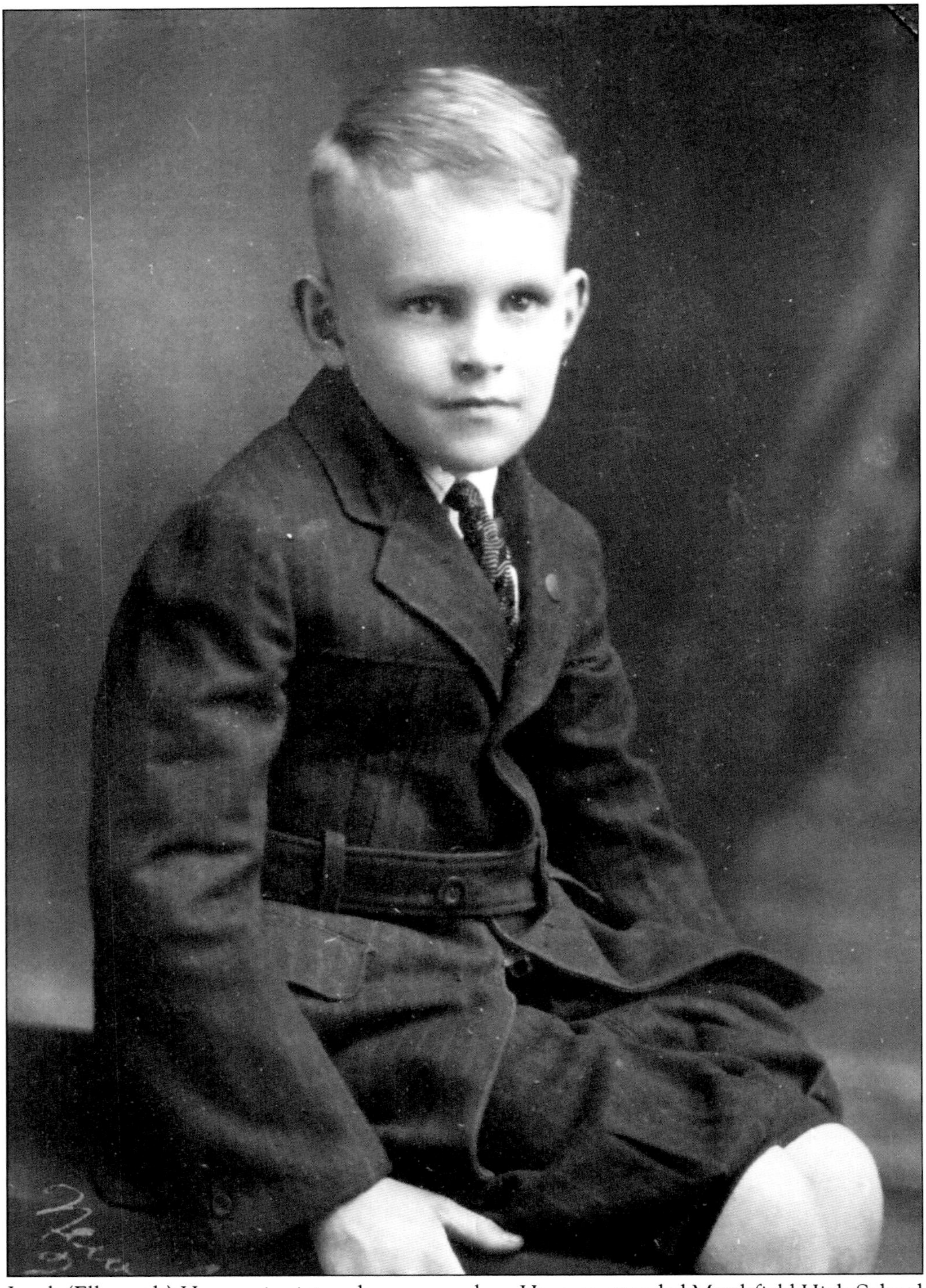

Jacob (Ellsworth) Haymes is pictured as a young boy. Haymes attended Marshfield High School for one term in September 1892, after which he entered the University of Missouri and graduated from the military department in 1894. After law school, Haymes entered practice with Webster County prosecuting attorney James Case. He was later elected as prosecutor in 1904 and again in 1908. (Courtesy of the Webster County Historical Museum.)

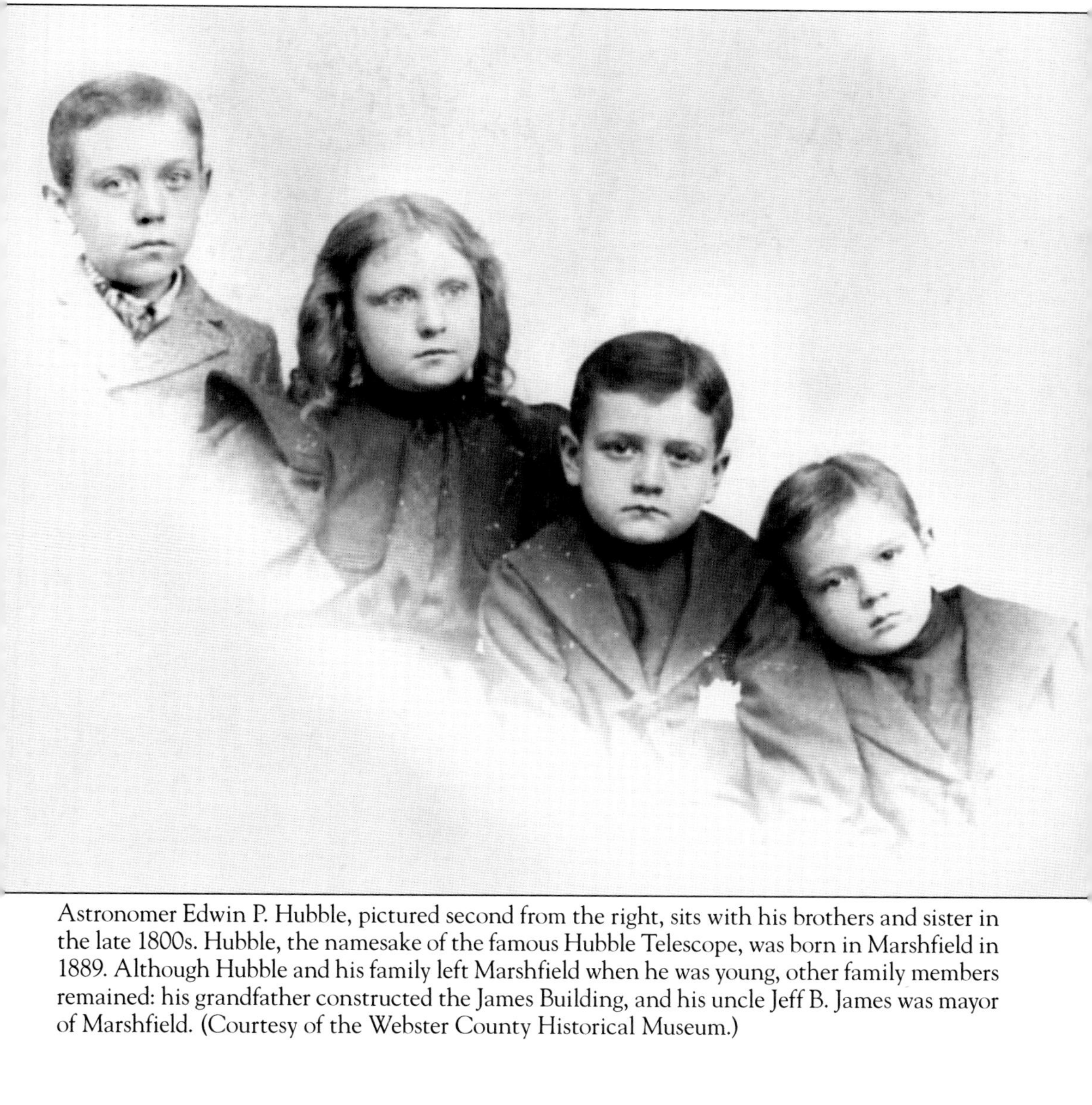

Astronomer Edwin P. Hubble, pictured second from the right, sits with his brothers and sister in the late 1800s. Hubble, the namesake of the famous Hubble Telescope, was born in Marshfield in 1889. Although Hubble and his family left Marshfield when he was young, other family members remained: his grandfather constructed the James Building, and his uncle Jeff B. James was mayor of Marshfield. (Courtesy of the Webster County Historical Museum.)

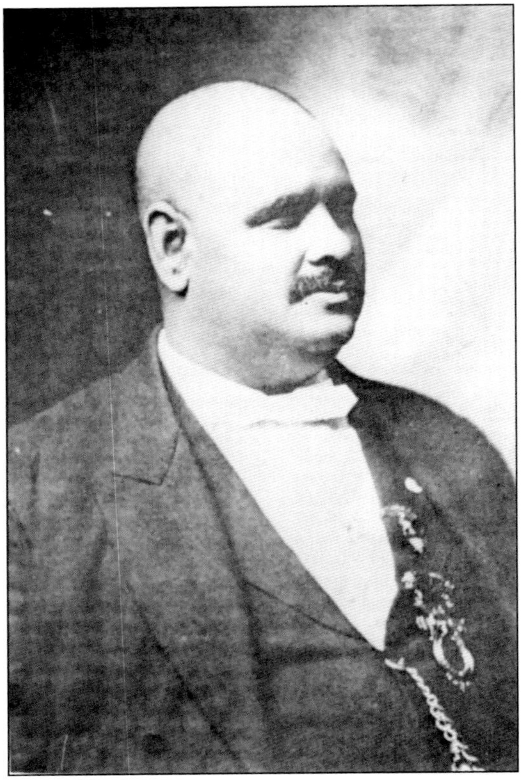

John Williams "Blind" Boone is shown in a portrait from the early 1900s. Boone composed "The Marshfield Tornado," a song thought to re-create emotions connected with the Marshfield cyclone. While the song closed many of Boone's performances nationwide, today it is long gone. Boone refused to record the song, and it was last played on May 31, 1927, at Boone's final performance in Virden, Illinois. (Courtesy of Randy Clair.)

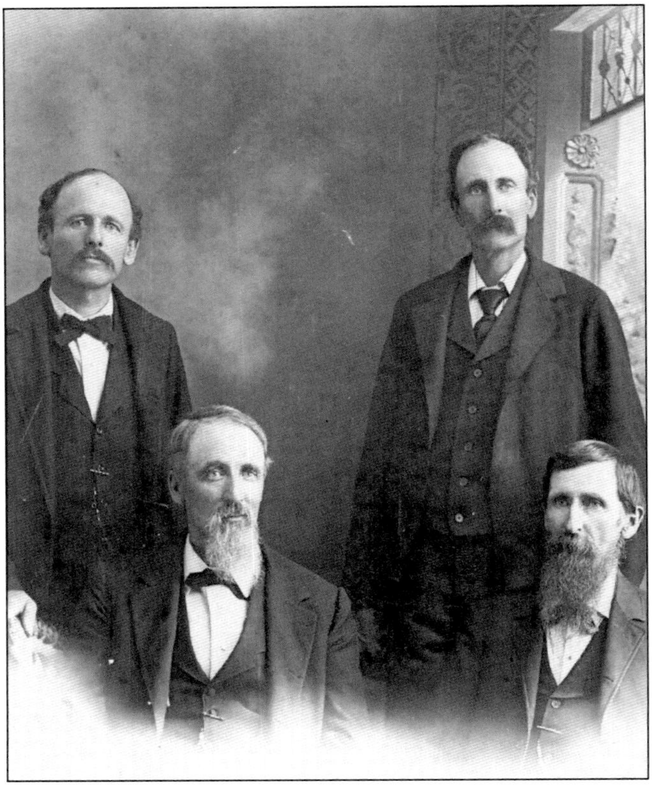

Four of the Brooks brothers are pictured in a formal portrait. From left to right they are (seated) Christopher Williams and William; (standing) John Kerr and Dr. Andrew J. The family moved to Webster County in 1854 with their parents, sisters, and numerous slaves. The family helped form the Mt. Olive Cemetery, and C.W. Brooks was the founder of a namesake mercantile in Marshfield. (Courtesy of the Webster County Historical Museum.)

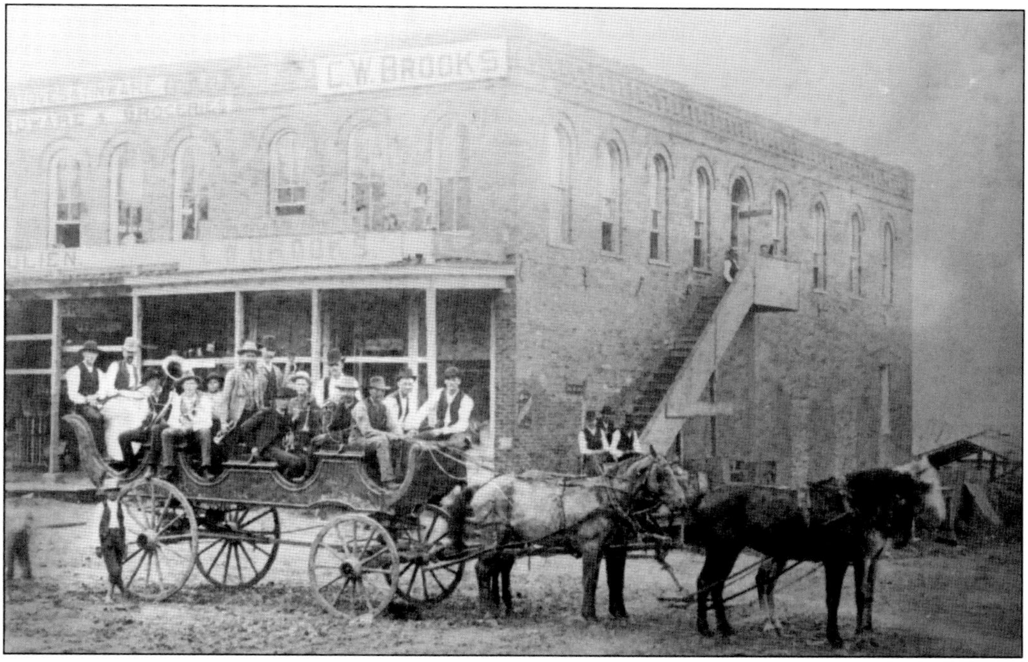

Members of the town band are shown riding on the town bandwagon in 1895. The band members are, from left to right, Frank Bollinger, Henry Gilbert, Charles Thompson, J.E. Thompson, Will Chitty, Ed Sutherland, Professor Smith, Charley Allgore, John Paul, Joe Hubbell, Royal Corbett, P.T. Johnson, R. Clay Florance, and Jim Bruce; the driver is Lou Avery. (Courtesy of Randy Clair.)

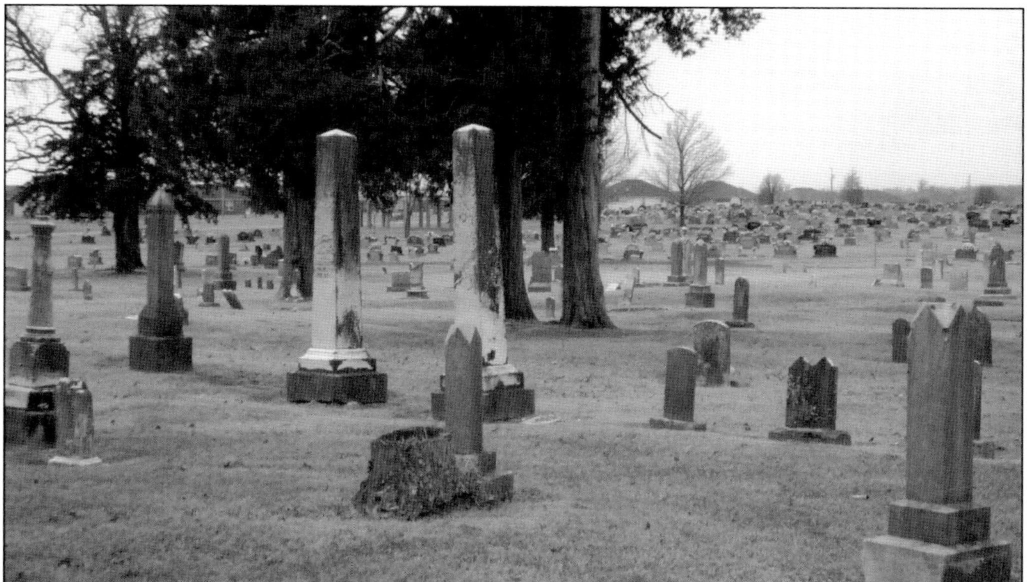

The Marshfield Cemetery began with the burial of Elizabeth Burford in 1879. At one time, there was a brick factory at the northwest corner that made many of the bricks used to construct local buildings. Memorial Day has typically been a holiday that was recognized at the cemetery. In years past, people would gather and eat picnic lunches on the grounds. (Courtesy of the Webster County Historical Museum.)

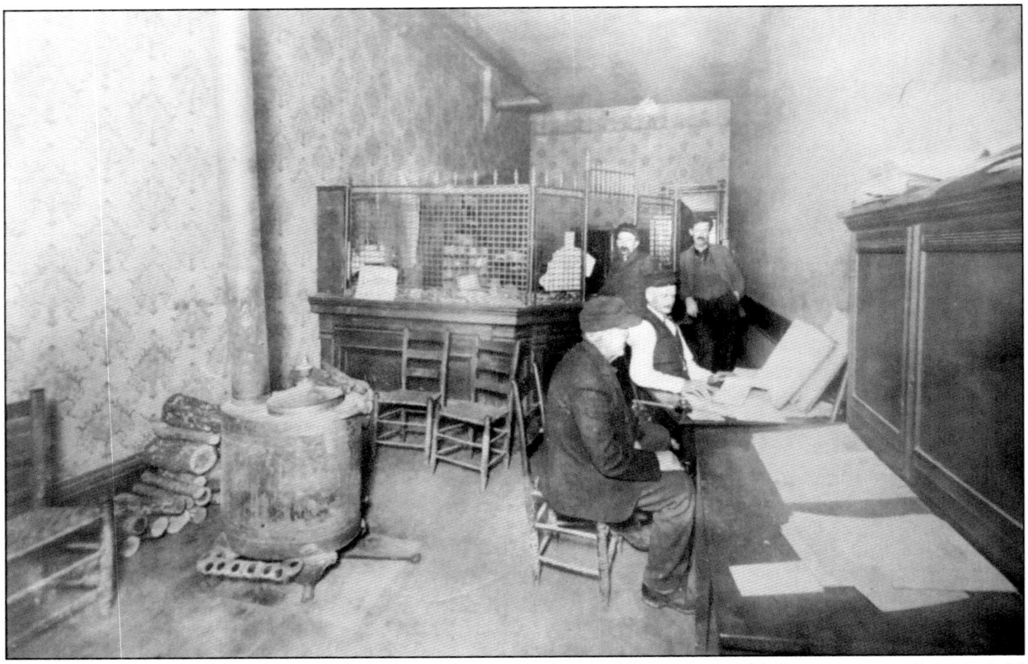

Marshfield's original post office is pictured in 1903. It was established in 1856, the same year Marshfield was founded, and Allen E. Goss served as postmaster. The current post office was dedicated in 1959 after a federal grant provided funding for its construction. (Courtesy of Randy Clair.)

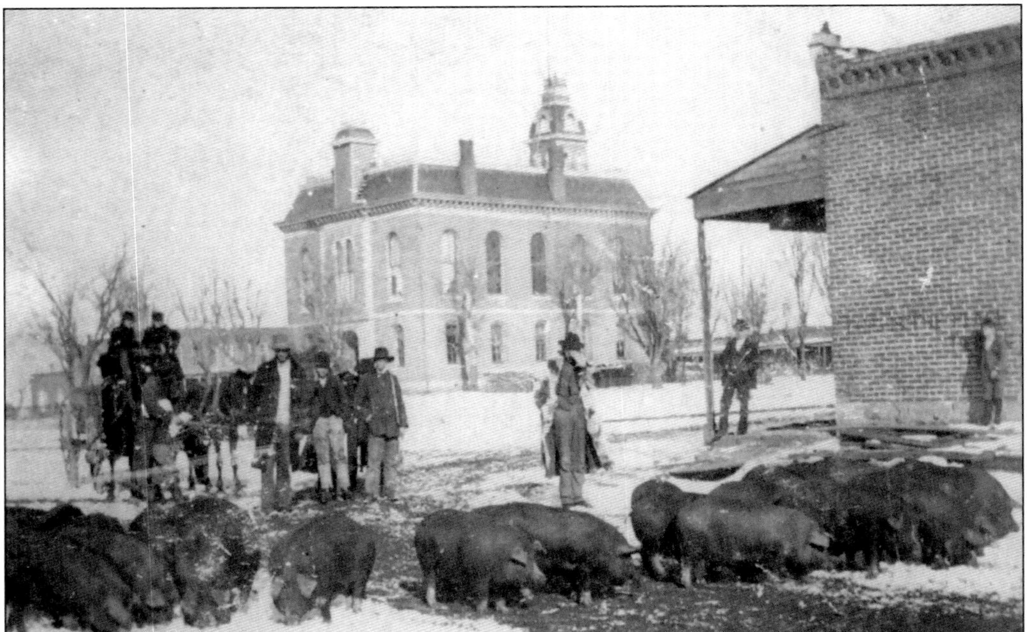

Agriculture has always been a large part of Webster County. This was never more evident than by the herd of seven-month-old pigs John Clift brought through the town square in the early 1900s. The only other identified man in this image is Sam Montgomery, who is standing in front of the horses wearing an open overcoat and hat. (Courtesy of Randy Clair.)

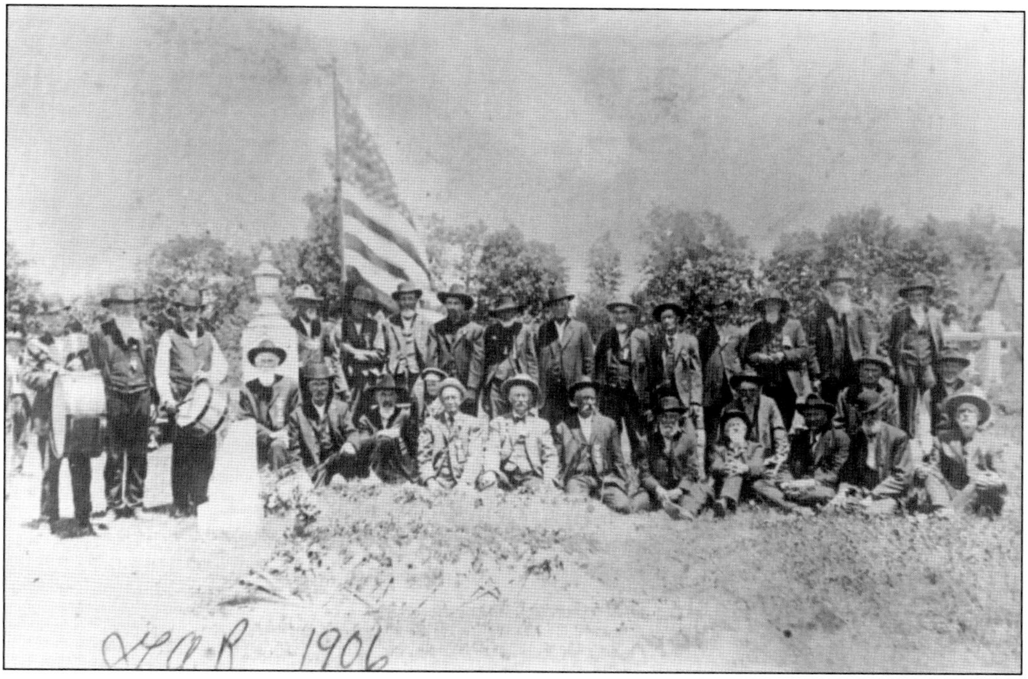

Members of the Grand Army of the Republic gathered for a graveside service of a former soldier in 1906. Comprised of former Union soldiers, Post No. 588 was "mustered" on July 7, 1908, and was the second GAR post to exist in Marshfield. One of the functions of the organization was to care for the members' fellow comrades and their widows. (Courtesy of Randy Clair.)

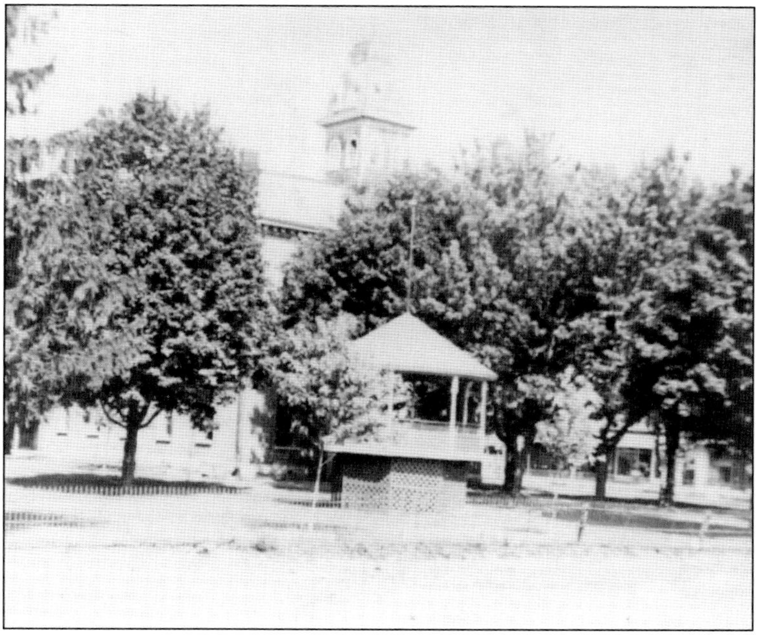

Pictured in 1929, Marshfield's gazebo has been a town icon since 1906. The structure was used for Marshfield's weekly band concerts and special events through the 1930s. However, construction of the new courthouse in 1939 found the gazebo up for auction. It sold for $18 and was removed. Portions of it were returned in later years as part of a new gazebo. (Courtesy of the Webster County Historical Museum.)

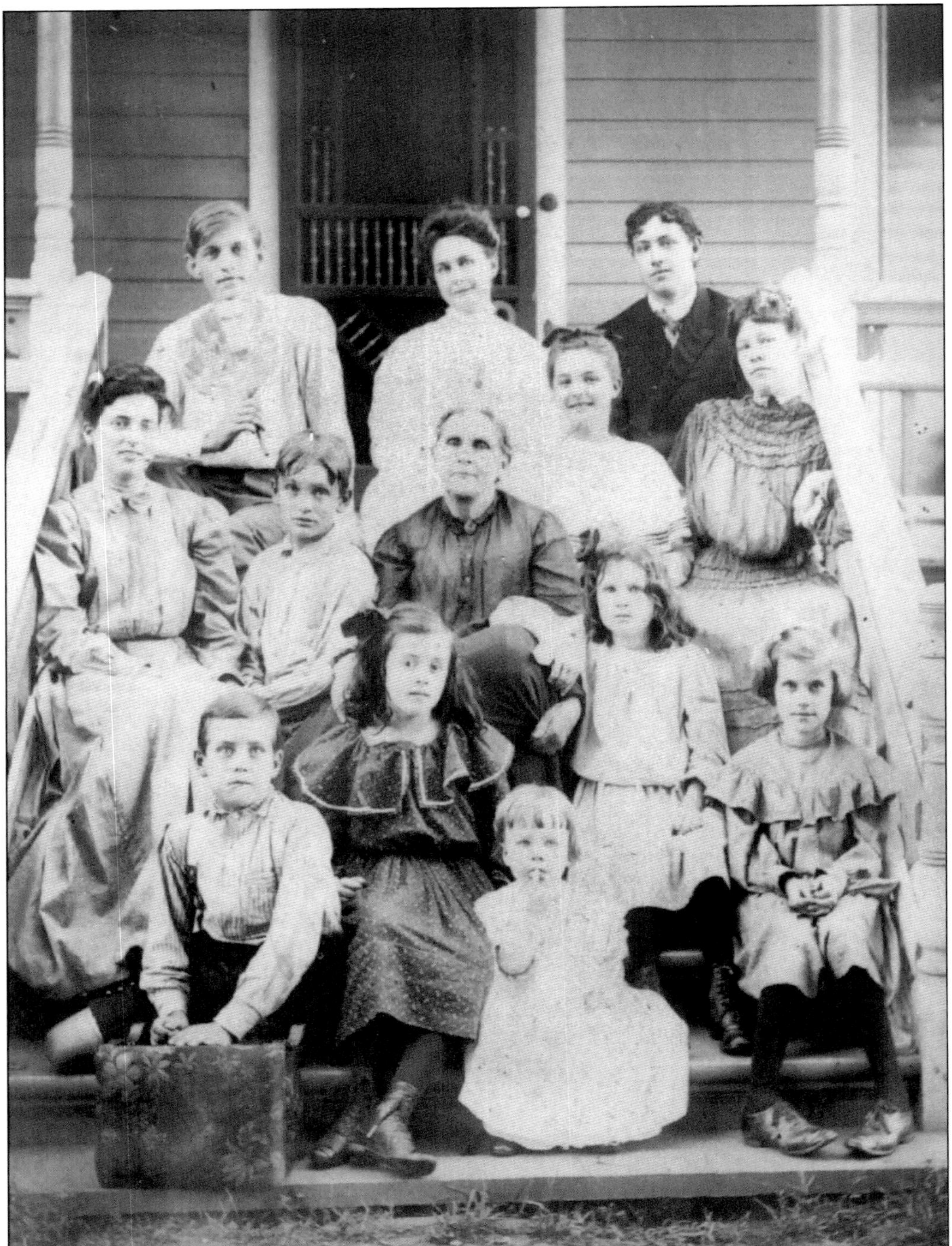

Mrs. Elizabeth Hoover Wallace is shown surrounded by several of her grandchildren in the early 1900s. At the top left corner is Ella Dickey, who would later serve as Marshfield's first librarian and whose family built the Dickey House in the late 1800s. (Courtesy of Lib Sims.)

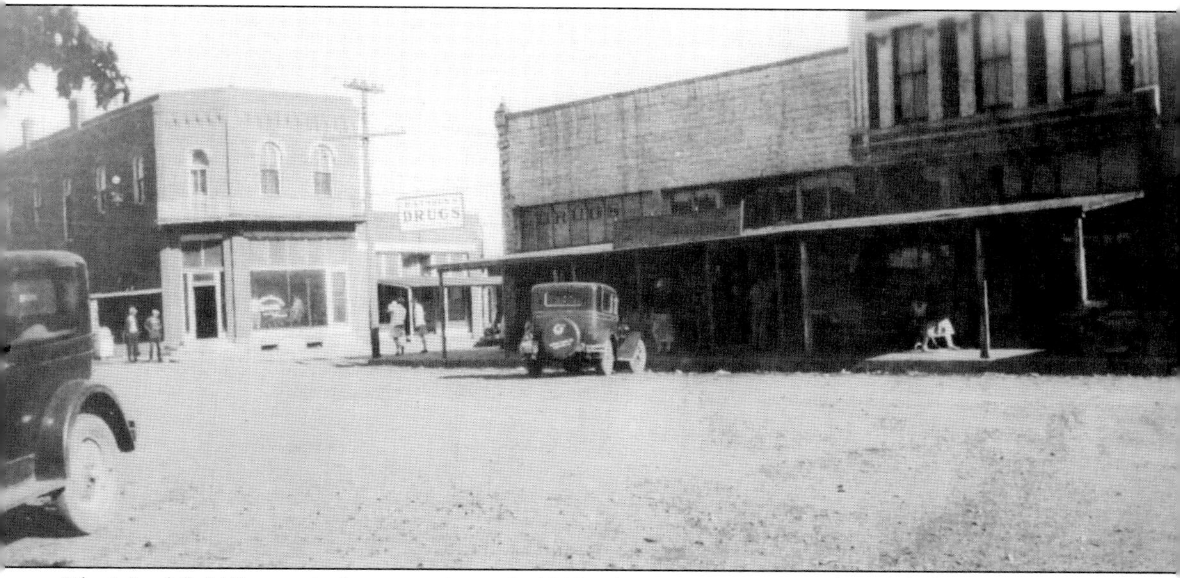

The Marshfield Square is shown in the early 1900s. A movement was made to lift the square "out of the mud" in 1907, when the streets were graded and macadamized. Prior to the modernizations, which included raising portions of the street as much as three feet, the square was virtually impassible in rainy weather. It was so deep that hogs wallowed under the wooden sidewalks. (Courtesy of Randy Clair.)

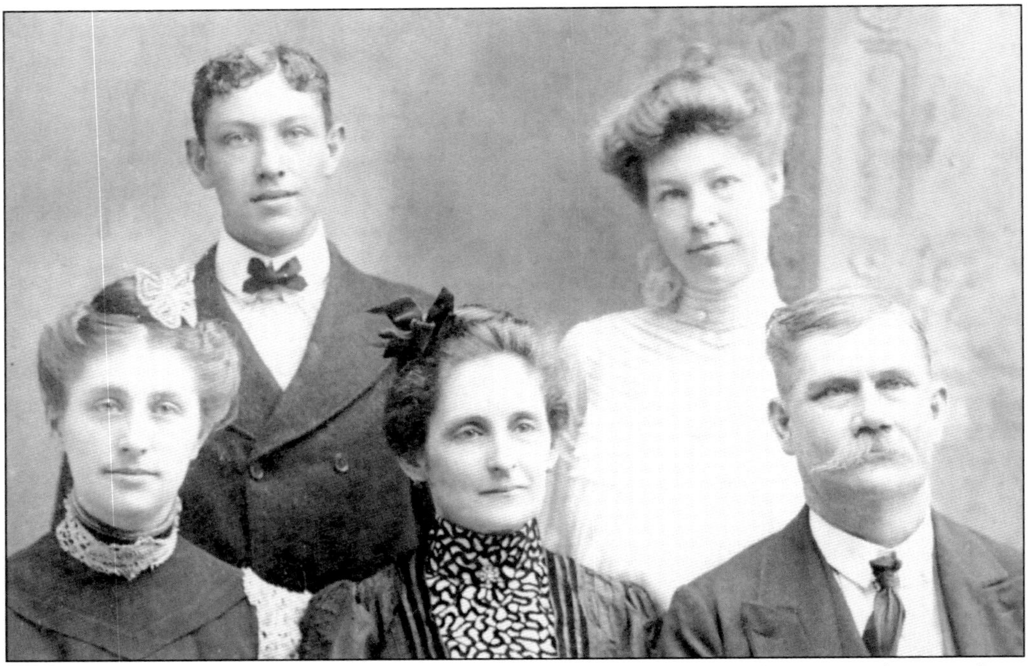

The Sam Dickey family is pictured during a formal portrait in the early 1900s. They are, from left to right, (first row) daughter Elizabeth, wife Sarah, and Dickey; (second row) son Charles and daughter Ella. Dickey served five terms as the local prosecuting attorney and was Marshfield's first city attorney. He died while serving as prosecutor in 1925. (Courtesy of Lib Sims.)

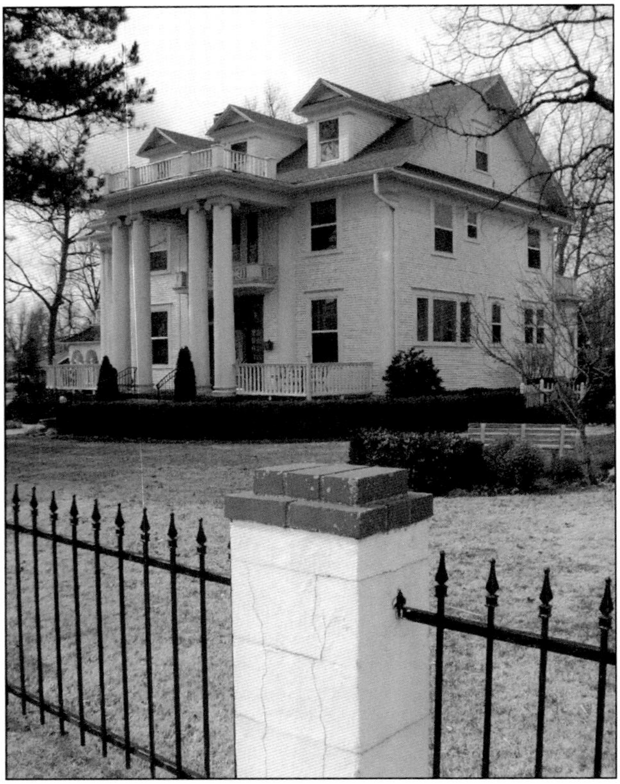

The Dickey House has set a standard of elegance dating back to the late 1800s. It was said that the mansion was built with fees attorney Sam Dickey earned defending a boxing-related death case. After his death, Sam's daughter Ella Dickey inherited the house; it became the location for her elaborate Halloween parties, family Christmas dinners, and spontaneous breakfast gatherings. (Courtesy of the Webster County Historical Museum.)

Shackleford Spring holds considerable distinction in Marshfield's history. It was the spring that prompted Marshfield's first family, the Flanigans, to settle nearby in 1856. After the 1880 cyclone, connections between Shackleford and other local springs were revealed. The water was declared to be medicinal after a man's eyes were healed after washing with it, and people flocked to reap its benefits. For several years, Marshfield became a health resort drawing people from across the country. (Courtesy of the Webster County Historical Museum.)

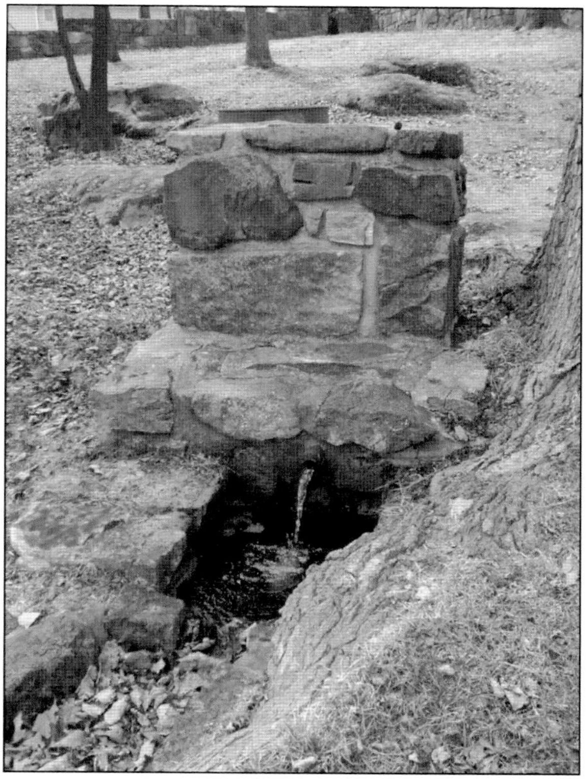

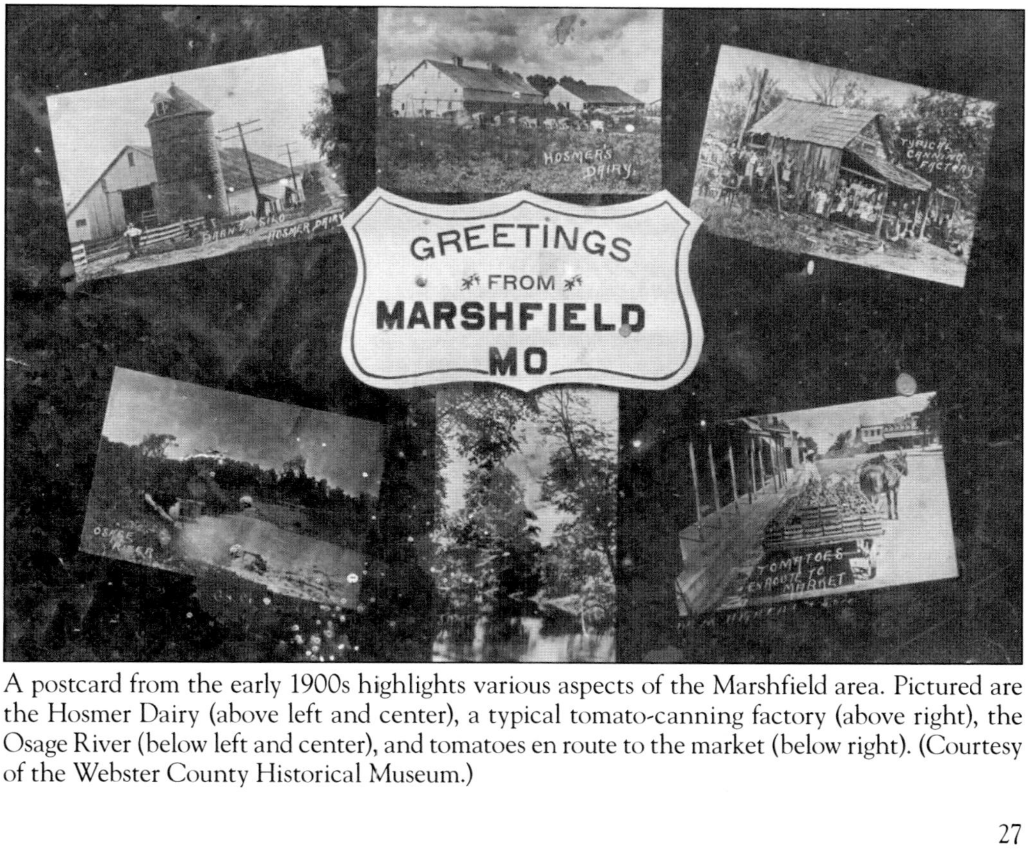

A postcard from the early 1900s highlights various aspects of the Marshfield area. Pictured are the Hosmer Dairy (above left and center), a typical tomato-canning factory (above right), the Osage River (below left and center), and tomatoes en route to the market (below right). (Courtesy of the Webster County Historical Museum.)

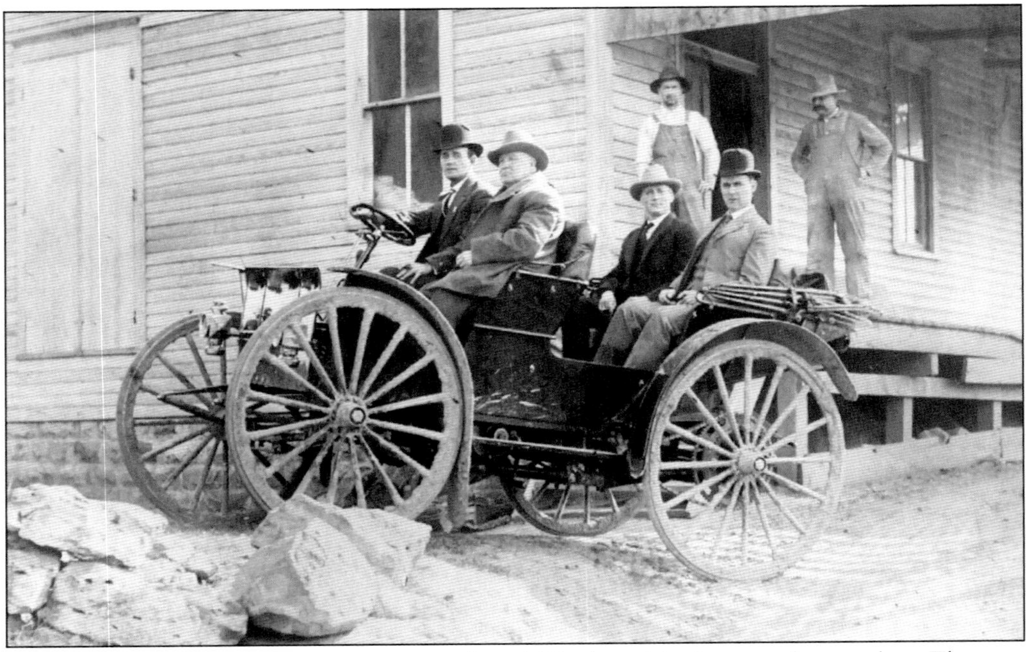

Four local men were heading out on a car ride in 1911 when this photograph was taken. The men are, from left to right, (front seat) Mr. Foster and Frank Hammell; (back seat) Cabe Shields and Monroe Andrews. On the platform of the old mill are Dan Wells and Mr. Kilpatrick, the miller. The men are riding in a High Wheel International automobile. (Courtesy of Randy Clair.)

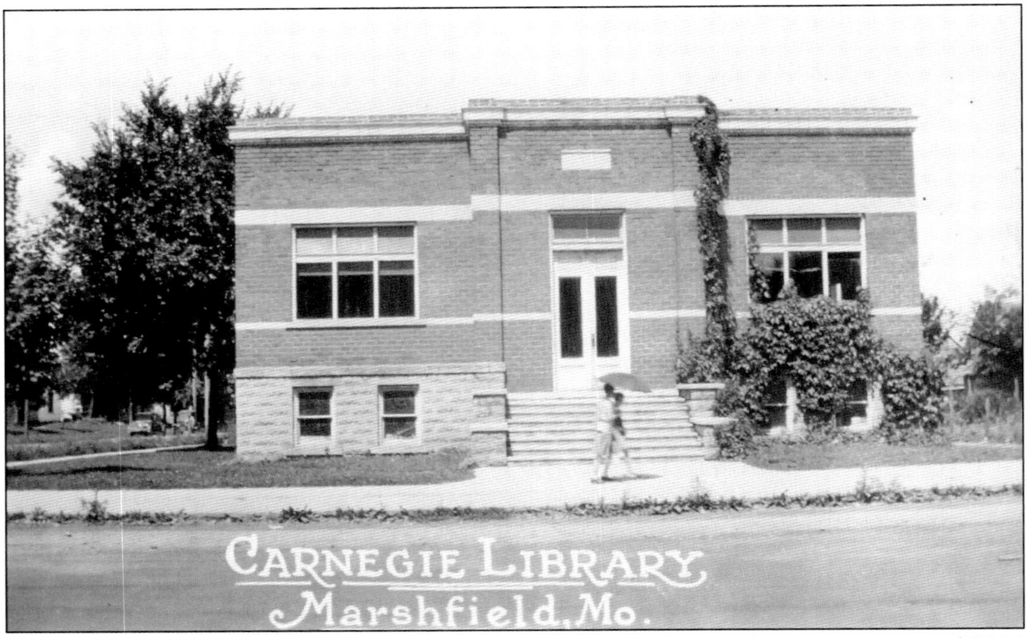

Marshfield's first library was completed in 1911 after philanthropist Andrew Carnegie gave $5,000 for its construction. Marshfield was nearly denied funding because Carnegie thought the town too small to tackle the tasks of donating the land and books and garnering support. Marshfield convinced him otherwise, and at the time it was said that Marshfield was the smallest town to receive funding for such a library. (Courtesy of the Webster County Historical Museum.)

A mule trader, W.T. Popejoy married Mary Ann Rader in 1874 at age 25. In a newspaper article written shortly before his death, Popejoy "expressed himself as ready and willing to go." At the time, "His only regret was leaving his beloved companion." He and Mary Ann were married for 56 years when he passed away on October 10, 1931. (Courtesy of Jennifer Hartman.)

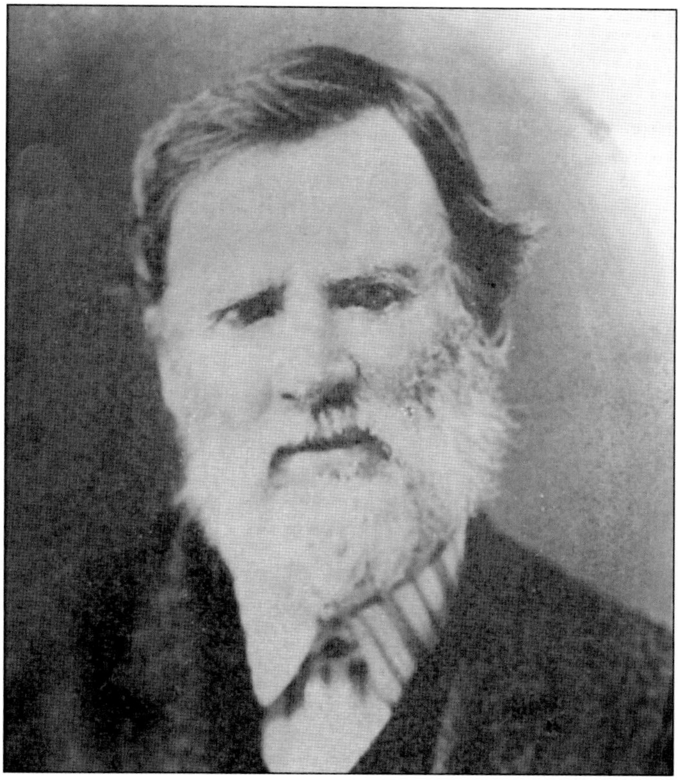

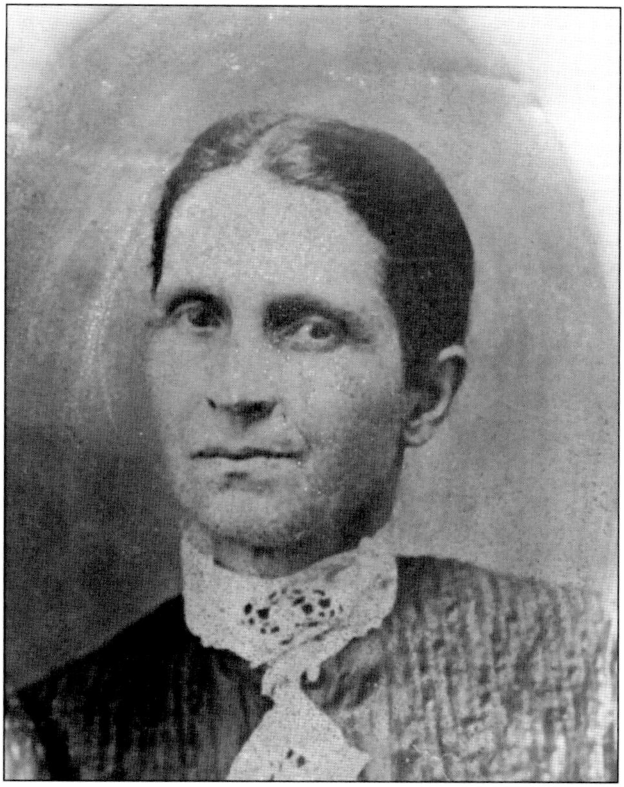

In 1874, Mary Ann Rader Popejoy's life was set to change after she married W.T. Popejoy. During her lifetime, Mary Ann bore 11 children: Elmer, Ruth, Ed, Nora, Minnie, Ola, Vida, Jim, Maggie, Nanny, and Lizzie. Mary Ann was born in 1856 near Knoxville, Tennessee, and moved with her family at a young age to Rader. Reared a Lutheran, she became a Baptist upon her marriage. (Courtesy of Jennifer Hartman.)

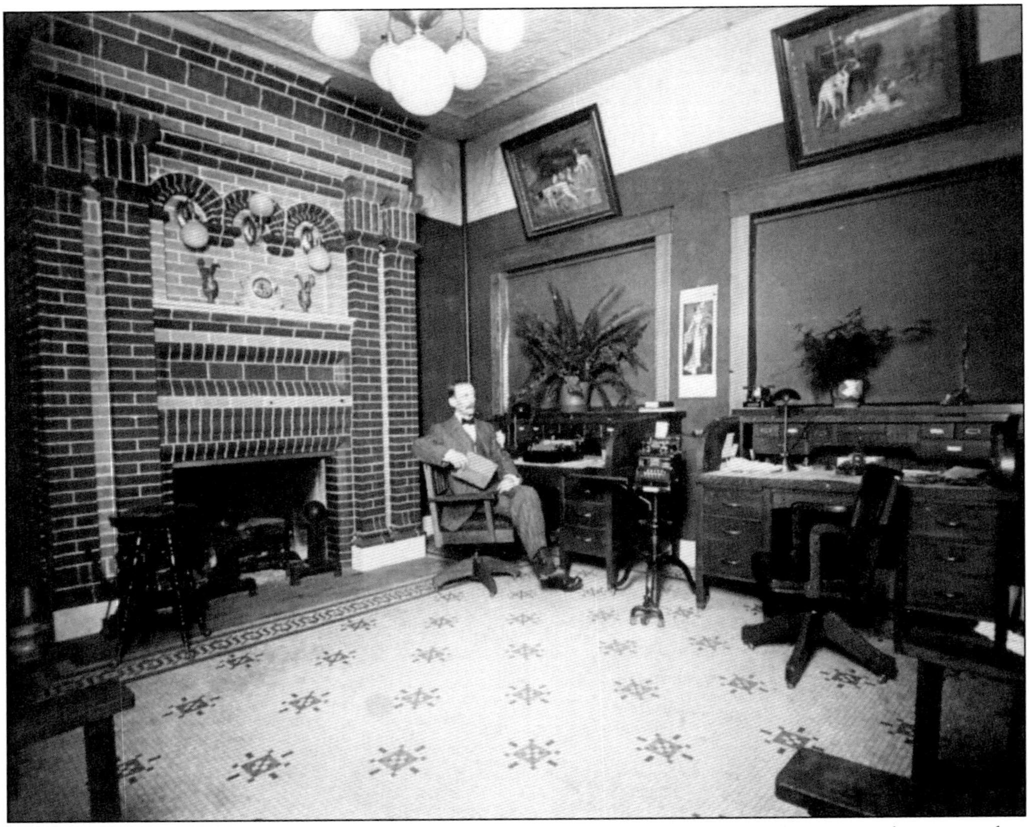

Jeff B. James is pictured in his office in 1926. In addition to owning a jewelry store adjacent to his office, James also served as Marshfield's mayor from 1904 to 1910, 1912 to 1916, and again from 1922 to 1924. James's father, Dr. W. H. James, constructed the building around 1875 to house his medical practice. (Courtesy of Randy Clair.)

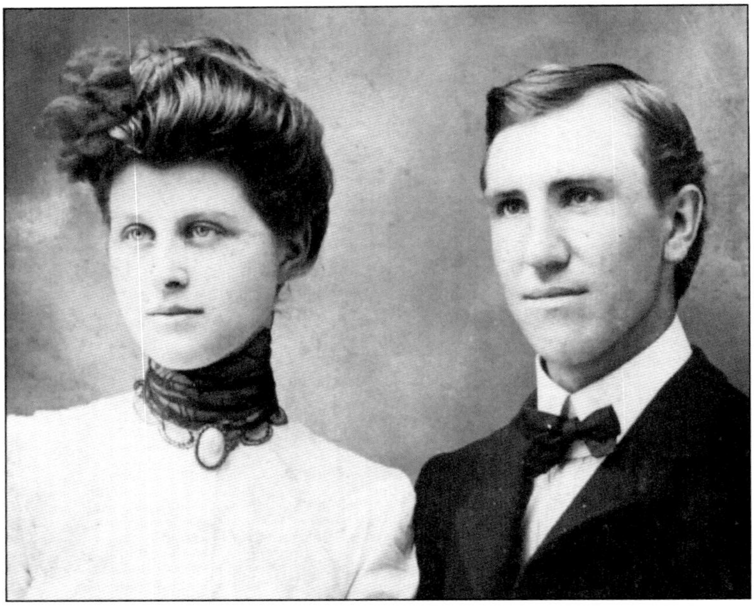

Minnie Brooks is pictured with her husband, Edward Winters Brooks, in the early 1900s. Minnie's father was Dr. Jolly, who served Marshfield as a physician for 50 years. Minnie, a member of the Methodist Episcopal Church, South, was also gained local fame as a musician; she played the piano at hundreds of funerals throughout her lifetime. (Courtesy of Ruth Brooks.)

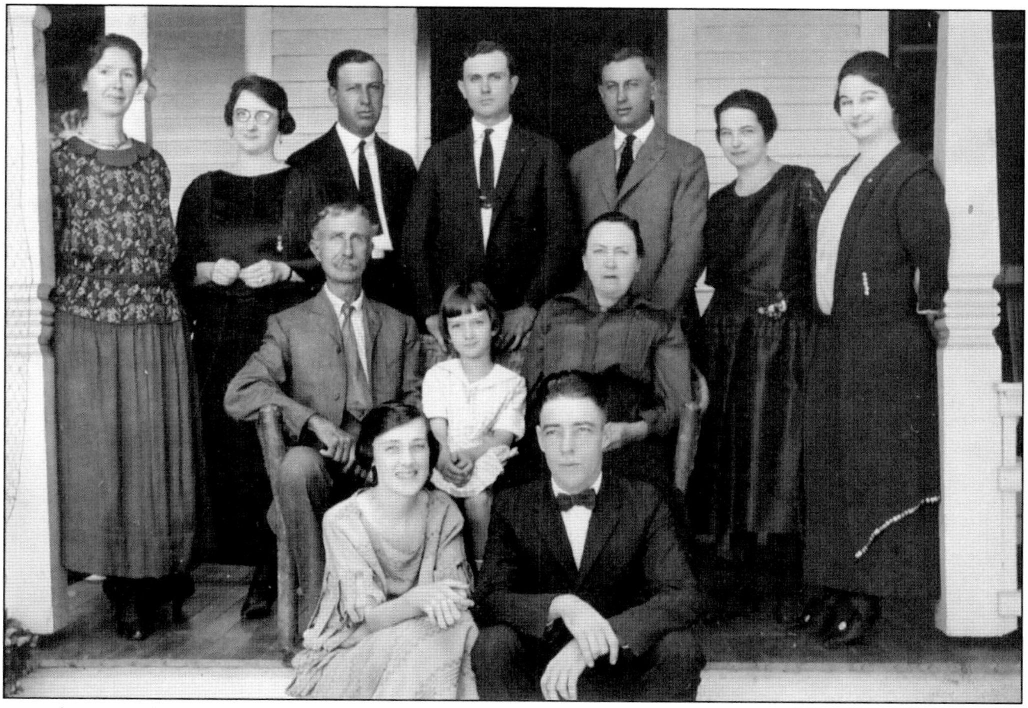

Members of the John and Arabelle Foster family are shown during a portrait from the 1920s. They are, from left to right, (first row) Frank and Susan (Foster) Renne; (second row) John B. Foster, Helen (Dennis) Foster, and Belle Foster; (third row) May Foster, Helen and Morris Foster, Bill Foster, John and Elizabeth (Fyan) Foster, and Ana Foster. (Courtesy of the Webster County Historical Museum.)

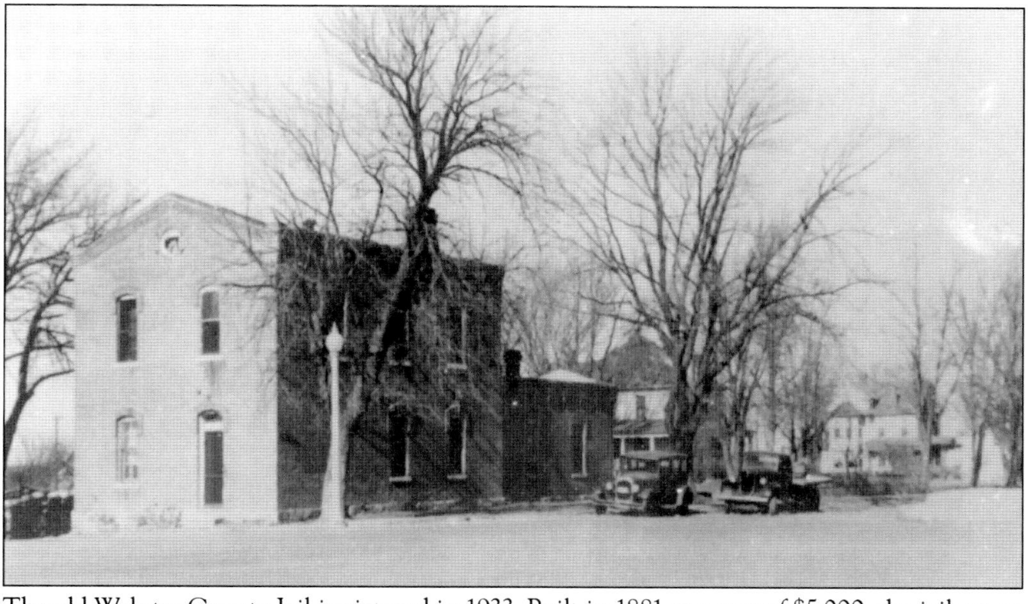

The old Webster County Jail is pictured in 1933. Built in 1881 at a cost of $5,000, the jail sat on the corner of Clay and Jefferson Streets in Marshfield for 60 years. The jail was used until 1941, when it was moved to the newly constructed courthouse. It was eventually torn down to make way for Marshfield's new post office, which opened in 1959. (Courtesy of Randy Clair.)

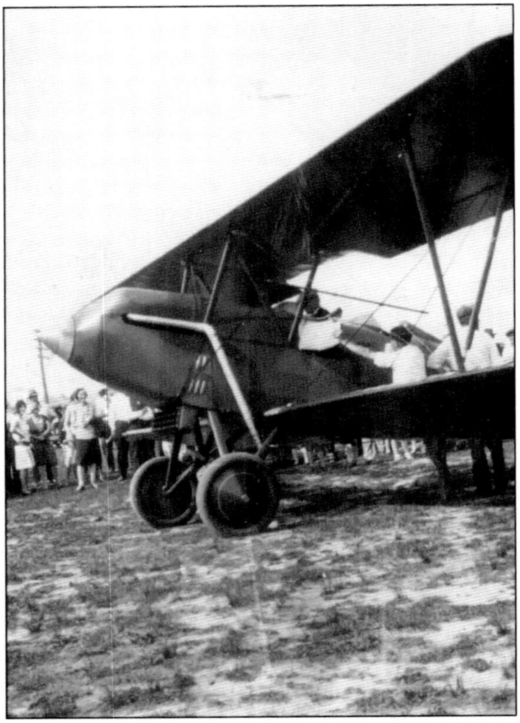

W.T. Popejoy is shown taking his first plane ride in 1936 shortly after his 81st birthday. According to a local newspaper, "Uncle Bill" enjoyed the ride very much; he even said that the plane did not go as high as he would have liked. He also earned the distinction of being the oldest person at the time to fly from that particular field. (Courtesy of Jennifer Hartman.)

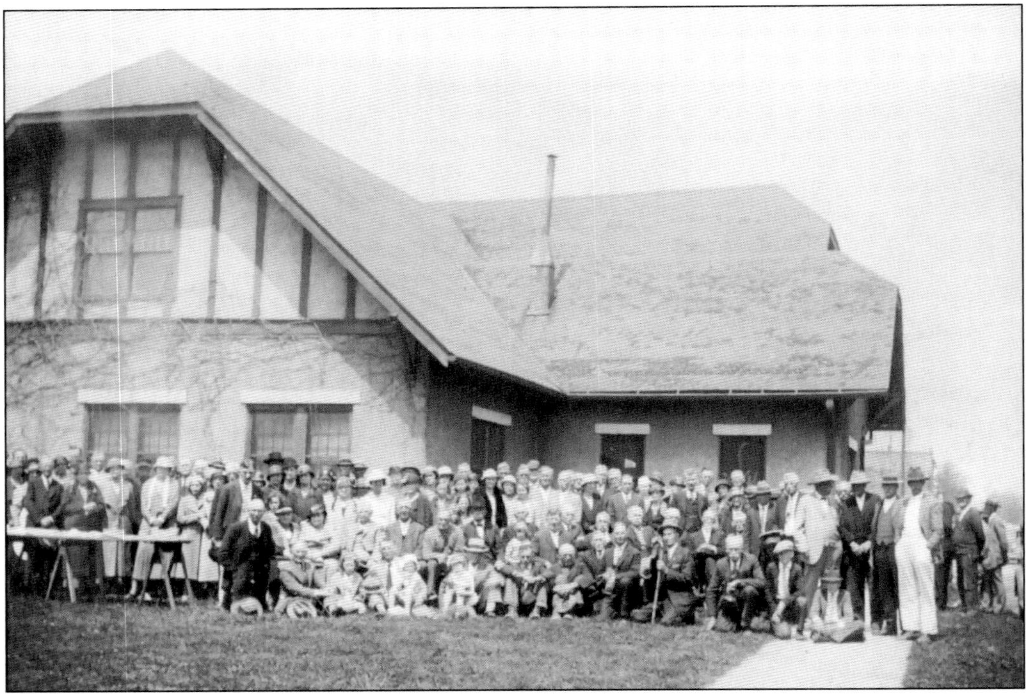

Beginning in 1930, survivors of the Marshfield cyclone gathered annually for a reunion. In 1938, however, the *Marshfield Mail* reported, "Very little mention of the storm was made this year. With H.E. Banning, head of the Marshfield Tornado Survivors organization, in Indiana . . . no reunion of survivors was held." *The Marshfield Mail* made no mention of it in 1939. (Courtesy of the Webster County Historical Museum.)

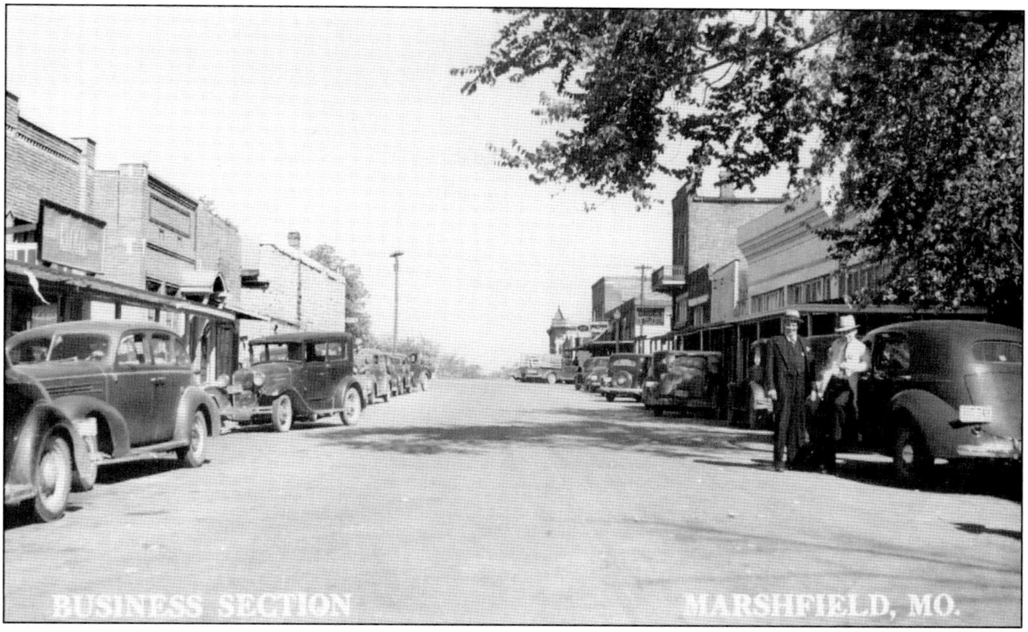

Crittenden Street is pictured sometime in the 1930s. On the left side of the street is the Kroger grocery store, as well as the Robertson Block building at the end of the street; on the right side of the street is the *Marshfield Mail* office and Rathbun's Drug Store. (Courtesy of Randy Clair.)

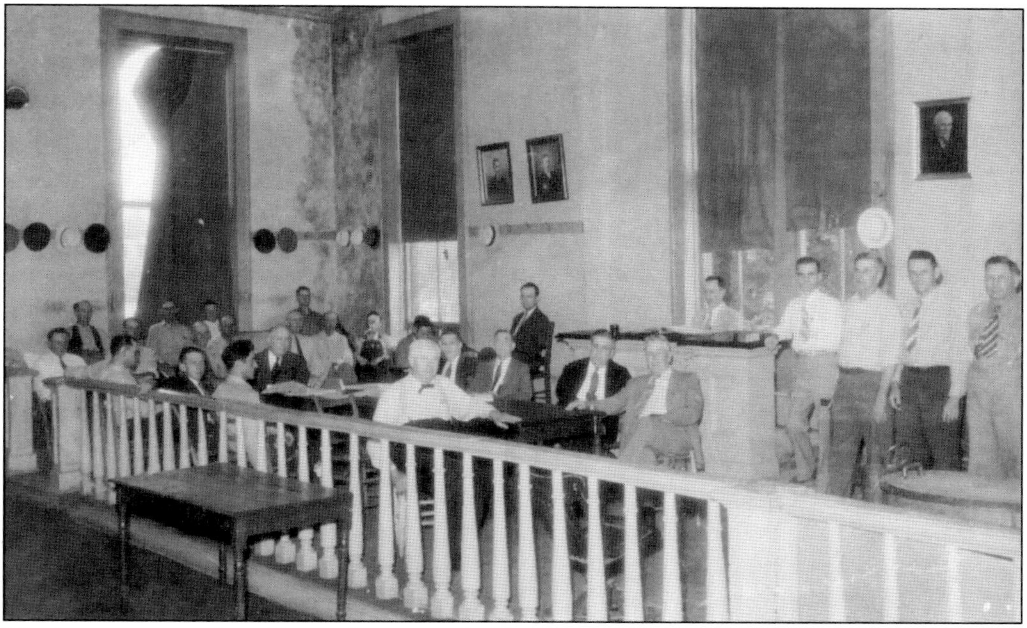

The last session in the old courthouse was held in June 1939. Bittersweet for many people, Paul Watters snapped this final photograph shortly before the structure was razed. The courthouse had been condemned and partially vacated nine years earlier; however, sessions moved back there after Redmen Lodge Hall, where the court was temporarily meeting, burned in 1932. (Courtesy of Randy Clair.)

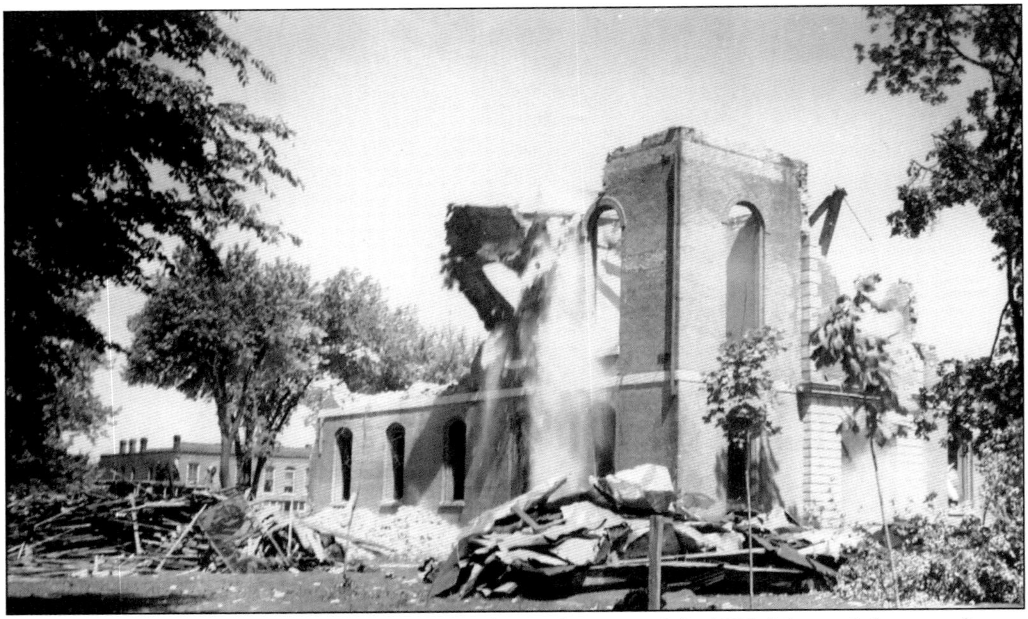

Demolition of the old Webster County Courthouse began in July 1939. Many of the courthouse offices moved to the Foster Building in the first week of July. Independence Day attendees were given one last look at the building before demolition began the next week. A temporary building, to house construction offices and tools, was soon constructed on the west side of the lawn. (Courtesy of Randy Clair.)

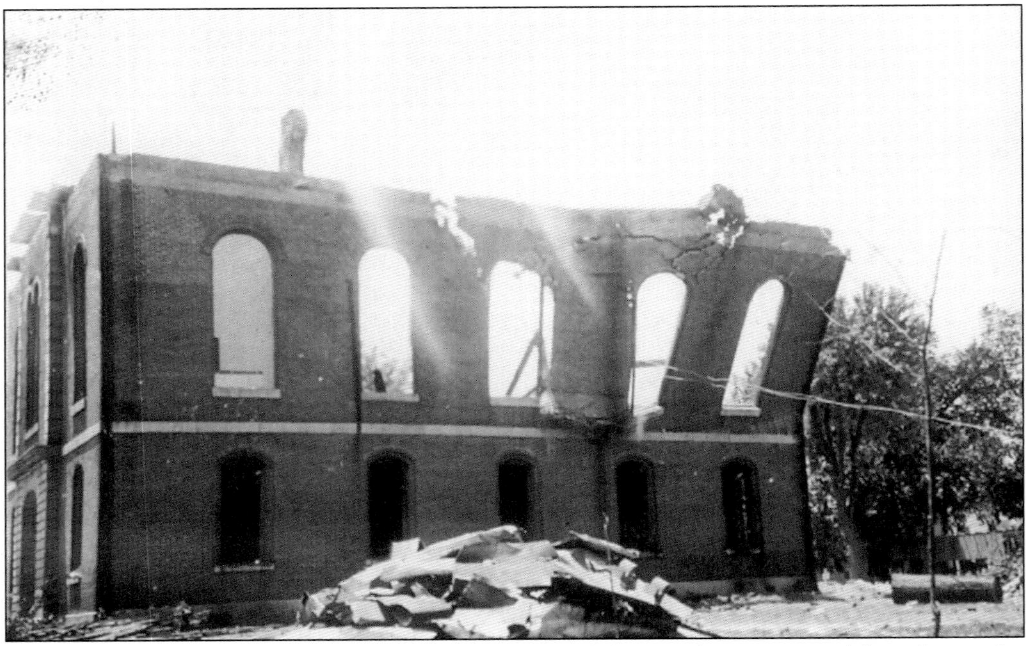

The city's road grader was used to pull down the walls of the courthouse's second floor during the demolition process. Several surprises occurred during the progression, including the discovery of a raised floor filled with gravel beneath the judge's platform, which was possibly created to deaden sound. Also, many historic papers, including ballots from when Abraham Lincoln was elected president, were also unearthed. (Courtesy of Randy Clair.)

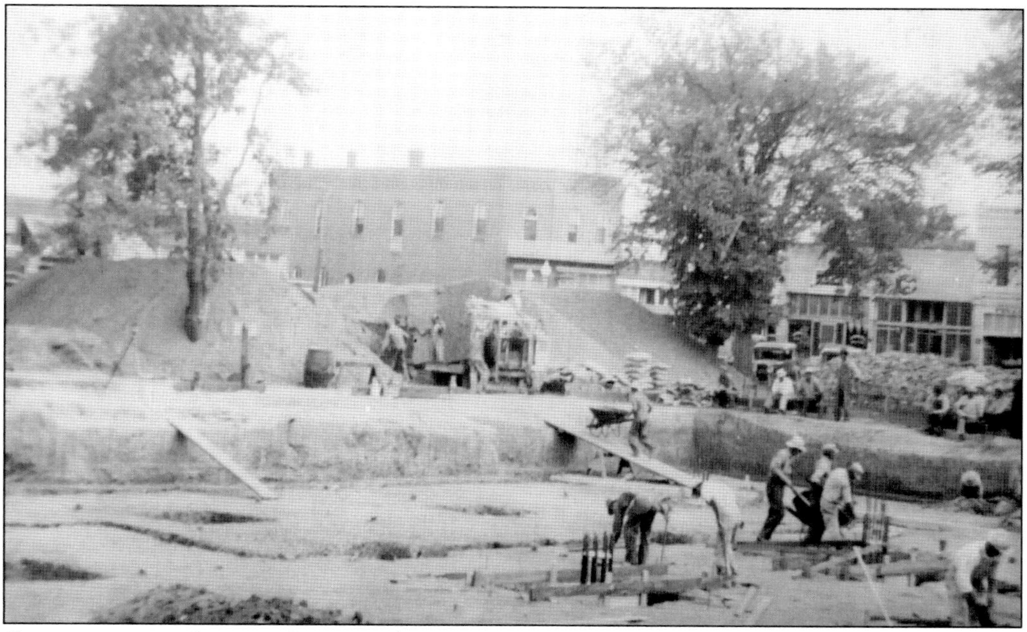

Construction workers are shown in the process of pouring beams for the new courthouse. After the old courthouse was demolished in 1939, work on the new facility began shortly thereafter, and it was greatly aided by the efforts of the Works Progressive Administration (WPA). In the background is the Rathbun Building, as well as portions of the east and south sides of the square. (Courtesy of Randy Clair.)

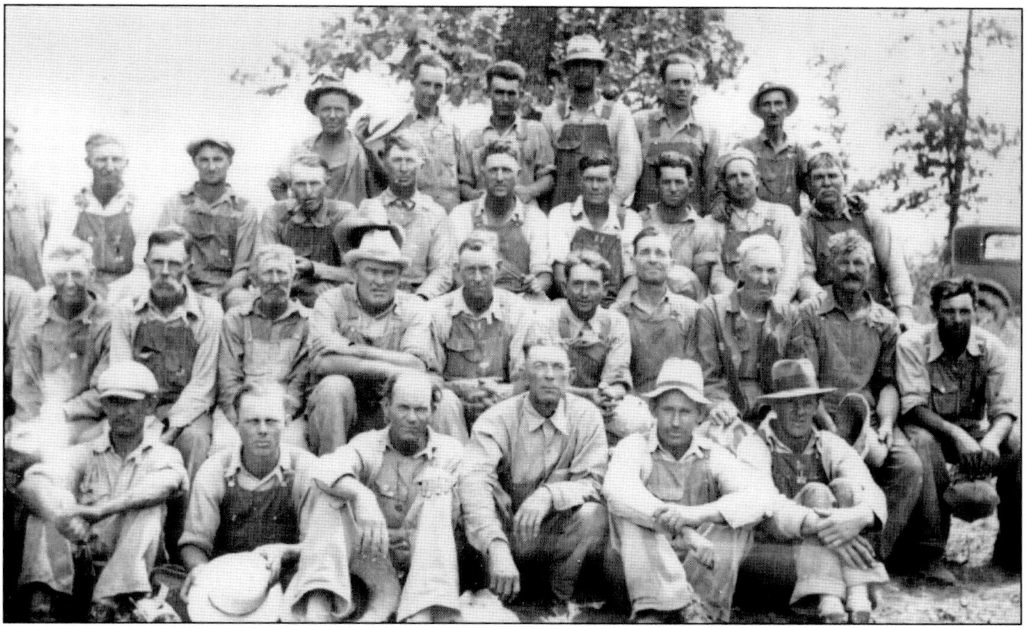

The WPA was instrumental in the construction of the Webster County Courthouse. Between 1939 and 1941, Marshfield saw WPA workers aiding in the construction of the new courthouse, as well as helping work on Marshfield's sewer system. At one point, more than 124 workers were assigned to the project, which consisted of digging and laying 10 miles of pipe throughout the town. (Courtesy of the Webster County Historical Museum.)

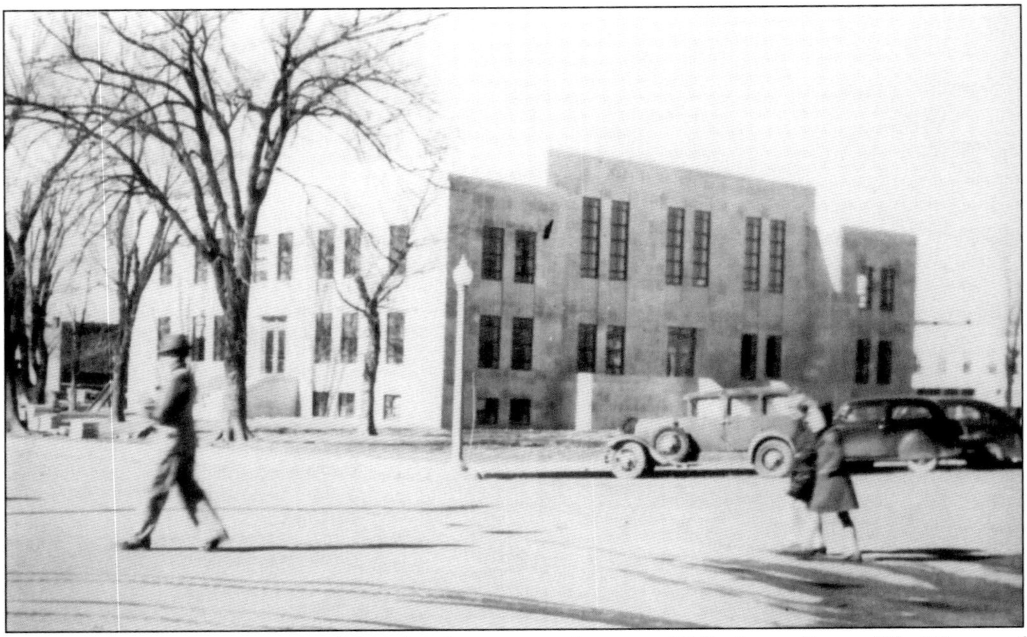

The new courthouse is pictured shortly after its completion in 1941. According to *The History of Webster County*, "The building [was] considered to be the most beautiful and modern for its size of any in the state of Missouri. . . . It [was] well landscaped, and with its velvety green lawn, and beautiful shade trees and shrubbery, it [was] much enjoyed by all the people of Webster County." (Courtesy of Randy Clair.)

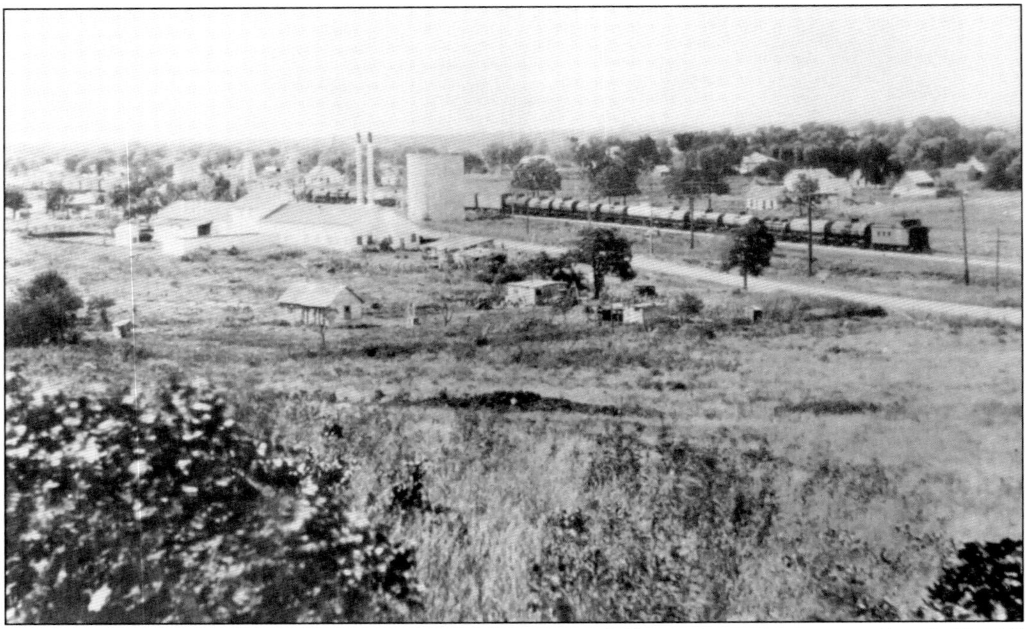

A view from Bald Hill to Marshfield in 1942 was quite different from the view today. Bald Hill was the site of Webster County's only legal hanging in 1872, when Charles Waller was executed for the murder of William Newlon, his wife, and baby. The hanging was a public event; according to the *Marshfield Citizen*, "Never so large a crowd has ever assembled in the southwest." (Courtesy of Randy Clair.)

Bert and Ola "Ollie" Blunt are pictured here on a typical Saturday afternoon in Marshfield. The couple is standing in front of Shields' Pharmacy on the east side of the square. Its windows are laden with advertisements, ranging from Rexall Drugs and Ex-Lax to the store's very own sales and promotions. (Courtesy of Jennifer Hartman.)

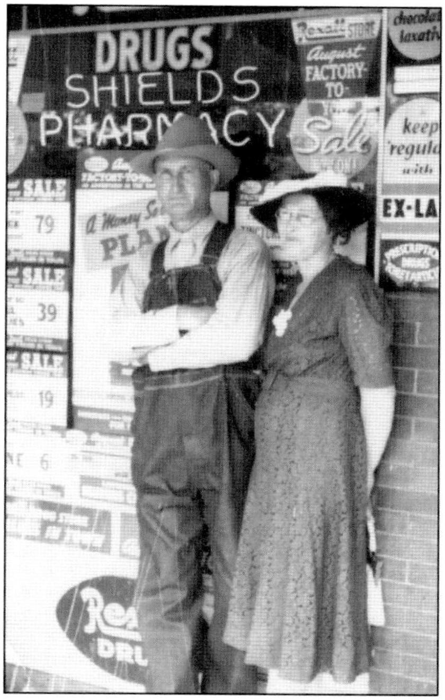

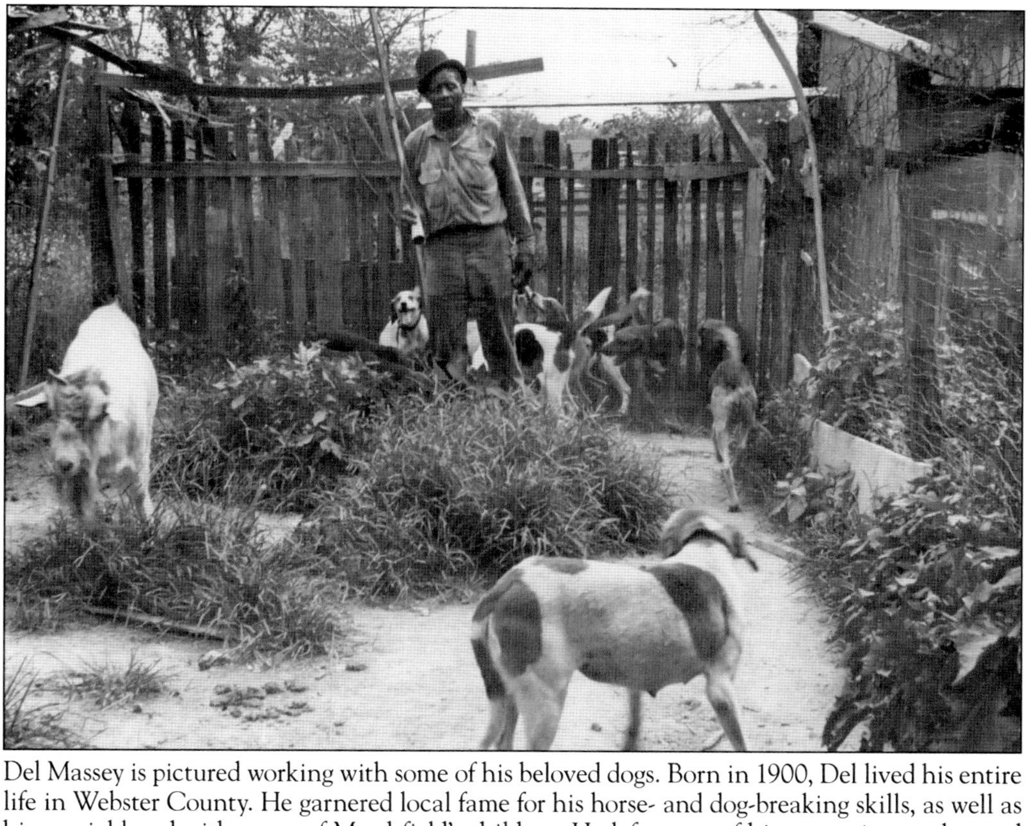

Del Massey is pictured working with some of his beloved dogs. Born in 1900, Del lived his entire life in Webster County. He garnered local fame for his horse- and dog-breaking skills, as well as his special bond with many of Marshfield's children. He left many of his possessions to be used for the betterment of the community's youngsters, ultimately resulting in Marshfield's Massey Park. (Courtesy of Randy Clair.)

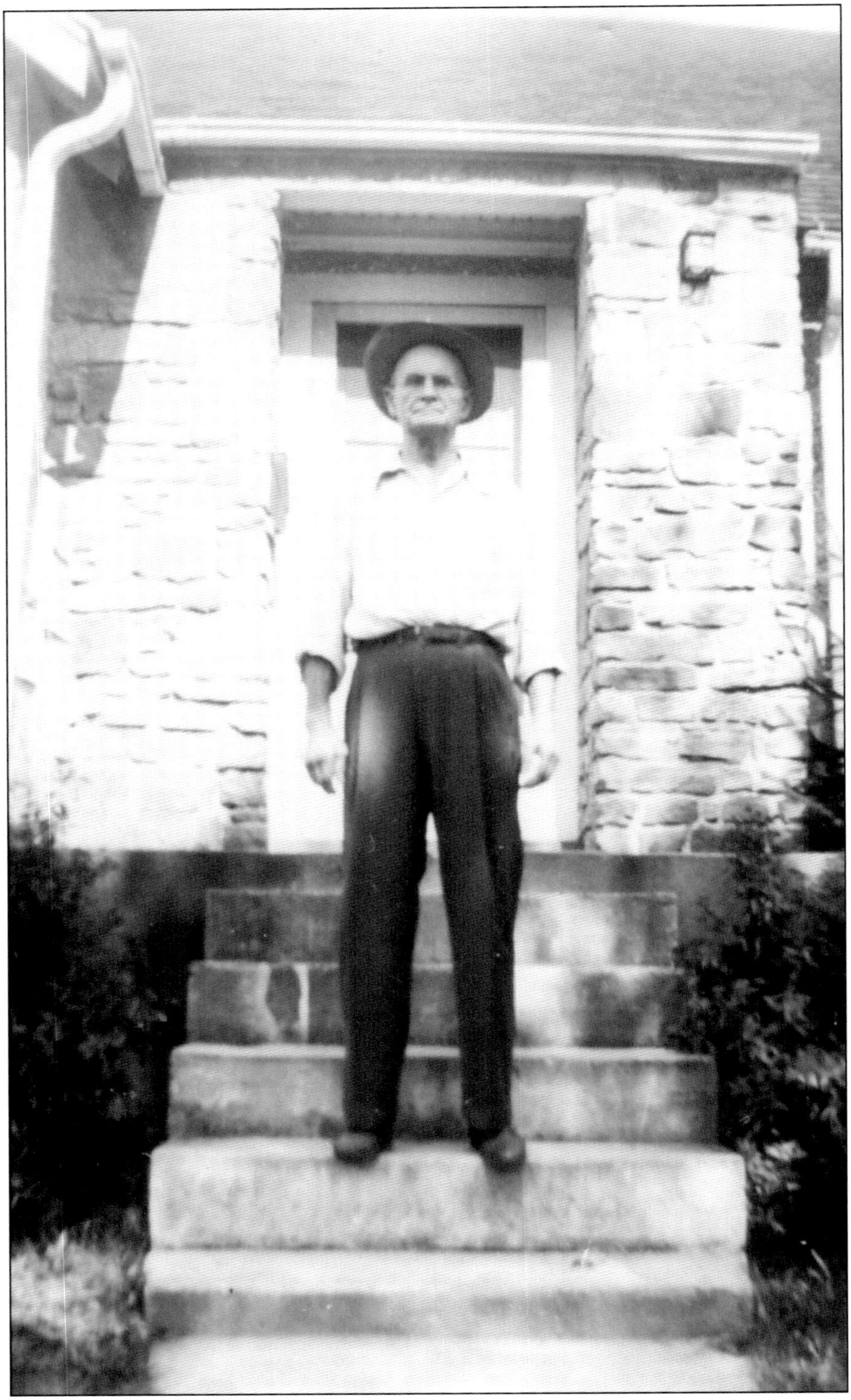

Frank Crittenden Day stands in front of his home on, coincidently, Crittenden Street. Day owned a dry goods store on the Marshfield Square at various times throughout the early to mid-1900s. His grandfather John Day was one of Webster County's earliest settlers and a member of the Marshfield Home Guard during the Civil War. (Courtesy of Jennifer Hartman.)

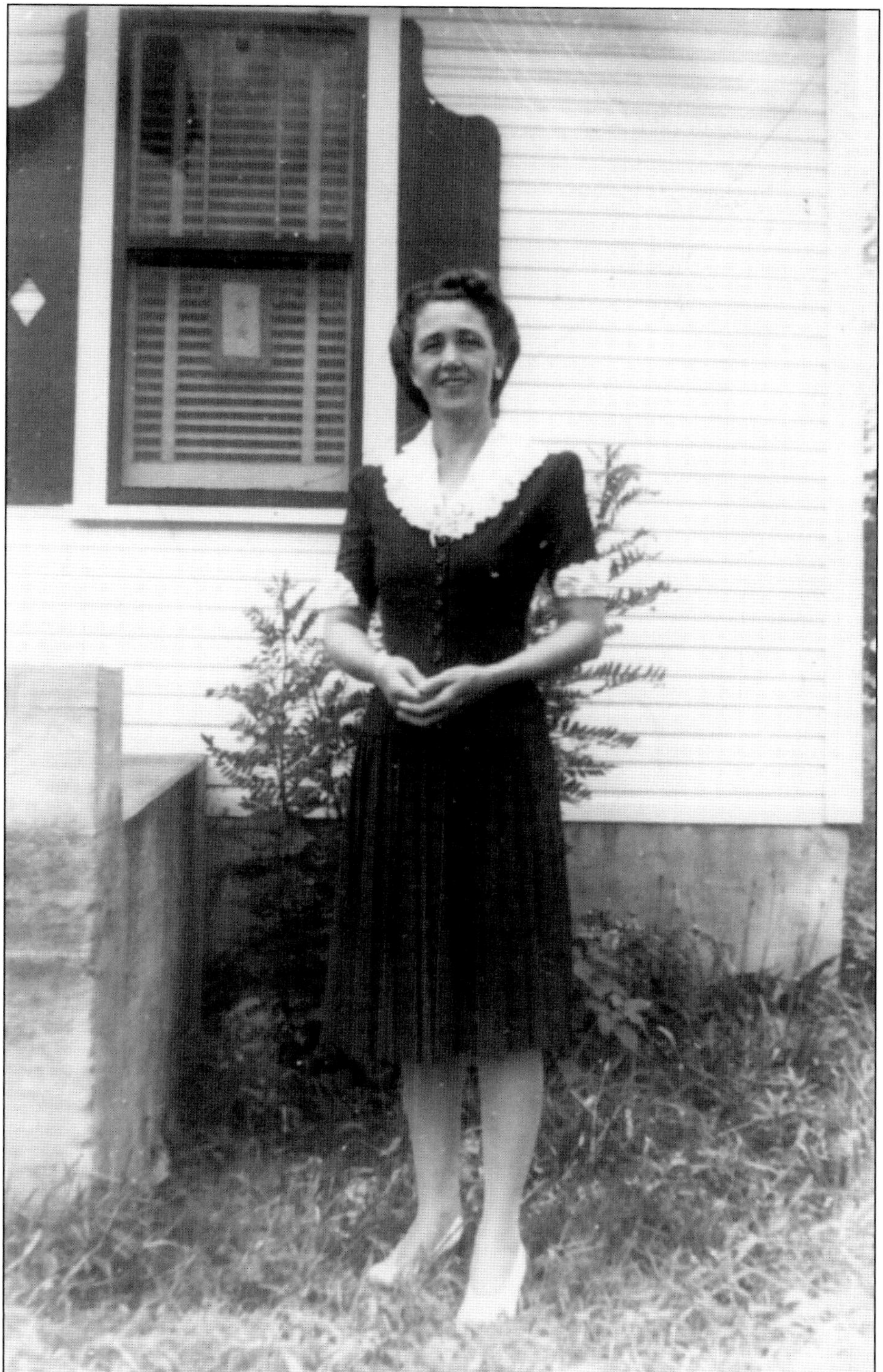

Delphine Popejoy poses for the camera in front of her home in Marshfield in the early 1940s. The two blue stars hanging in the window were in honor of her son Jim Popejoy and her son-in-law Bob Day, who were serving in the military during World War II. (Courtesy of Jennifer Hartman.)

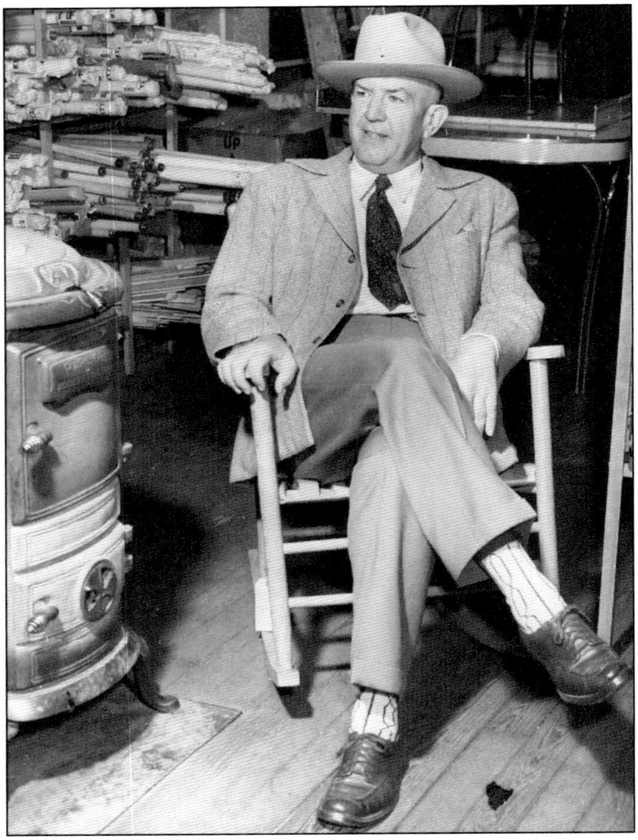

State representative and businessman Murray Thompson is pictured taking a moment to relax. Former owner of Thompson's Furniture Company, Thompson decided to enter politics after meeting Albert Reeves, a federal district court judge from Kansas City who suggested that the best way to get the country back under control was to have businessmen, such as Thompson, involved. He was elected to the state legislature in 1940 and later went on to run unsuccessfully for governor in 1948. (Courtesy of the Webster County Historical Museum.)

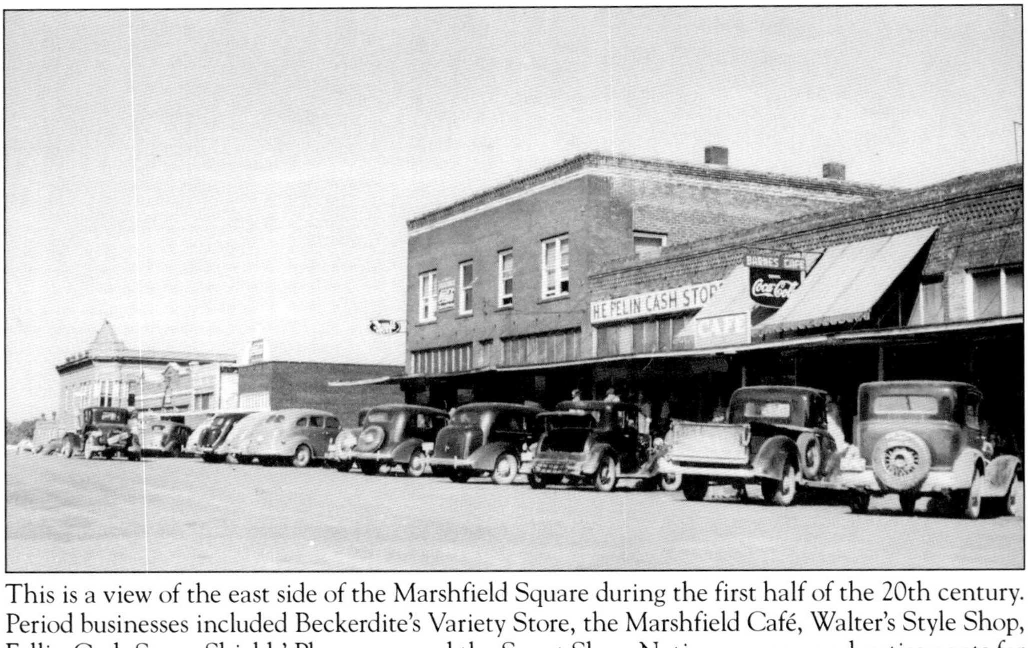

This is a view of the east side of the Marshfield Square during the first half of the 20th century. Period businesses included Beckerdite's Variety Store, the Marshfield Café, Walter's Style Shop, Fellin Cash Store, Shields' Pharmacy, and the Sweet Shop. Notice numerous advertisements for Coca-Cola, Rexall Drugs, and the people who have gathered to talk in front of Fellin Cash Store. (Courtesy of the Webster County Historical Museum.)

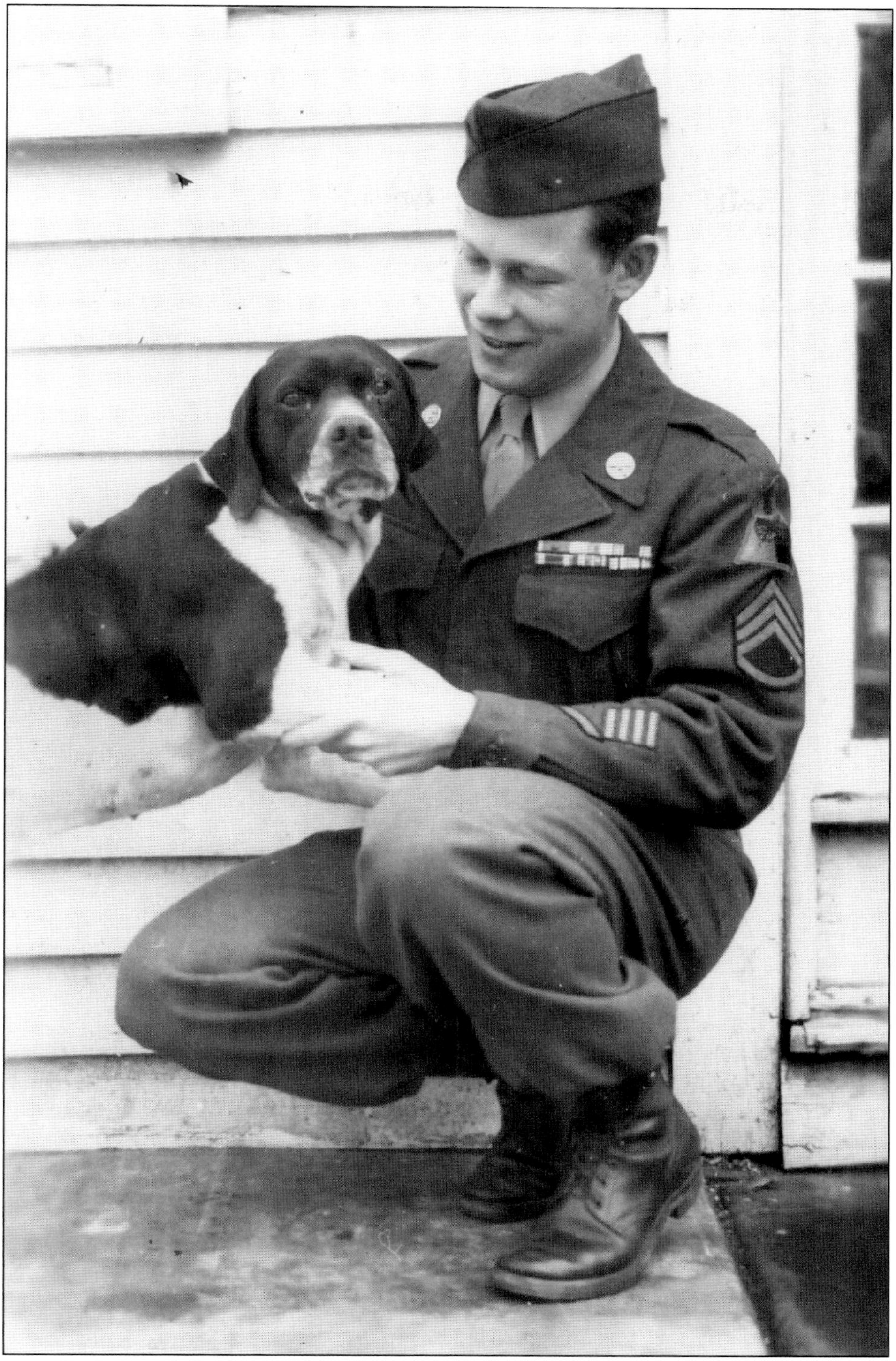

A young Dr. Tommy Macdonnell is pictured in the mid-1940s after returning from service during World War II. In just a few short years, he would join his father's medical practice in Marshfield and become one of the town's most beloved and longtime doctors. He was also elected to the state legislature from 1986 to 1994. (Courtesy of Dr. Tommy Macdonnell.)

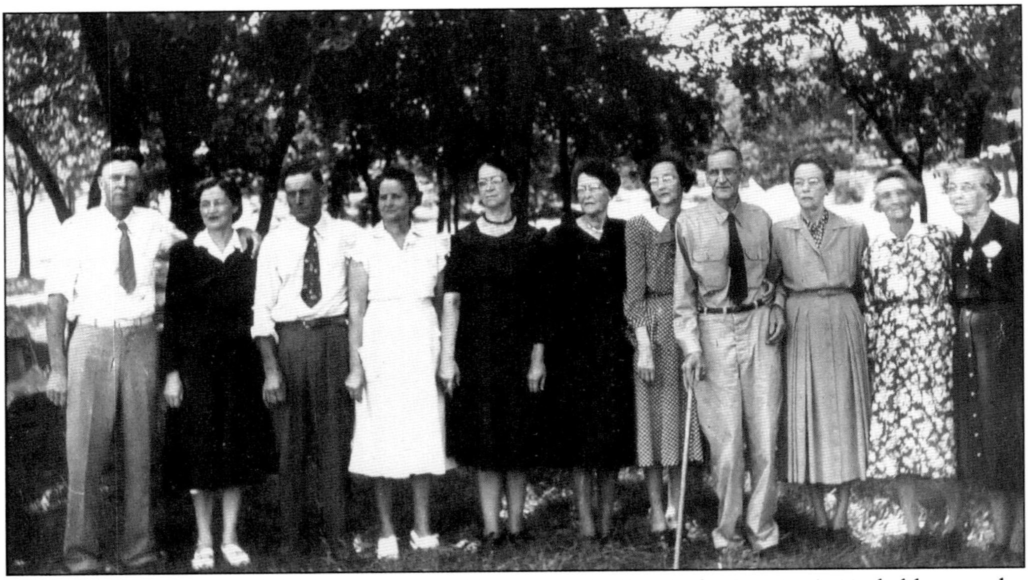

A reunion of William "Bill" Torrence and Mary Ann "Polly" Rader Popejoy's 11 children at the Marshfield City Park was held in 1948. They are, standing from left to right and youngest to oldest, Elmer Popejoy, Ruth Carter, Ed Popejoy, Nora King, Minnie King, Ola Rogers, Vida Gerhardt, Jim Popejoy, Maggie Davis, Nannie Hewett, and Lizzie Myers. (Courtesy of Jennifer Hartman.)

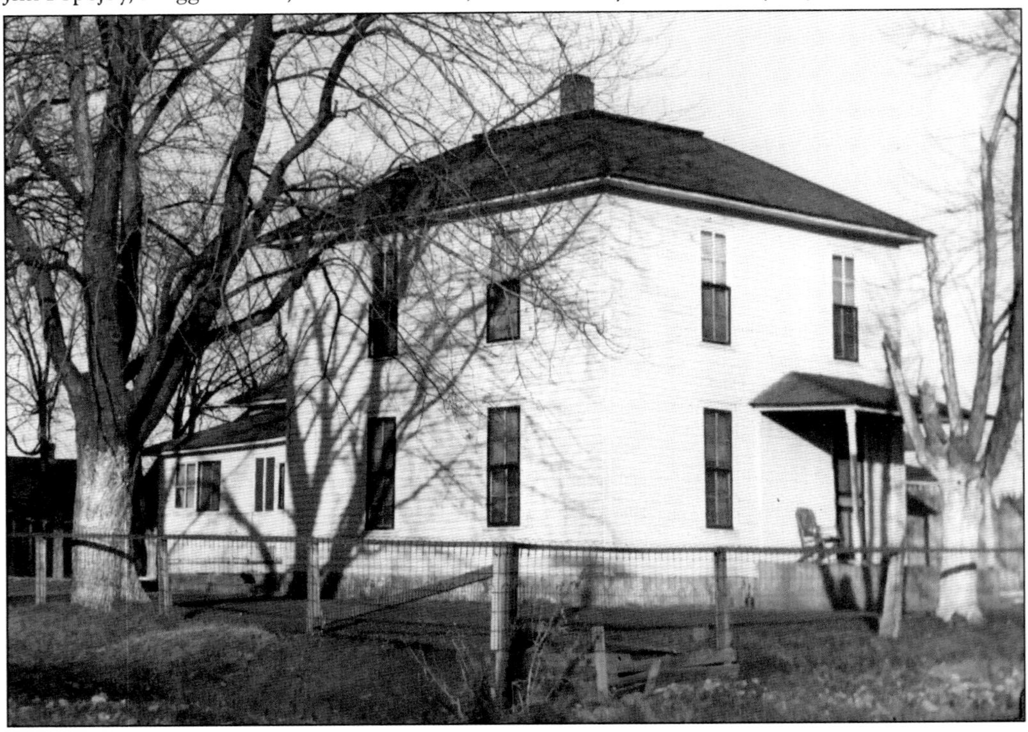

The Webster County Poor Farm caretaker's residence is pictured in the late 1940s. For many years, the poor farm housed the area's poor, indigent, and mentally incompetent. The original poor farm was built in 1884 and was self-sufficient; residents were expected to earn their keep by working around the farm. Eventually the work was eliminated and a nominal fee was charged instead. (Courtesy of Dr. Tommy Macdonnell.)

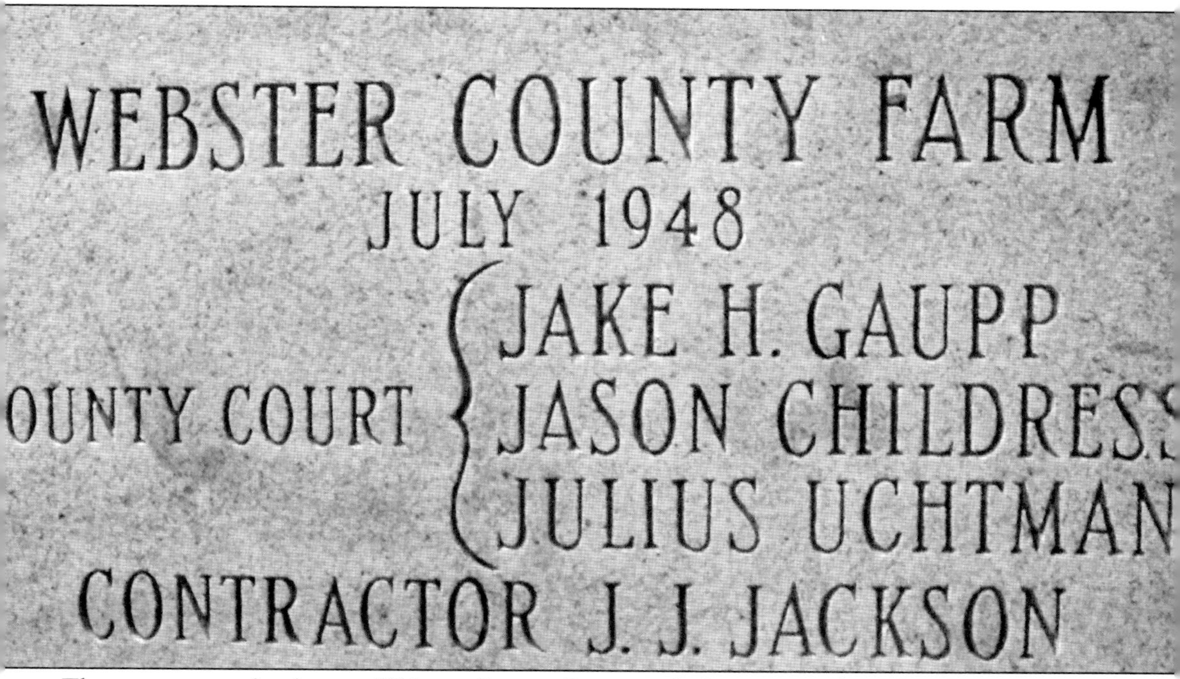

The cornerstone for the new Webster County Farm was laid in 1948. After a bond was passed, construction was soon complete on a new, "modern" facility. There was one problem—the bond paid for the building, but not any furnishings. The issue was solved with help from several Marshfield organizations, including the Marshfield Business and Professional Women's (BFW) and Lions Clubs, which raised the funds for immediate necessities. (Courtesy of the Webster County Historical Museum.)

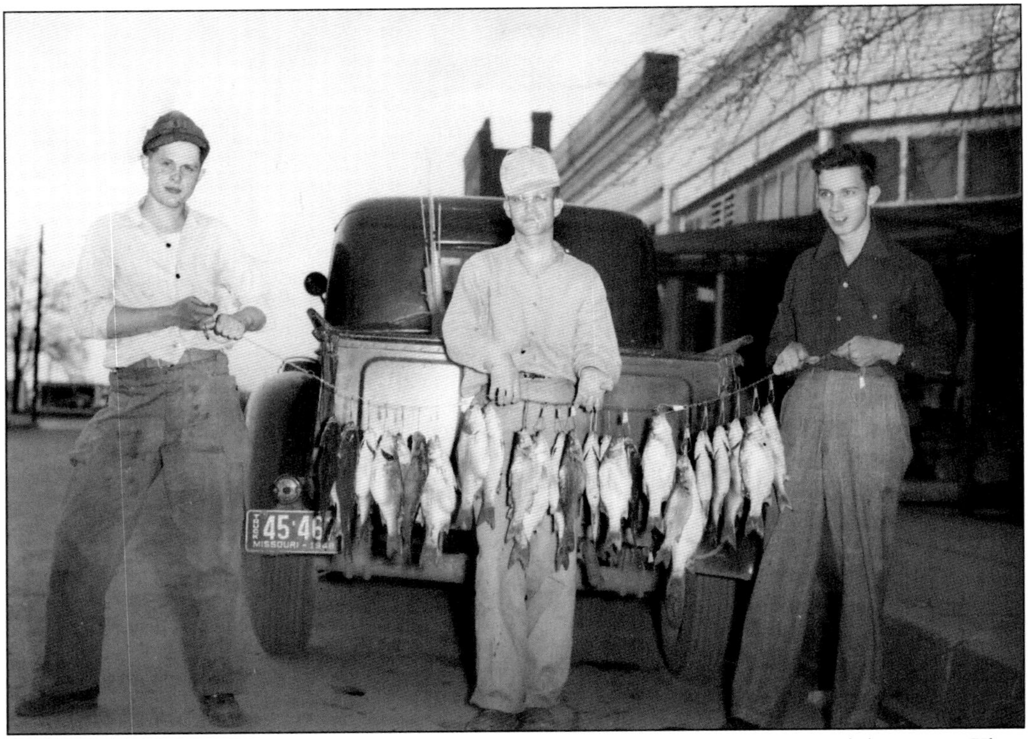

Three friends take a quick break for a photograph in 1948 after returning from a fishing trip. They are, from left to right, Bill Brooks, H.K. Campbell, and Johnnie Andrews Jr. The trio often fished together, traveling to places such as Forsyth and Tecumseh. (Courtesy of Ruth Brooks.)

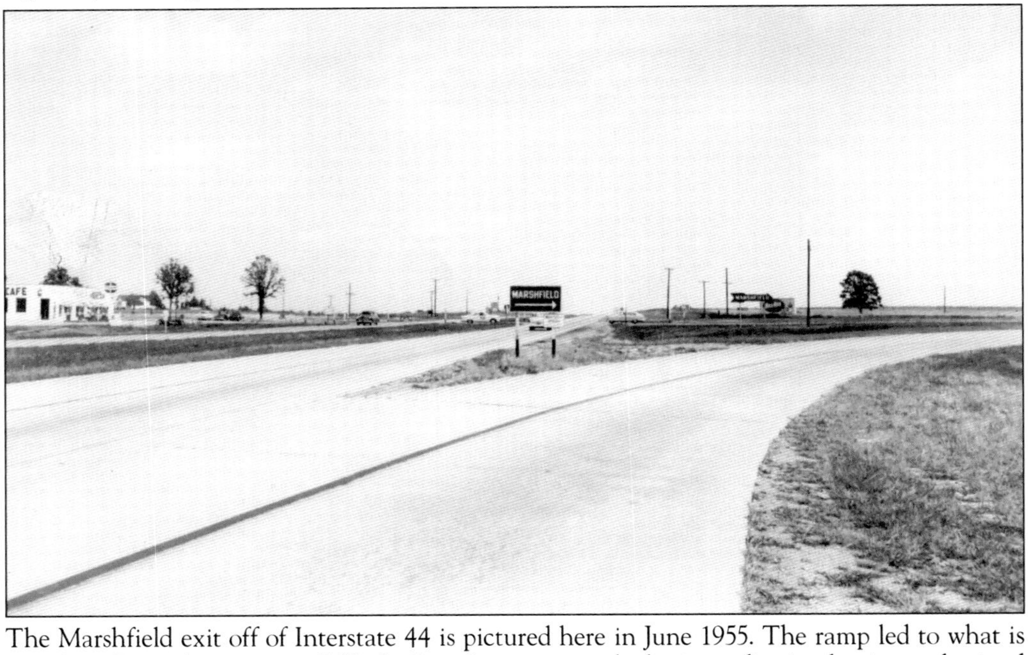

The Marshfield exit off of Interstate 44 is pictured here in June 1955. The ramp led to what is now Spur Drive; however, in 1955, the "spur" was not yet the business district that it was destined to become. On the left is the Spur Café, which was owned and operated by George and Jean Barnes. (Courtesy of Randy Clair.)

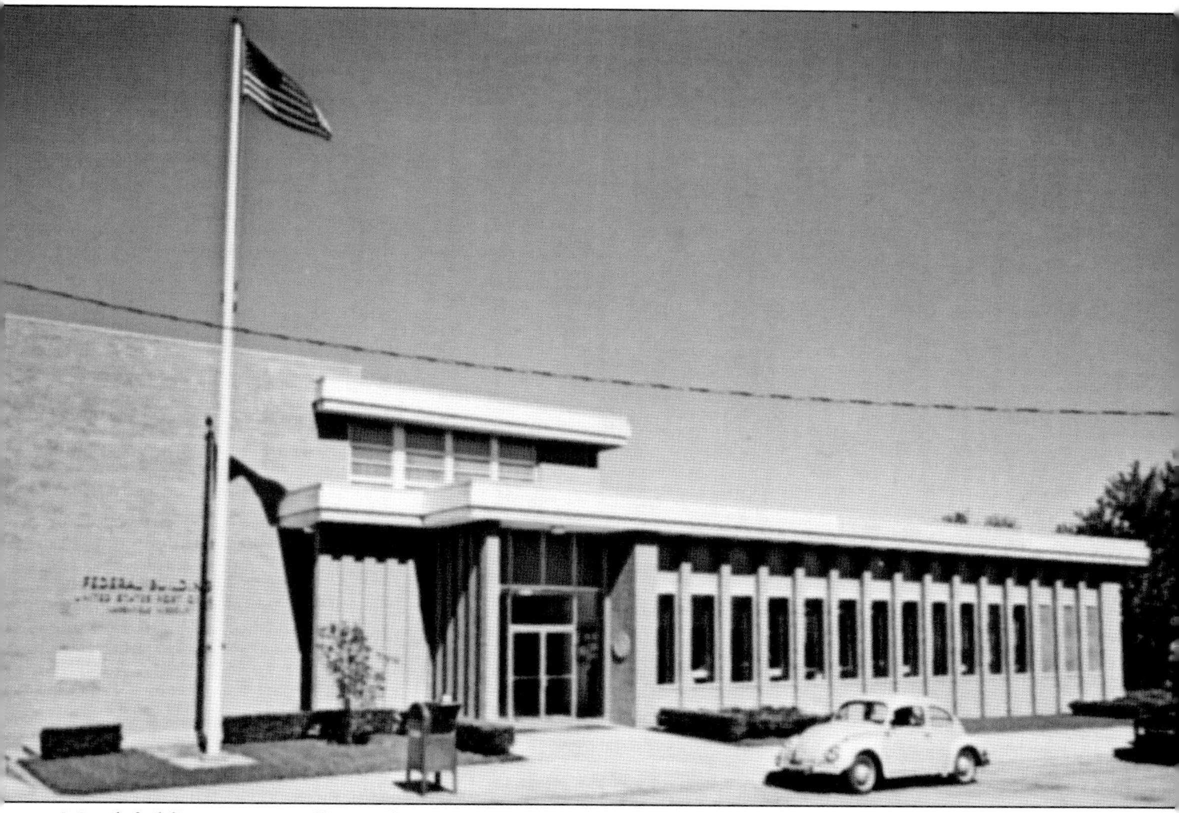

Marshfield's new post office is featured on this penny postcard that was available at Beckerdite's Variety Store. In 1938, the town received land for the construction of a new post office at the corner of Clay and Jefferson Streets, and the ground-breaking was held after the Independence Day parade in July 1958. The building was dedicated on July 4, 1959, and is still in use today. (Courtesy of Randy Clair.)

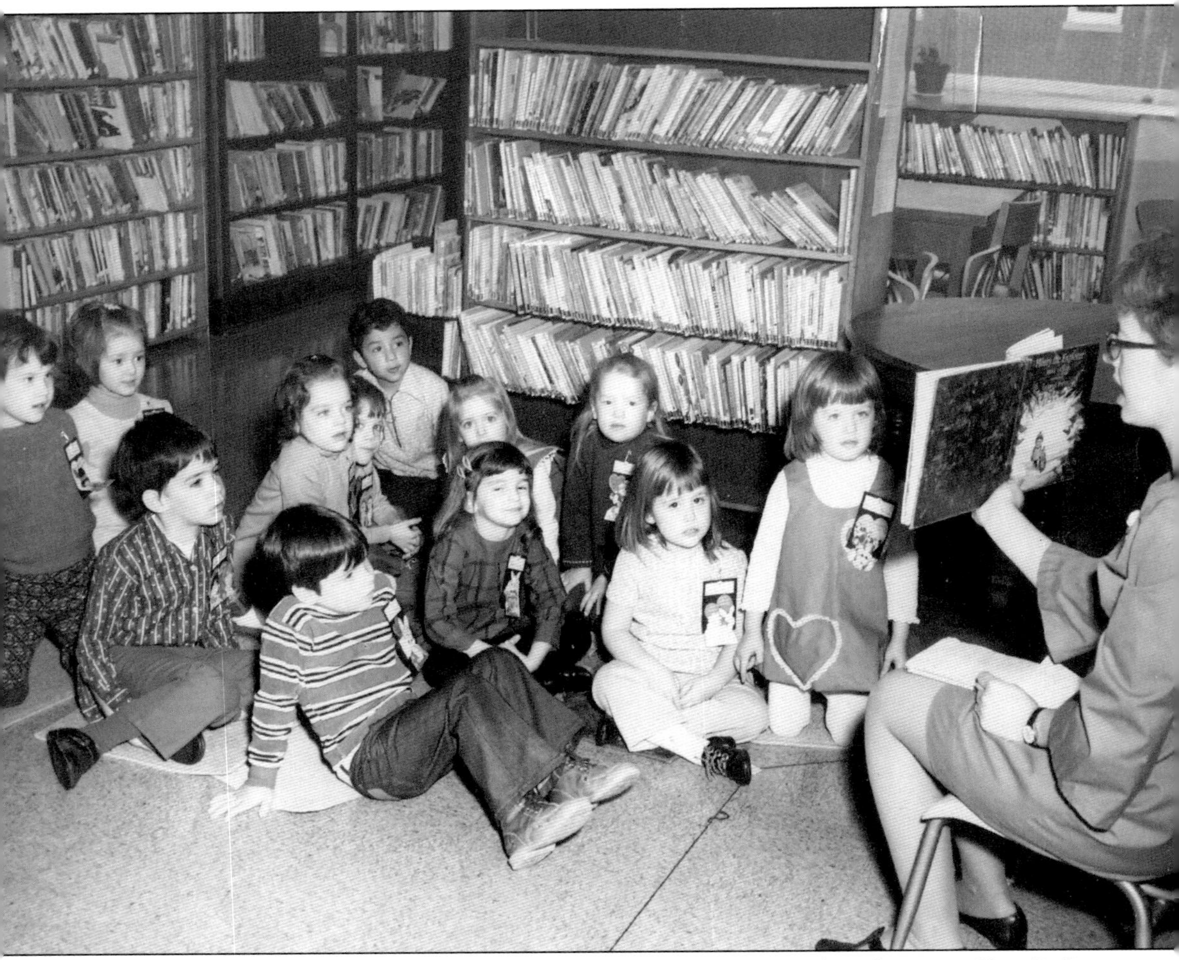

Pictured in February 1973, a group of children attending morning story hour listens to Clara DePriest reading a book. In no particular order are Rodney Bennett, Doug Greer, Marta Case, Carol Terry, Jennifer Brown, Amy Highfill, Angie Myers, Sally Pekarek, Kenneth Dishman, Jonathan Gutierrez, Sabrina Lewis, and Linda Casarotta. (Courtesy of the Webster County Historical Museum.)

Two

THE RISE OF INDUSTRY

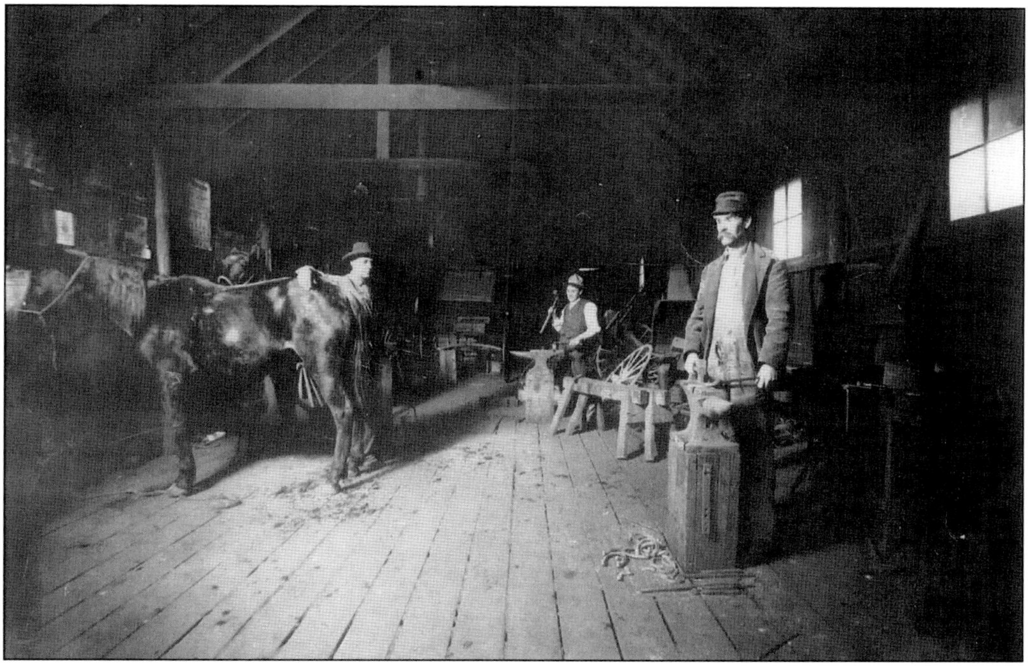

John McVay stands in Marshfield's blacksmith shop during the late 1800s. As many other rural communities, Marshfield's early days saw the presence of a town blacksmith to deal with equine issues and various other metal construction. McVay, who married Nancy "Nanny" Hamilton, came to Marshfield at the age of one. He relocated with his father, Pleasant McVay, from Tazewell, Tennessee; his mother died en route to Marshfield. (Courtesy of Jennifer Hartman.)

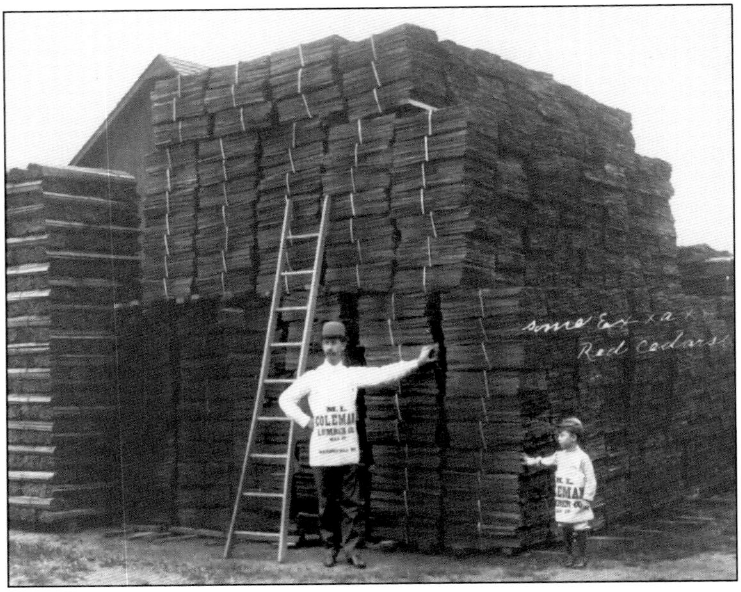

Ahrend Muehring, manager of the Coleman Lumber Company, is pictured in September 1909. The note written on the image indicates that Muehring is standing next to extra red cedars. The aprons worn by Muehring and the young boy also served as advertisements, stating, "M.L. Coleman Lumber Co. Has It. Marshfield, MO." (Courtesy of the Webster County Historical Museum.)

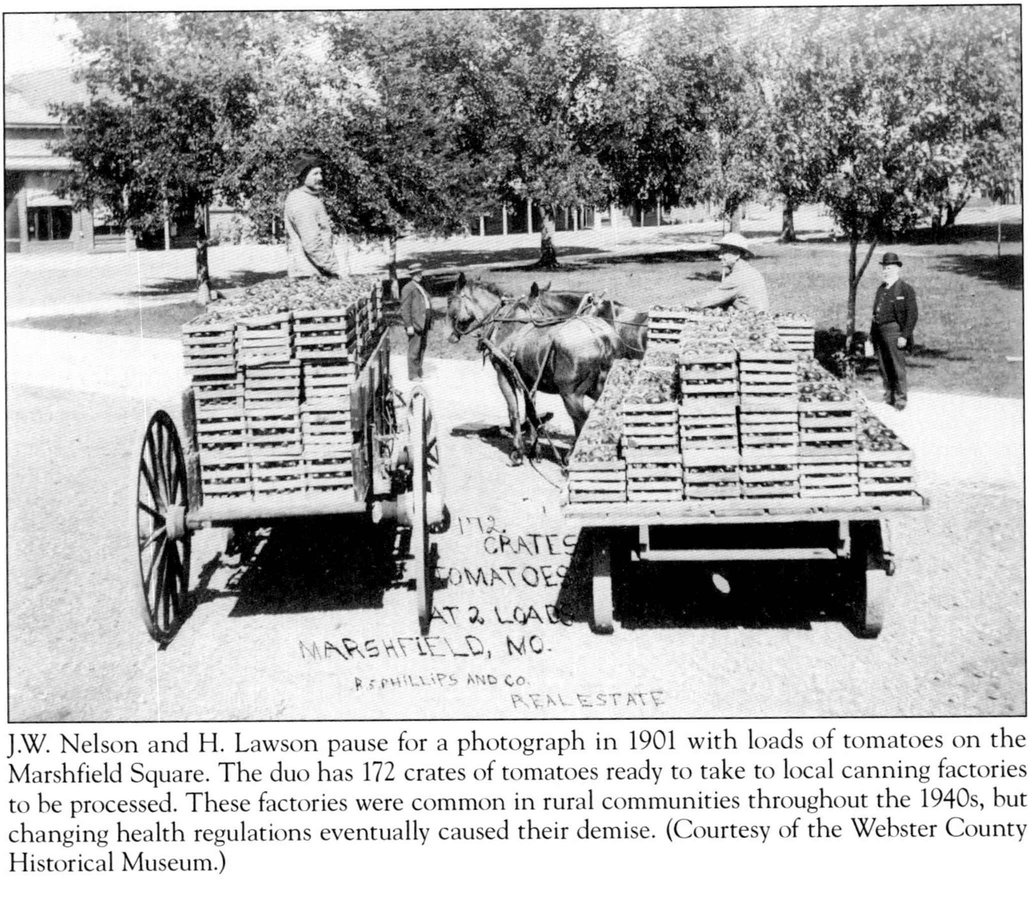

J.W. Nelson and H. Lawson pause for a photograph in 1901 with loads of tomatoes on the Marshfield Square. The duo has 172 crates of tomatoes ready to take to local canning factories to be processed. These factories were common in rural communities throughout the 1940s, but changing health regulations eventually caused their demise. (Courtesy of the Webster County Historical Museum.)

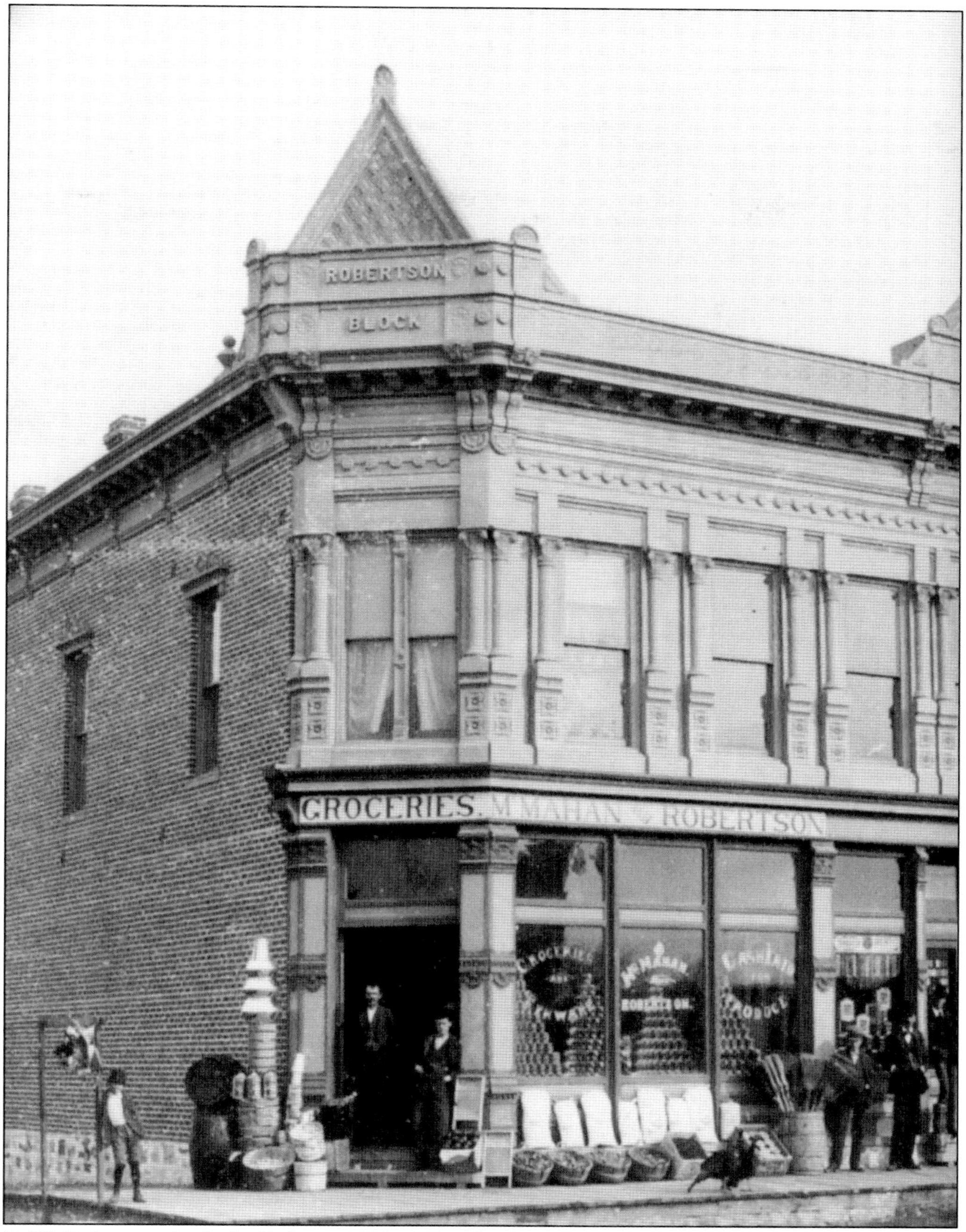

D. W. Robertson built the Robertson Block Building in 1894. Robertson was involved in numerous enterprises in the community, including hardware and lumber businesses. In the early 1900s, he created a lake in Marshfield by damming up water from the nearby Shackleford Spring. In the summer it was a popular recreation spot, and in the winter it provided ice for Robertson's icehouse. (Courtesy of the Webster County Historical Museum.)

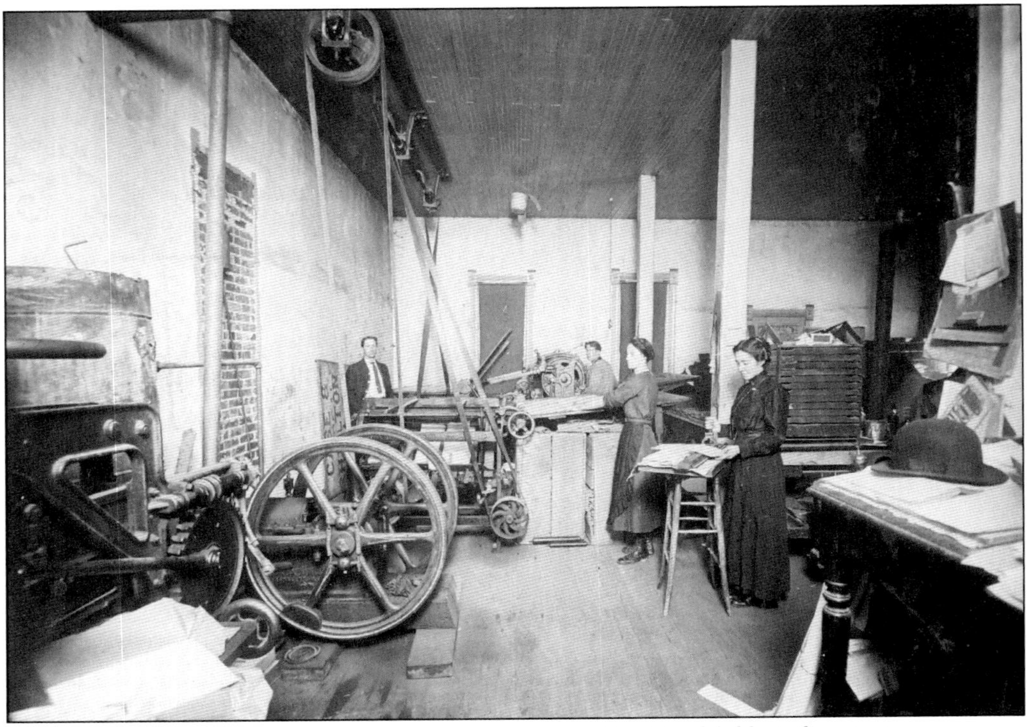

The *Marshfield Mail*'s printing press and workroom is pictured in 1913. Dating back to 1892, the *Marshfield Mail* is the city's oldest business in operation. The paper began on the second floor of the Brooks Building and moved numerous times thereafter, spending many years on Crittenden Street before moving to Clay Street in 1967. (Courtesy of Randy Clair.)

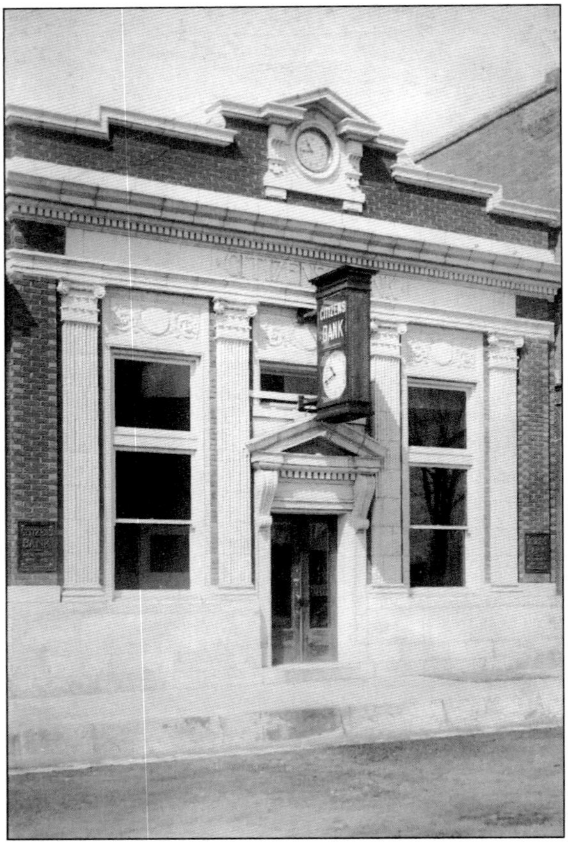

The Citizens Bank of Marshfield is shown in 1919. Founded in 1896, the bank began with a capital stock of $10,000 and was located on the south side of the square. In 1934, it reorganized under a state charter as the Citizens State Bank of Marshfield after the bank holiday in 1933 during the Depression. After moving to the west and then north sides of the square, the bank eventually merged with Metropolitan National Bank. (Courtesy of Randy Clair.)

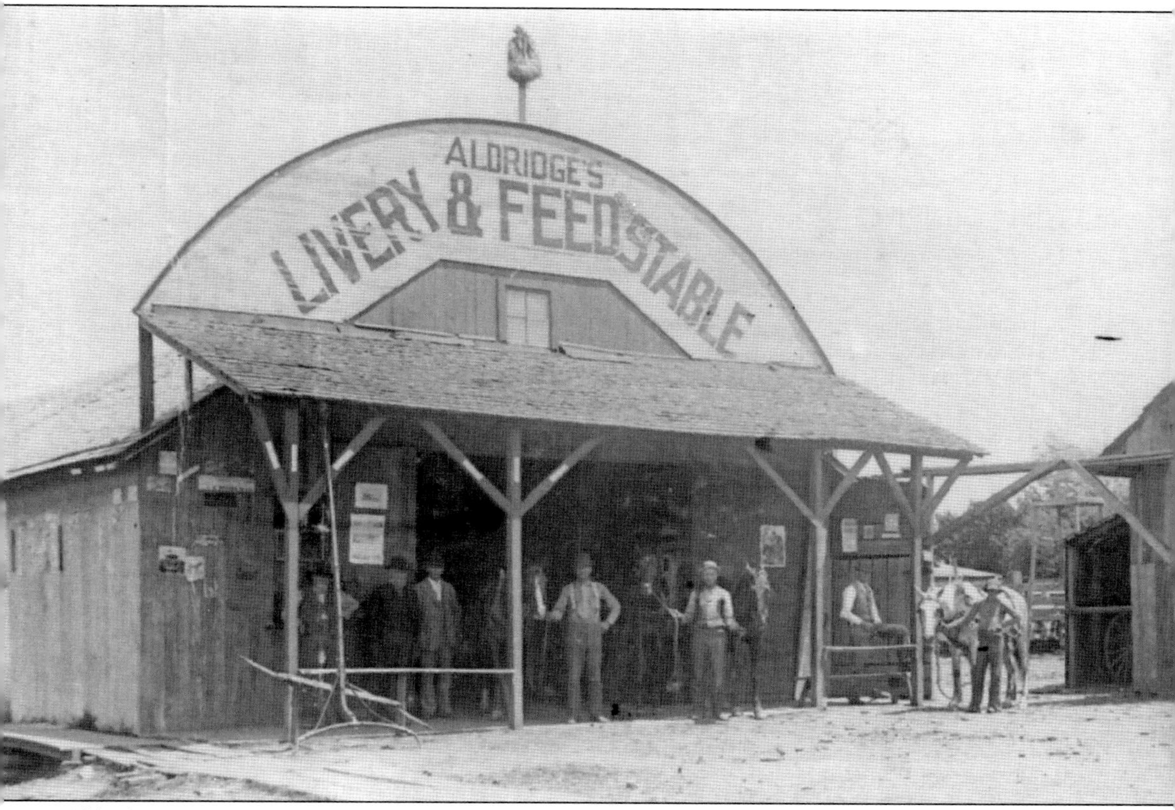

Aldridge's Livery and Feed stable was once near what would later be the location of the Marshfield Mill. At one time, Marshfield was home to five livery stables, with four of them located on Jackson Street. Farmers who came in for regular "tradin' " at the stores often left their horses at a livery to have them fed and watered. (Courtesy of the Webster County Historical Museum.)

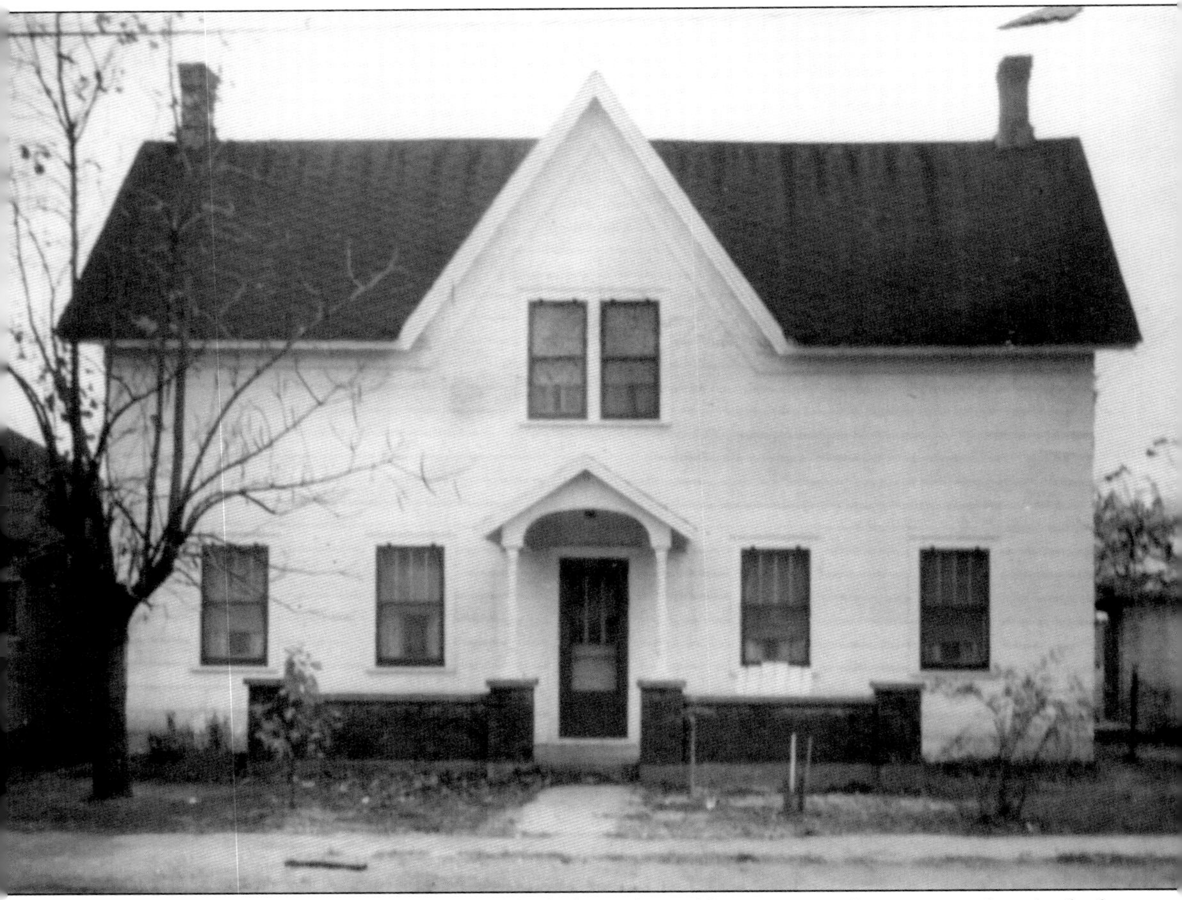

The City Hotel was located about a block from the public square and was a popular abode for travelers. It began operation in 1892 and contained rooms that could be rented by the day, week, or month. The 1924 "Message to the Homeseeker," a promotional booklet for the community, stated, "Leading commercial men who visit Marshfield make the City Hotel their headquarters." (Courtesy of the Webster County Historical Museum.)

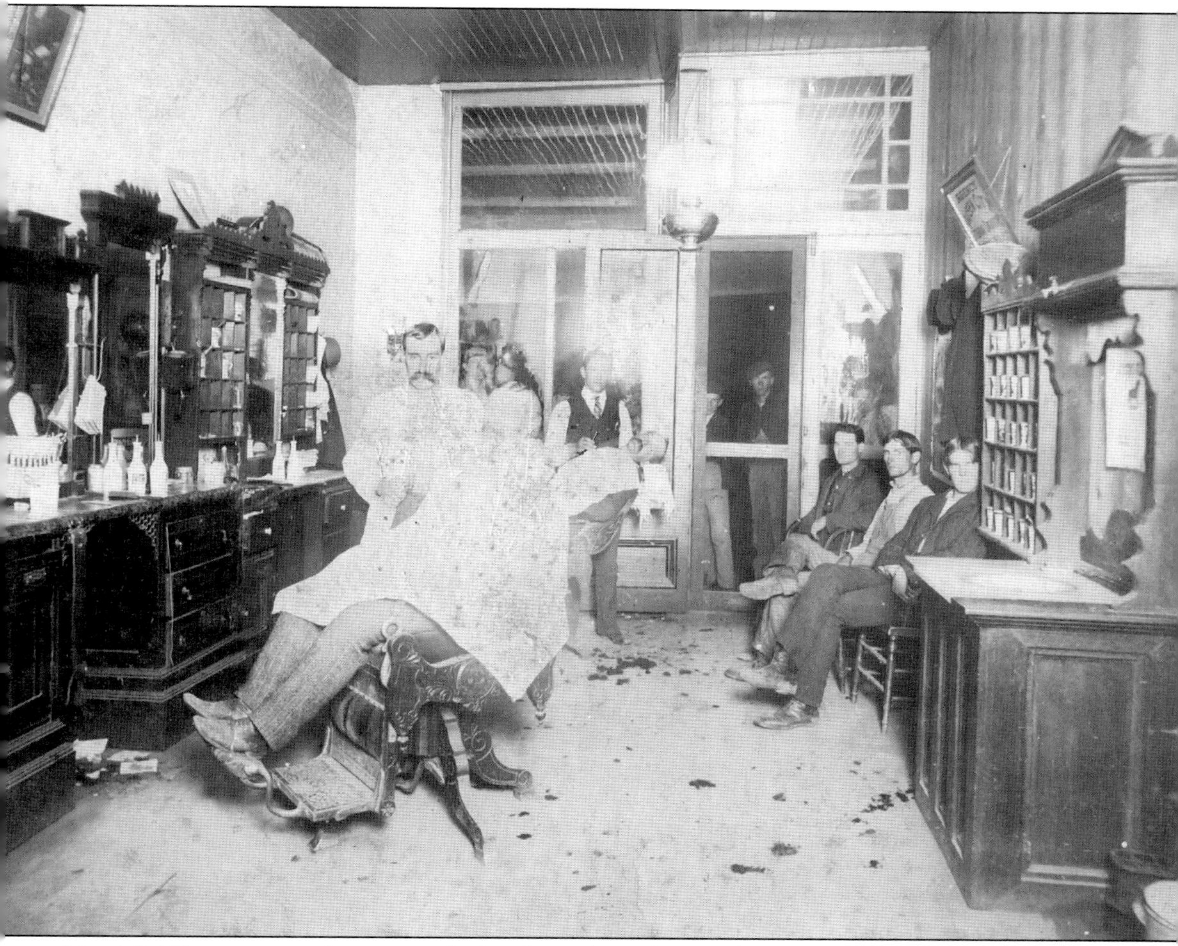

Marshfield has supported numerous barbershops throughout its history, and this one was located on the east side of the Marshfield Square. The barber in the back is Theron Watters, who later became famous throughout Marshfield for his role in the town concert band, as well as with the *Marshfield Mail.* An item of note is Watters's trombone, at the ready and placed on top of the shelving unit. (Courtesy of Randy Clair.)

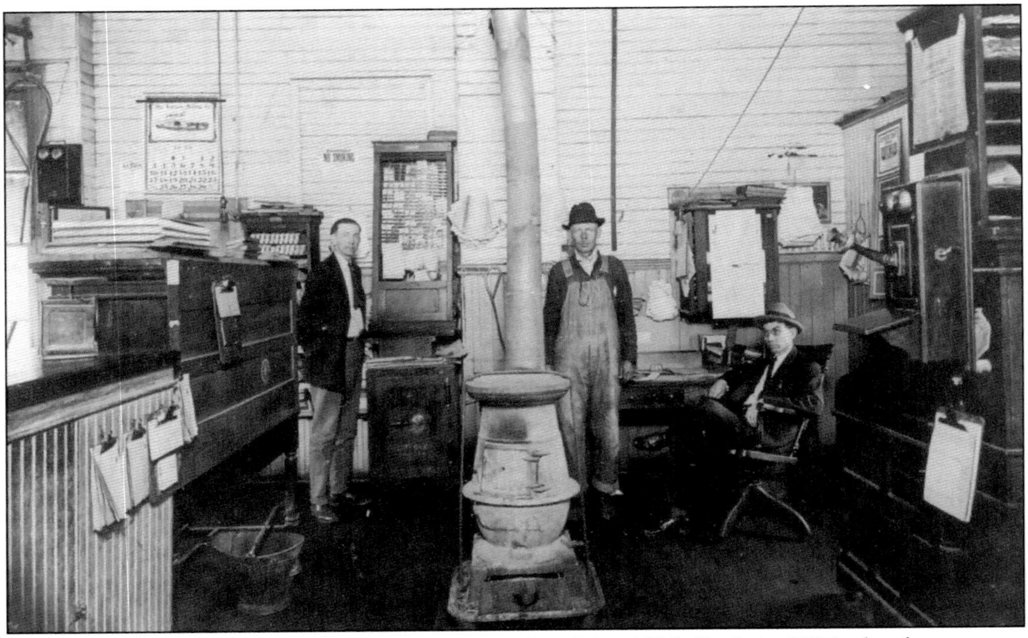

The interior of the Marshfield Depot is pictured in May 1925. Built in 1886, the depot was a hub of activity throughout its existence, both for transportation and social reasons. Paralleling Jackson Street, it was constructed after the San Francisco–St. Louis Railroad Company, adding a line running through town. (Courtesy of the Webster County Historical Museum.)

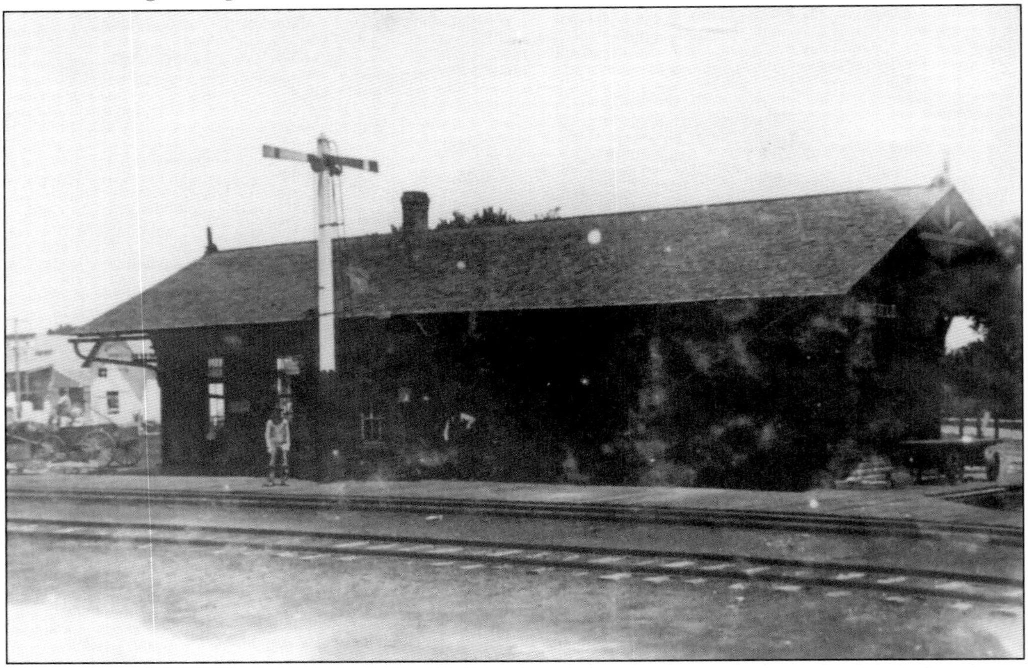

This is the exterior of the Marshfield depot as it appeared in the early 1900s. The depot saw many of the area's tomatoes, as well as butter from Marshfield's Sugar Creek Creamery, shipped nationwide. Passenger trains stopped twice daily: the 8:00 a.m. train headed to Oklahoma, while the 4:00 p.m. train went to St. Louis. The last passenger train rolled through town on May 13, 1967, and the depot officially closed in 1971. (Courtesy of the Webster County Historical Museum.)

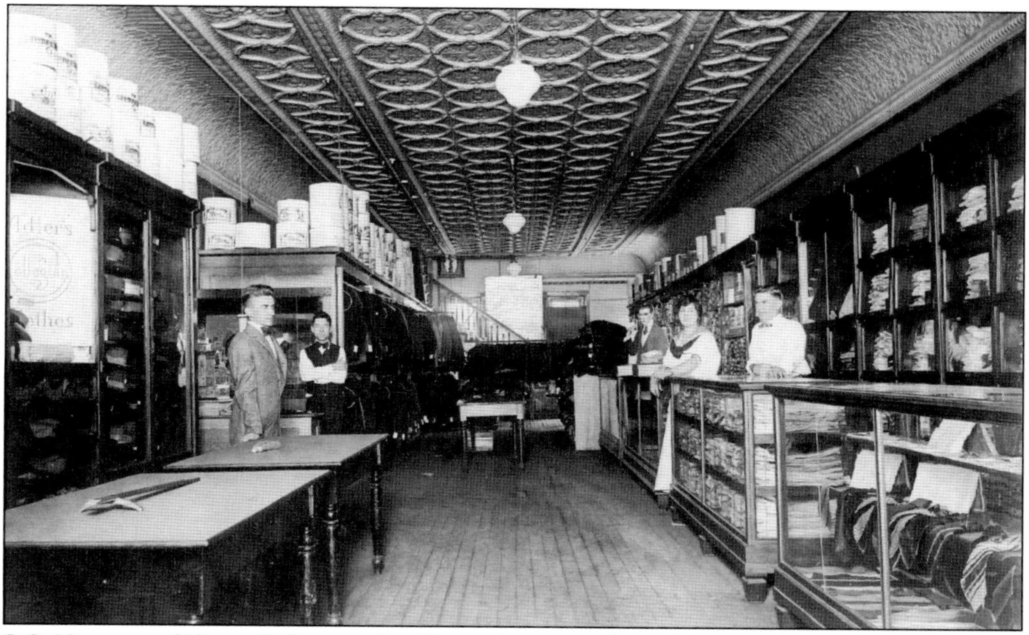

S.C. Hoover and Henry Fellin stand in Hoover's store in the early 1920s. The business eventually became the Fellin Cash Store in 1936 when Fellin and Eugene Pretti purchased it from Hoover. In 1924, a fire broke out nearby and gave quite a scare; most of the damage, however, was caused by frantic attempts to get the merchandise outside, where it was raining. (Courtesy of the Webster County Historical Museum.)

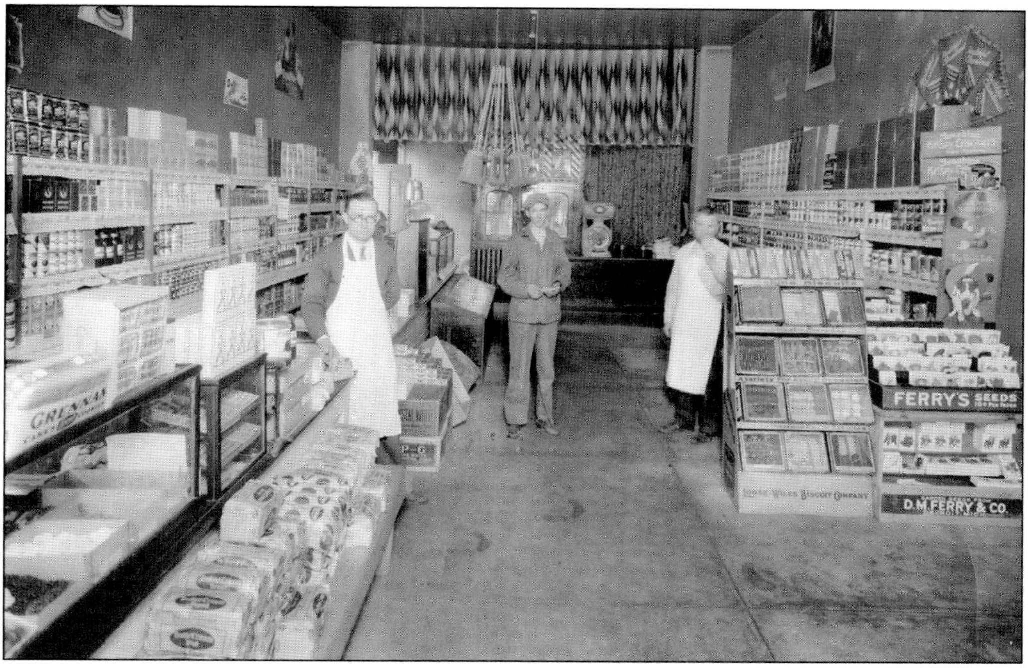

Olan Day (left) and Clyde Hargus (center) are pictured in Frank C. Day's grocery store in February 1929 on the northwest corner of the Marshfield Square. A 1938 advertisement stated that the store was "the home of quality, headquarters for the best the market affords." It also pointed out that Day's store "had to be good to stay [in business] that long." (Courtesy of Randy Clair.)

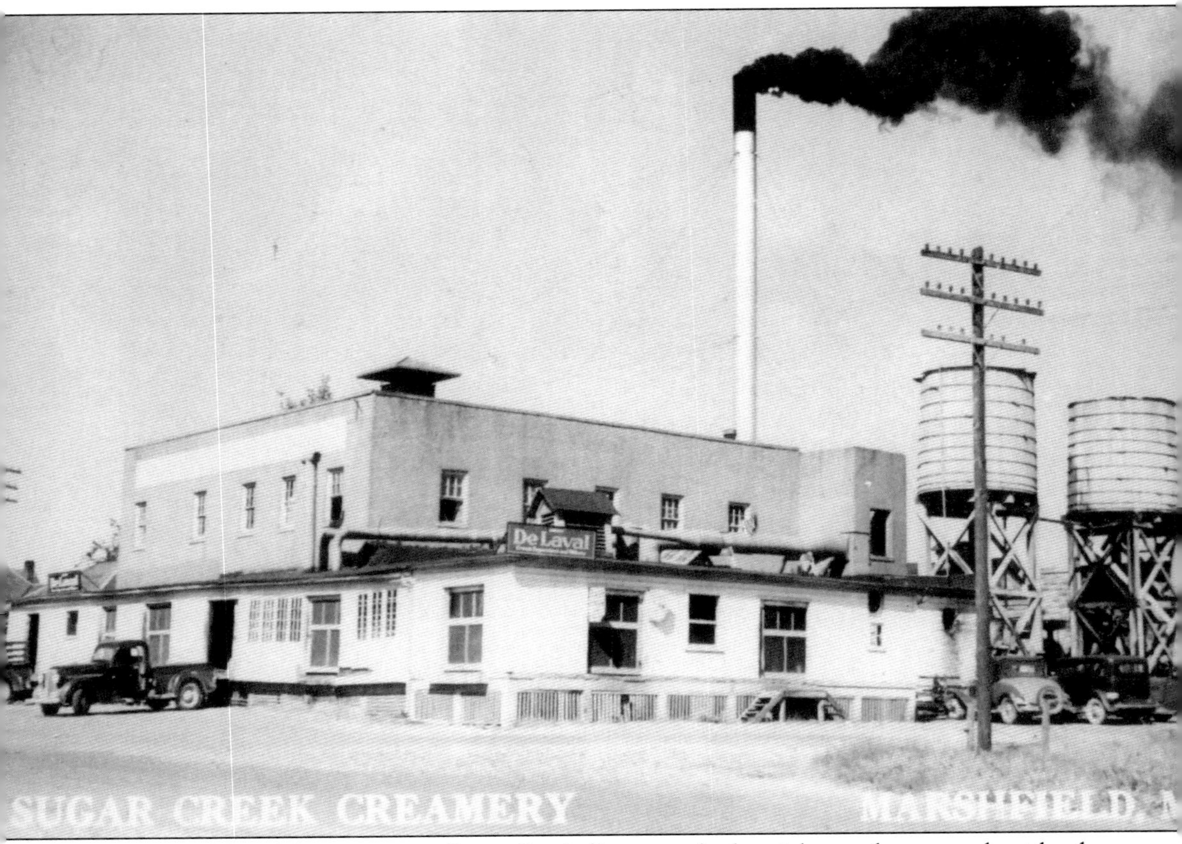

In the middle of dairy country, Sugar Creek Creamery had a niche market to work with when the business opened in 1923. Initially, the plant only manufactured butter, relying heavily on area farmers to supply the necessary cream. Cheddar cheese was added to the roster in 1941, and Sugar Creek began buying whole milk from farmers to accommodate the addition. (Courtesy of the Webster County Historical Museum.)

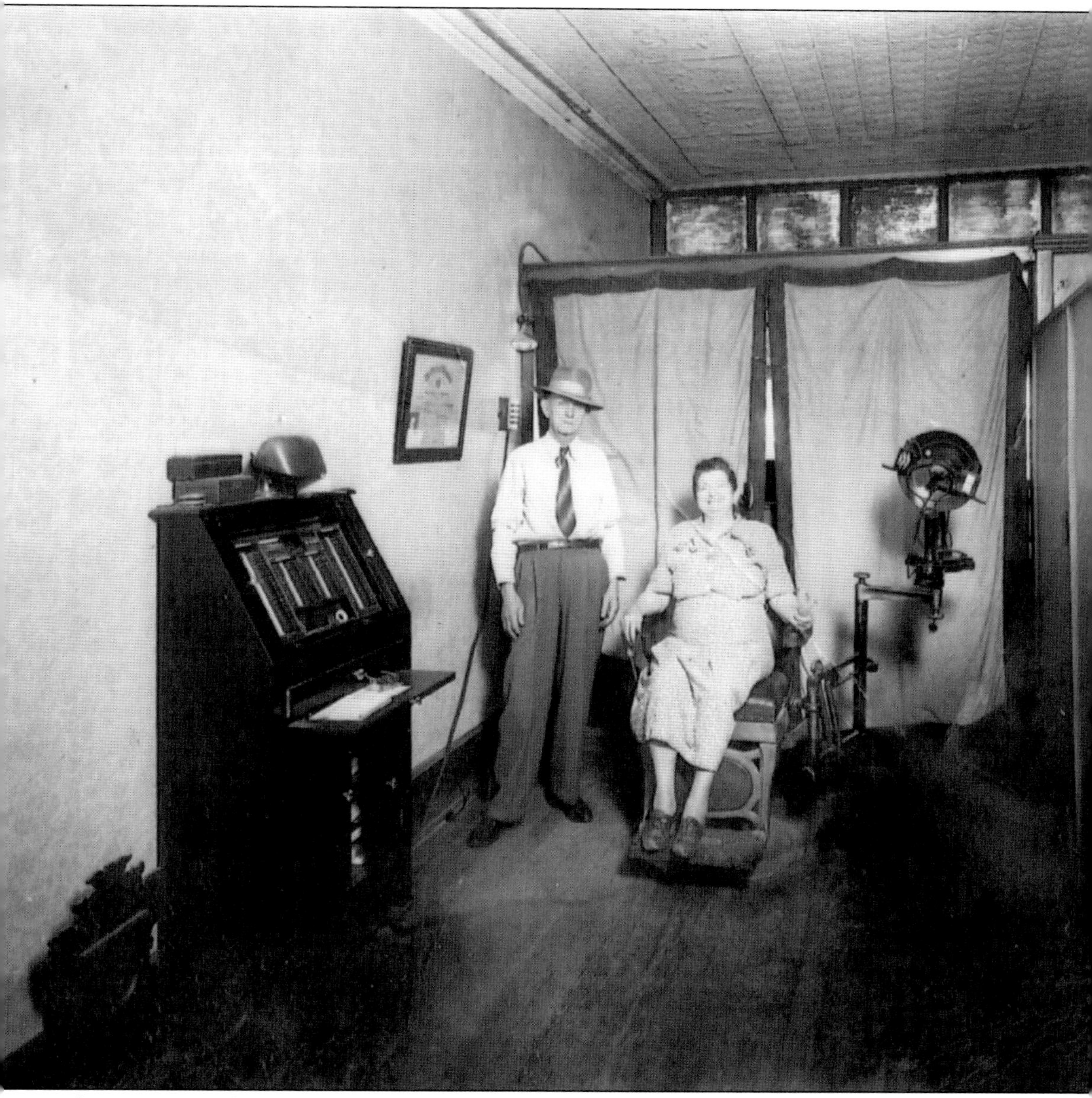

John W. Campbell and his wife, Dora, are pictured in his optometry office on the Marshfield Square. Campbell initially started in business as a barber, moved to watch repair, and eventually taught himself optometry. After originally setting up shop on the west side of the square, he moved his practice to the old Hosmer Building, where he also operated a jewelry store. (Courtesy of Diana Hudspeth.)

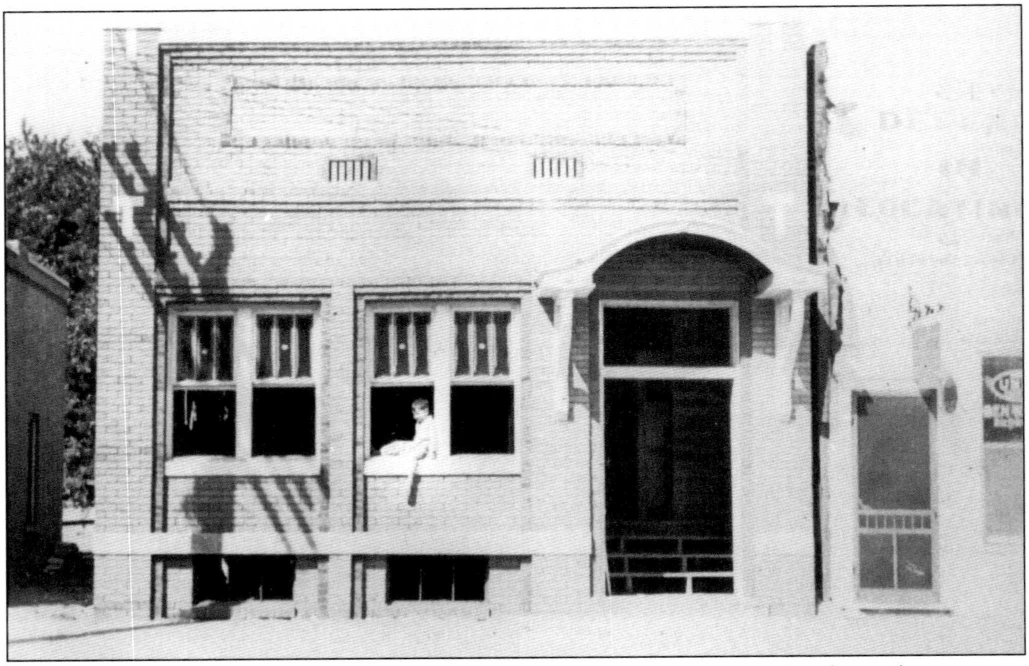

Gene Garst sits outside the Webster County Telephone Exchange on June 31 of an unknown year. The company dates back to 1915, when L.H. Garst and E.J. Frantz bought the telephone exchange and built a more modern system. In 1931, the brick building was constructed on Crittenden Street. The following year, Garst acquired full interest in the company. (Courtesy of Randy Clair.)

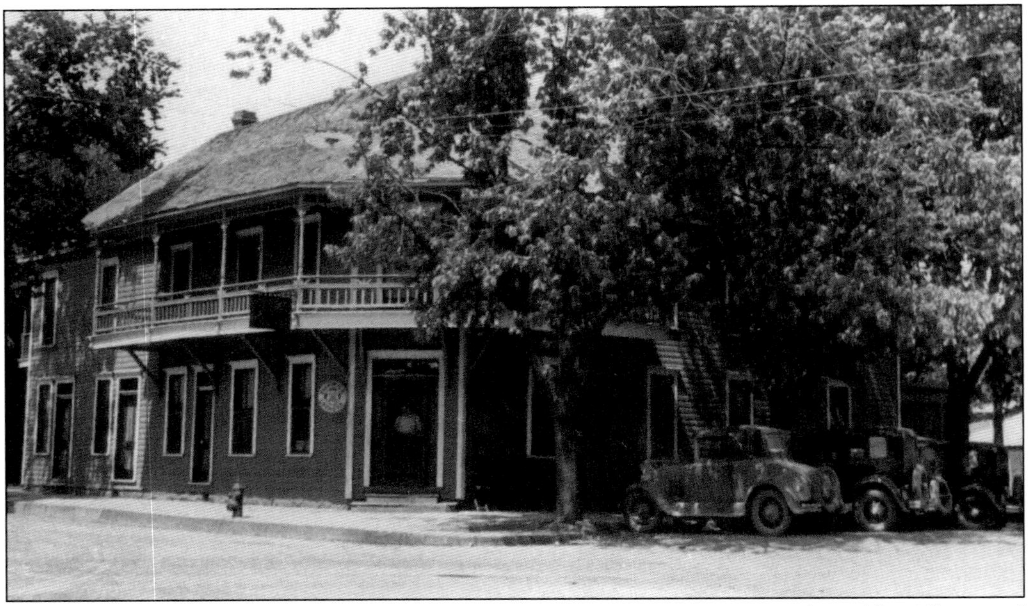

The Webster Hotel is pictured in 1929. Built in 1888, the building was purchased by Albert and Della Cardwell in 1905, who operated it as a hotel. After 35 years of the Cardwells' ownership, the hotel closed; however, the Cardwells' son Dr. O.L. Cardwell continued to house his dental practice there alongside fellow dentist Dr. William Bartow. The building also housed restaurants, a flea market, and was a Greyhound bus stop before it was destroyed by fire in 1999. (Courtesy of Randy Clair.)

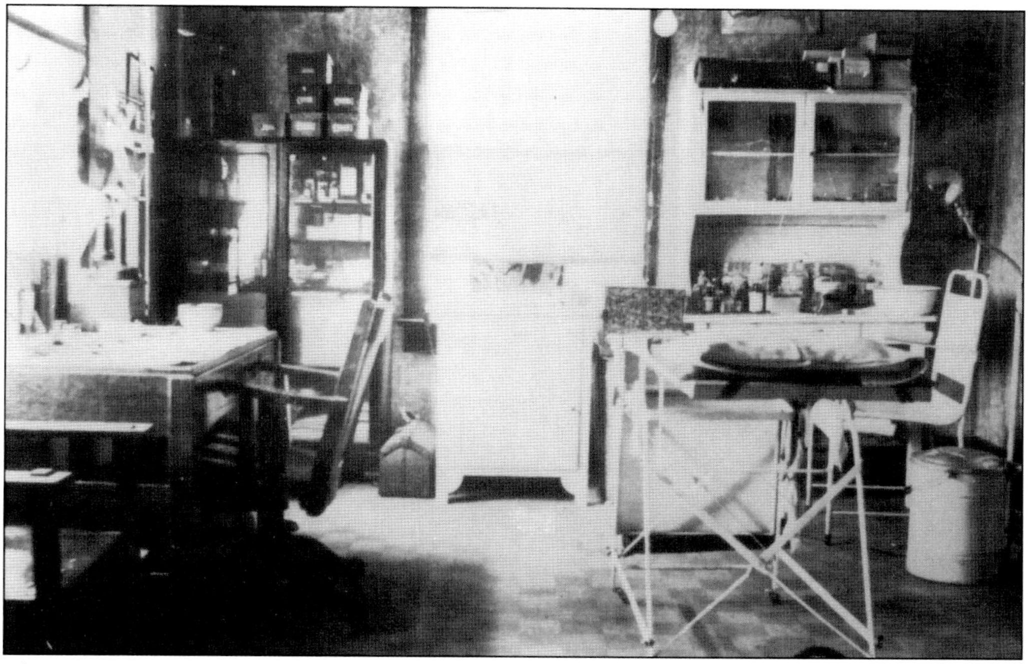

The interior of Dr. C.R. Macdonnell's office on the second floor of the Dickey Building is shown in June 1929. When Macdonnell visited Marshfield in late 1928, the young doctor quickly decided that the community would be a good place to set up a practice. He soon relocated from Higginsville, MO. (Courtesy of Randy Clair.)

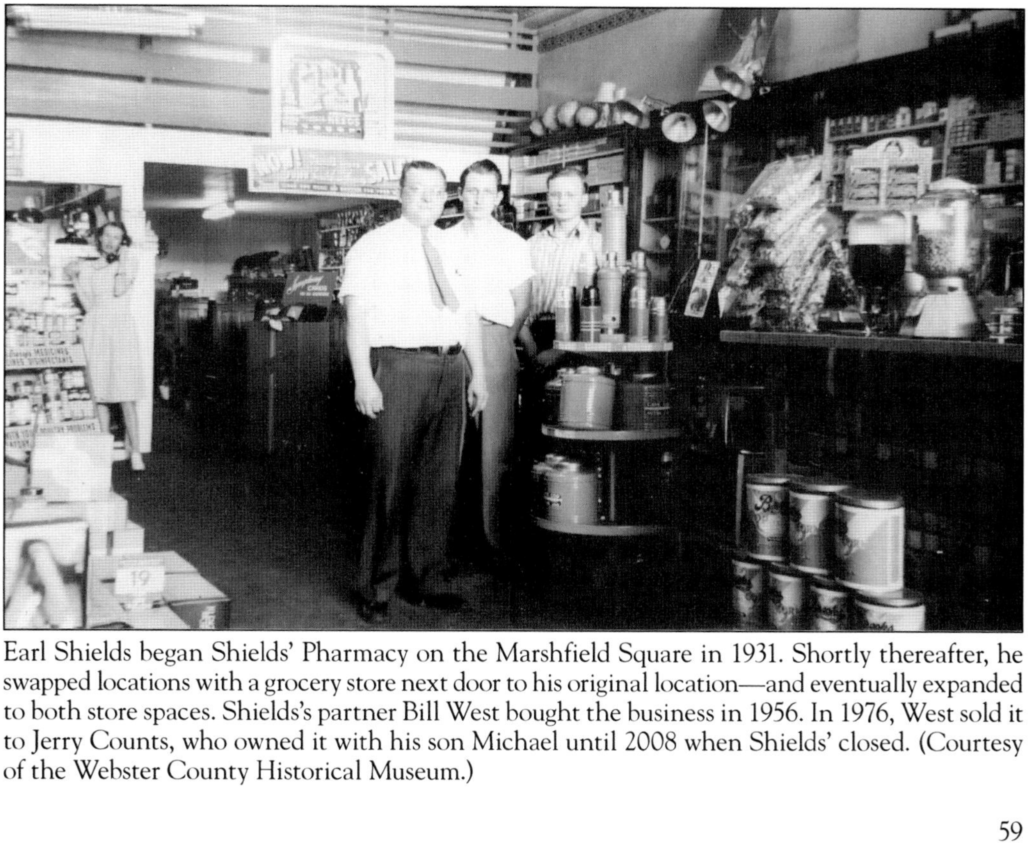

Earl Shields began Shields' Pharmacy on the Marshfield Square in 1931. Shortly thereafter, he swapped locations with a grocery store next door to his original location—and eventually expanded to both store spaces. Shields's partner Bill West bought the business in 1956. In 1976, West sold it to Jerry Counts, who owned it with his son Michael until 2008 when Shields' closed. (Courtesy of the Webster County Historical Museum.)

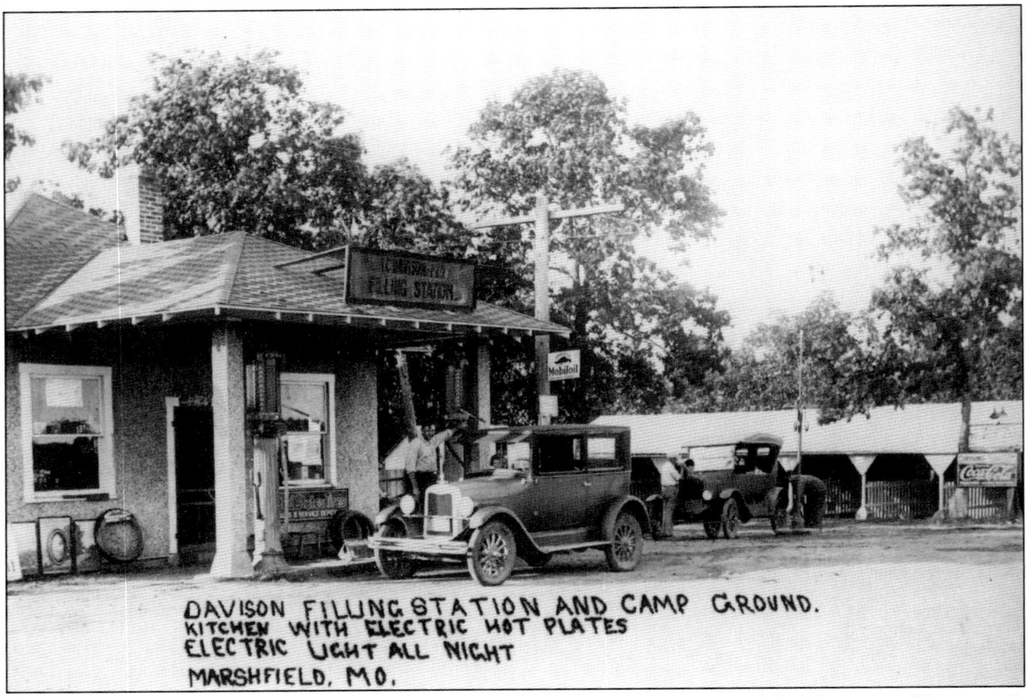

The Davidson Filling Station and Camp Ground was a stop on Marshfield's part of Route 66. Its perks were many for its day: a kitchen with electric lights, hot plates, and electric lighting all night were advertised as reasons to stay there. Also notice advertisements for Coca-Cola, Mobil Oil, and United States Tires. (Courtesy of Randy Clair.)

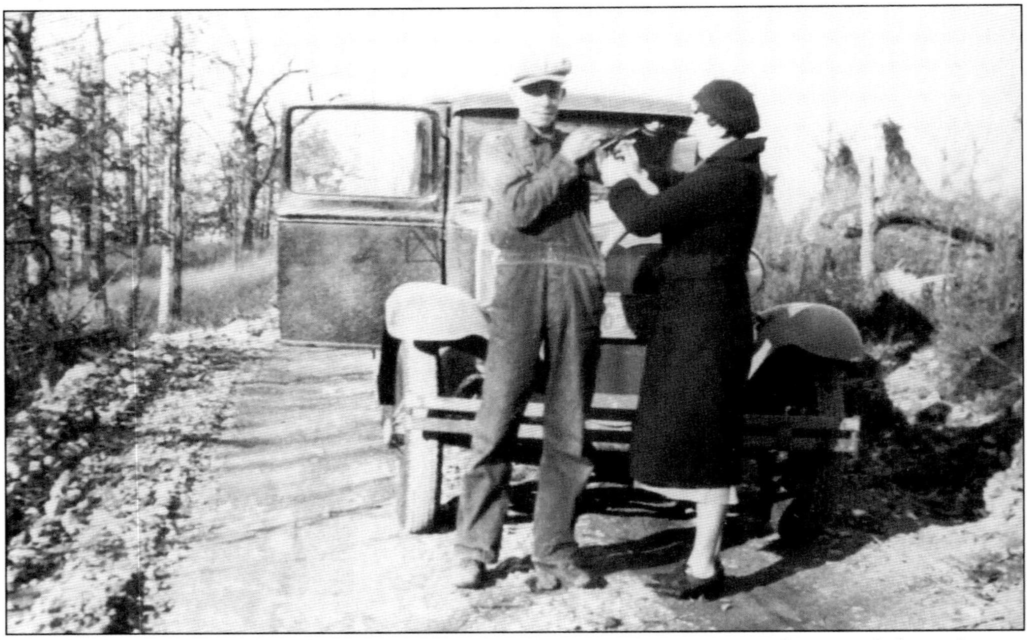

Dr. C.R. Macdonnell's nurse, Elnore Hackman, gives an injection to a farmer while making a run on the rural route in 1931. In addition to his office in the Dickey Building in Marshfield, Macdonnell also had a rural office to serve patients away from the town office. (Courtesy of Randy Clair.)

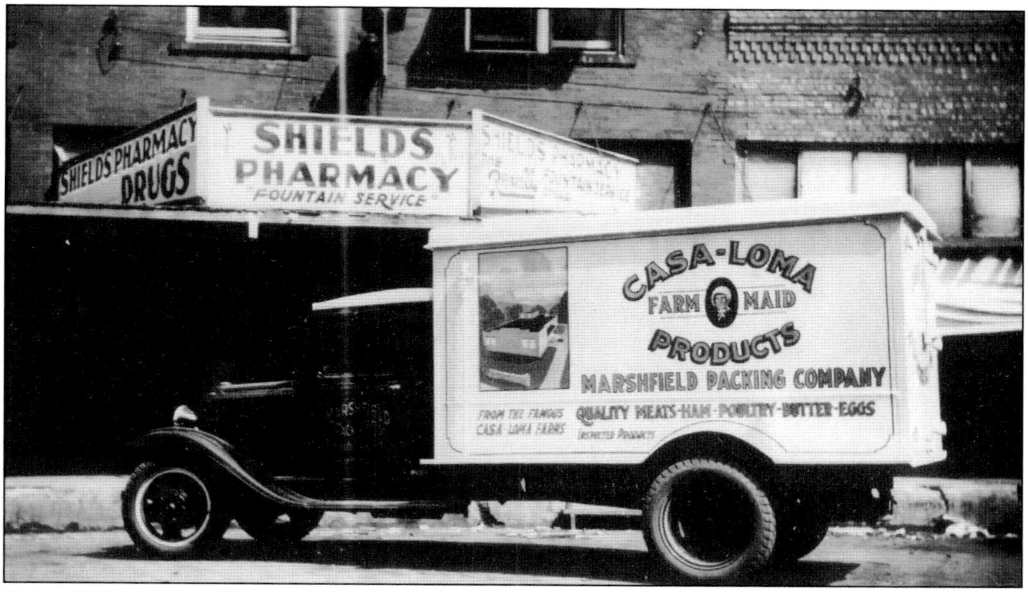

One of Casa Loma Farm's delivery trucks waits on the Marshfield Square. Founded by O.E. Jennings in 1932, the 2,000-acre estate included stables, a private racetrack, a large dairy barn, a rock crusher, and livestock including beef herds, hogs, and poultry. Marshfield Packing Company, a meat-processing plant and creamery, also existed on the premises. (Courtesy of Randy Clair.)

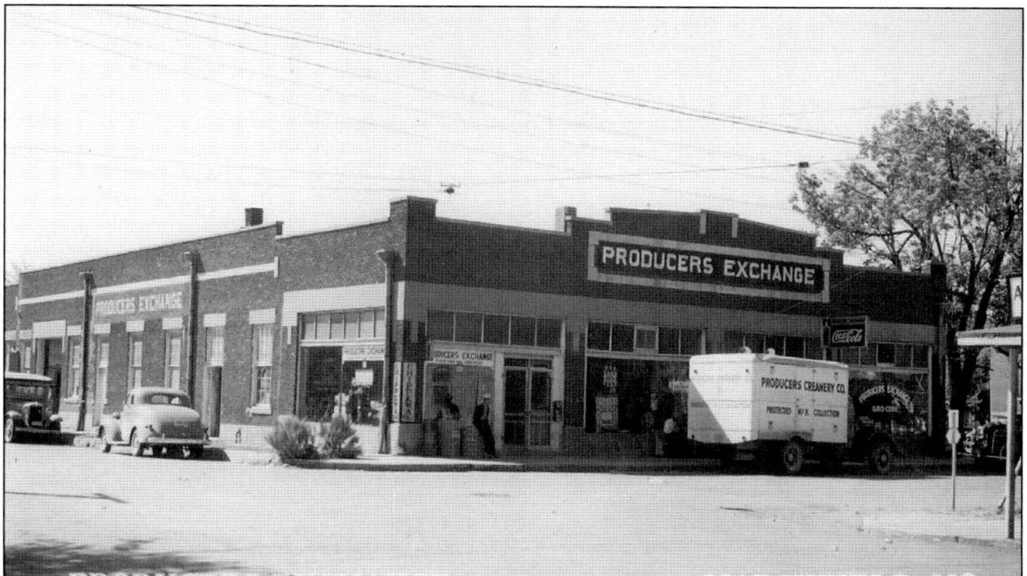

The Producers Exchange on Jackson Street is pictured in the early 1940s. Owned by 180 members from the Webster County Farmers Association, the cooperative business was a place for owners to bring their products to the store to sell. It was the policy of the exchange to buy products as high as possible and, in turn, resell them for as low of a price as possible. (Courtesy of Randy Clair.)

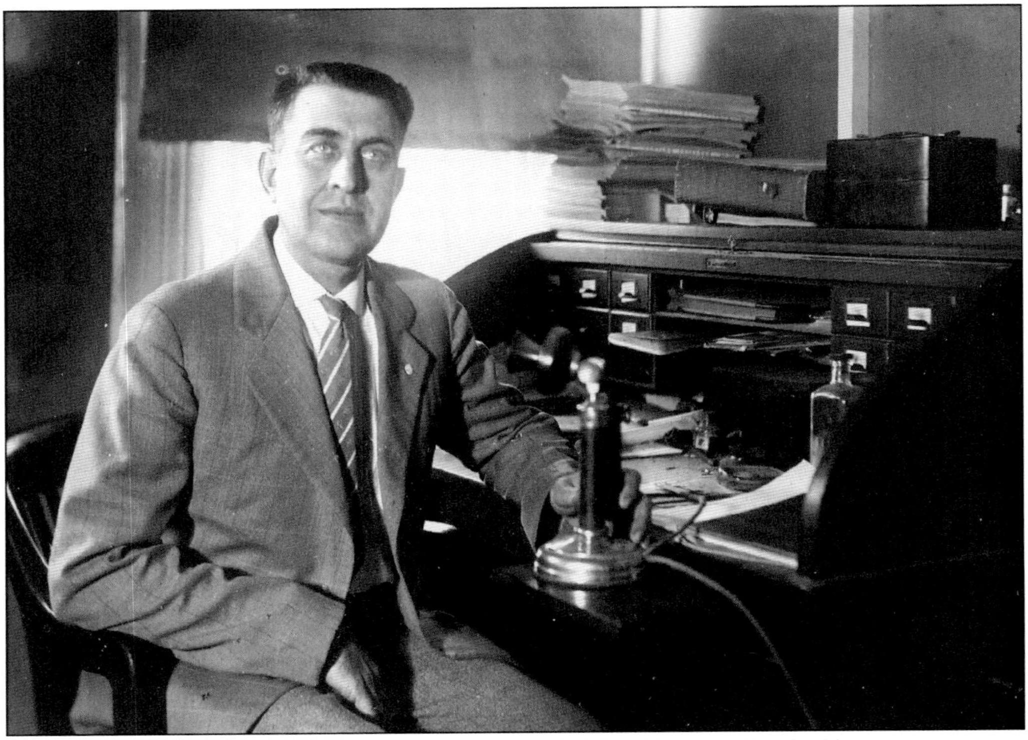

Dr. A.E. Todd is pictured making a call in his Marshfield office in 1927. Todd came to town in the 1920s after graduating from the St. Louis Chiropractic School. His early slogan, "The good effects will continue long after the cost is forgotten," helped spur a 38-year career, as well as a family legacy; both his son and grandson also set up shop in Marshfield as chiropractors. (Courtesy of the Webster County Historical Museum.)

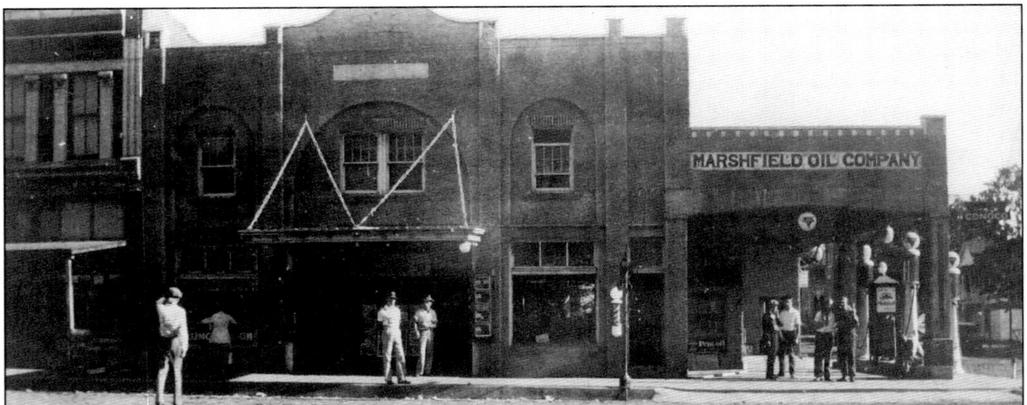

The Ritz Theater was a staple of many Marshfield's youth for over 50 years. Originally opened as the Universal in 1919, a fire ravaged the building in 1924; it reopened as the Ritz in 1927. In 1940, Charles Brooks purchased the theater, beginning memories of 10¢ giant-sized popcorns, the non-air-conditioning cooling system, and seeing the day's most popular movies. The Ritz was closed in 1975. (Courtesy of Randy Clair.)

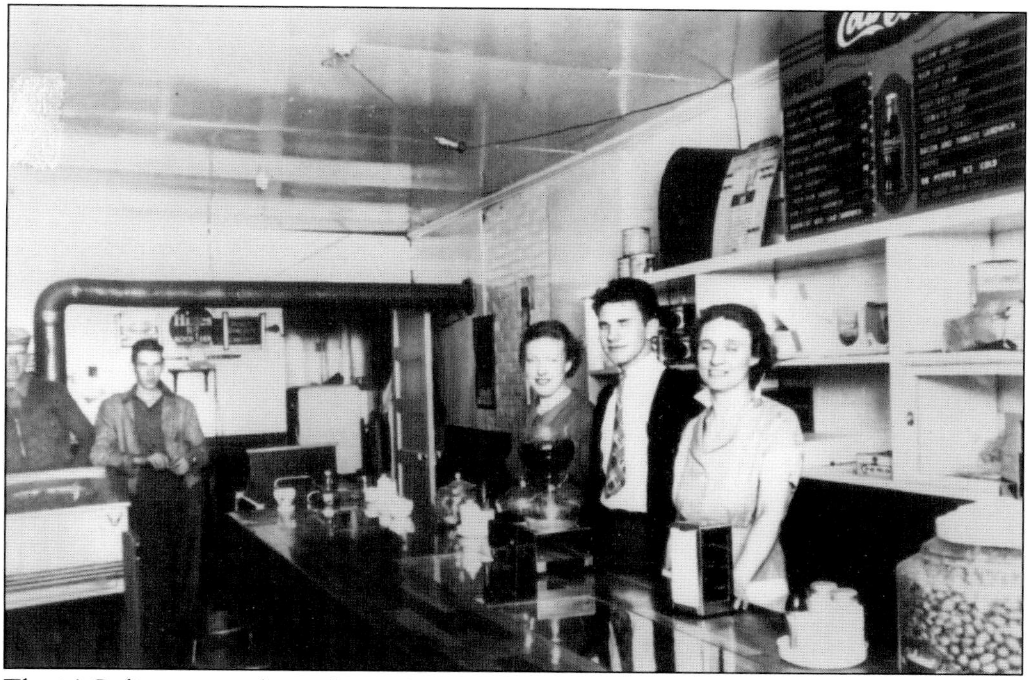

Thetis' Café was once located near Mary's Variety Store on South Crittenden Street. Lena (James) Jump, David Jones, and Thetis Jones appear in the photograph, while the two men standing in the back are unidentified. Various menu items at the time included ice-cold Dr. Pepper, buttered toast, bacon and tomato sandwiches, and oyster stew. (Courtesy of the Webster County Historical Museum.)

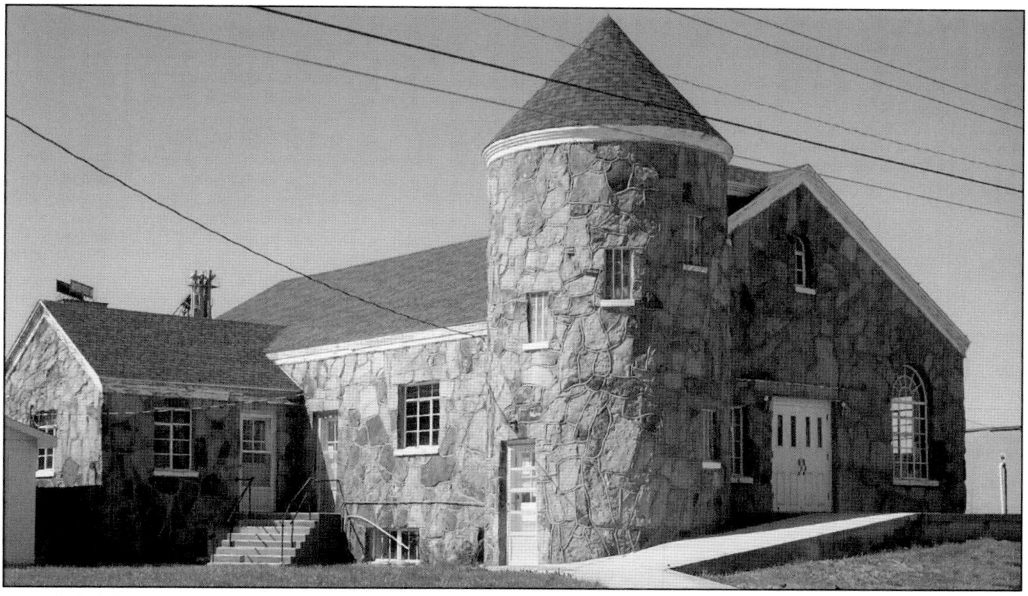

Marshfield's "rock castle" was originally known as the Rainey Funeral Home. Rex and Carmen Rainey constructed the building in 1938 as a new location for their funeral home. It was a novelty in its day; until that time, many funerals were either conducted in homes or in churches. The business changed hands several times, but it was consistently used as a funeral home until it closed. (Courtesy of the Webster County Historical Museum.)

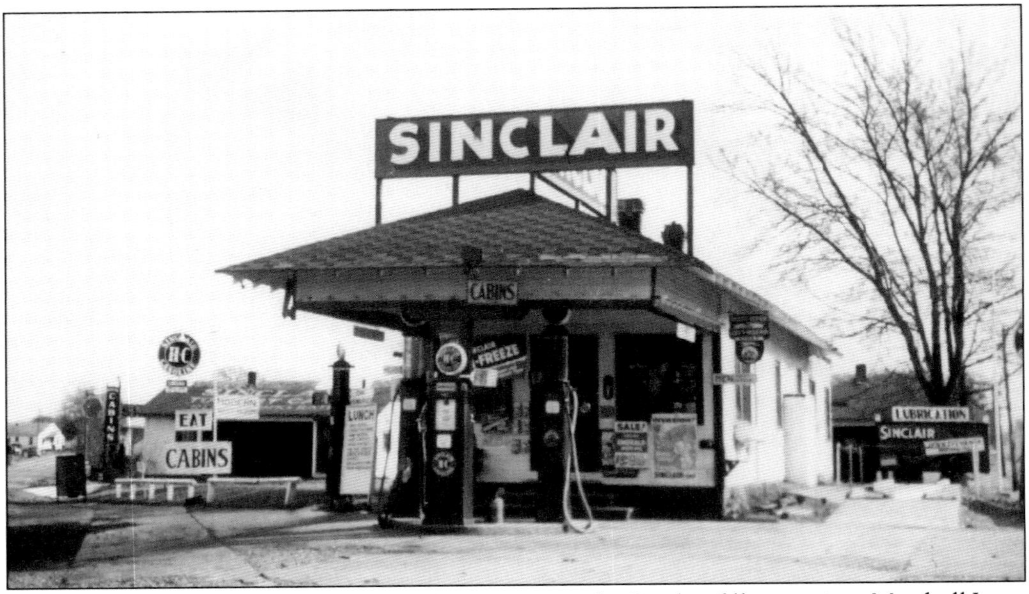

Another stop on Marshfield's segment of Route 66 was the Sinclair filling station. Marshall Lane bought the station in 1944, and after his son-in-law Bob Abbott returned from the service, a new station was built. Lane and Abbott eventually sold the station to Mrs. Jackson and her daughter Ethel. In 1950, the R and J Café and the bus station were located at the site. (Courtesy of the Webster County Historical Museum.)

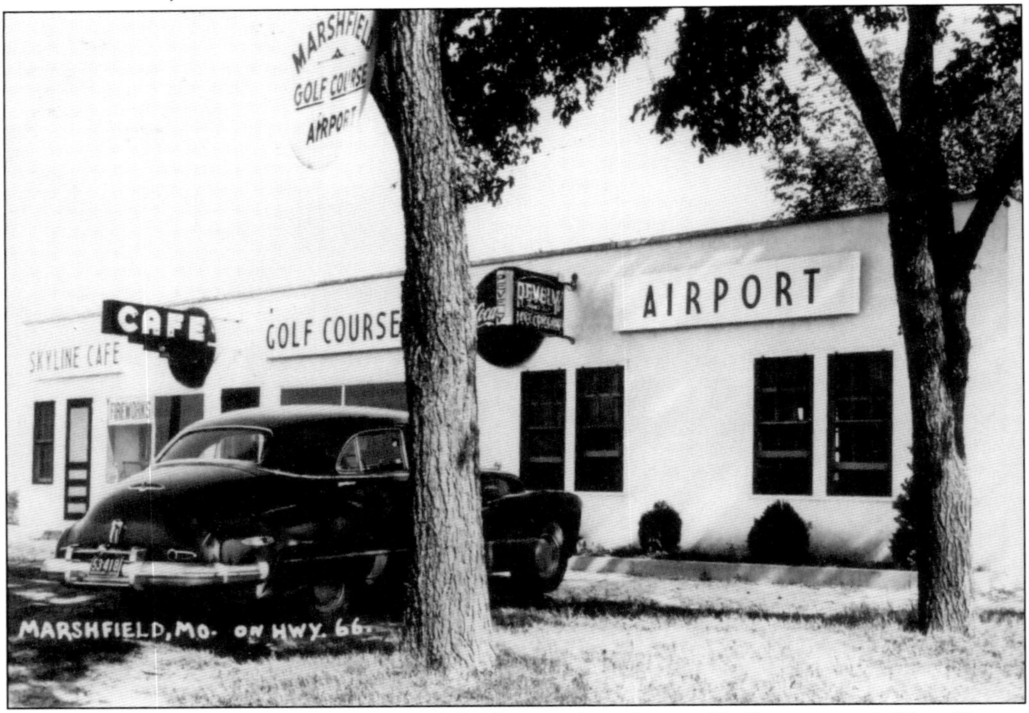

Skyline Café was built in 1947 on Marshfield's stretch of Route 66. Herman and Cleta Pearce built the café on the site of the Main Course filling station that existed from 1929 to 1931. The café was also adjacent to the Marshfield Airport and country club and was the highest point on Route 66 for a 900-mile stretch. (Courtesy of the Webster County Historical Museum.)

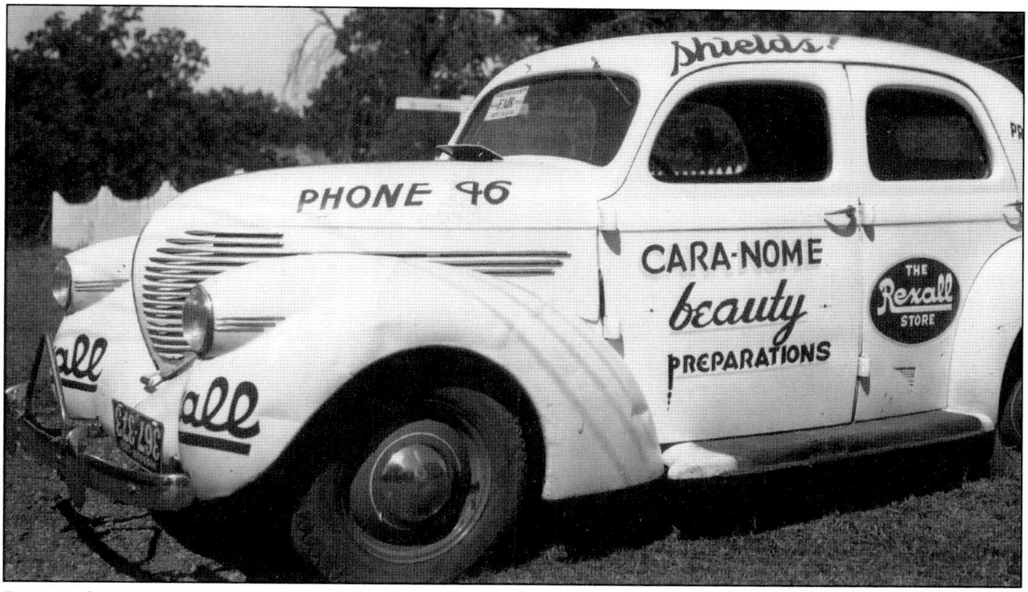

Pictured in 1942, the Shields' Pharmacy delivery car was known to many throughout the area. It did more than just make deliveries; adorned with advertisements for Cara-Nome beauty products and Rexall drugs, the pharmacy's phone number, and a flyer for the Webster County Fair taped to the windshield, it was also a moving billboard. (Courtesy of Randy Clair.)

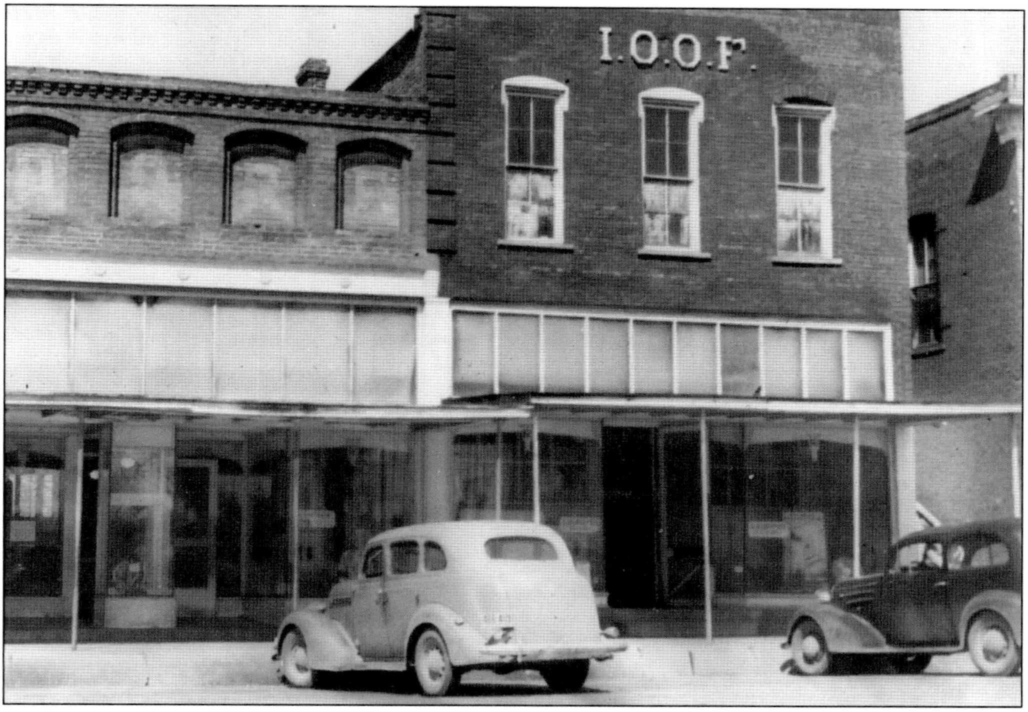

Looking north on the Marshfield Square in the 1940s, at left is Roper's Store, which began operation in July 1924 and carried a variety of clothing items. It was the second "Roper's" to open; the first was in Norwood, Missouri. The Marshfield store's first manager was Sallie Dorton. The Odd Fellows Lodge was housed on the second floor of the building at right. (Courtesy of Dr. Tommy Macdonnell.)

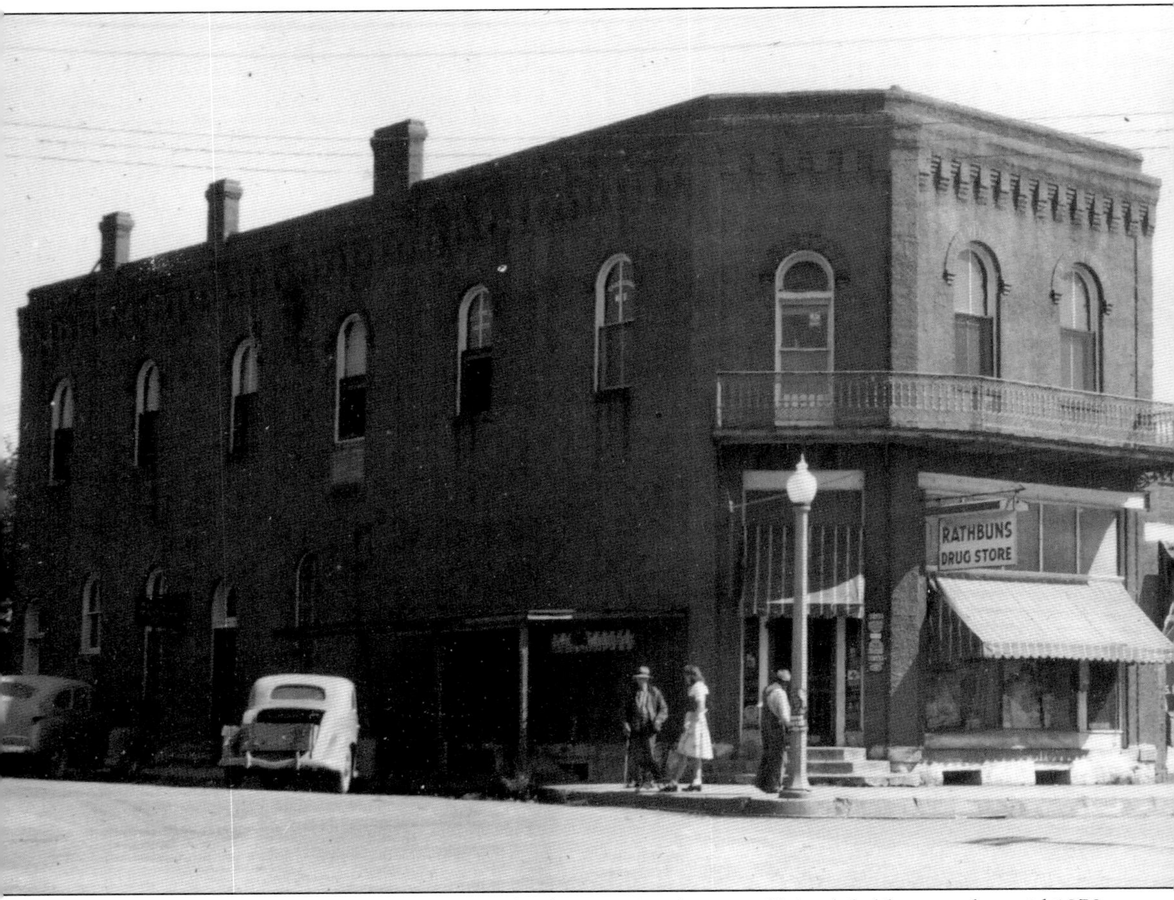

The Rathbun Building is pictured in the late 1940s. A part of Marshfield since the mid-1870s, the structure was previously known as the Alf D. Smith building. It was reconstructed after the 1880 cyclone. At various times, the basement housed a barbershop and a shoe-shine stand, while the second floor was primarily rented out to numerous local doctors. (Courtesy of Dr. Tommy Macdonnell.)

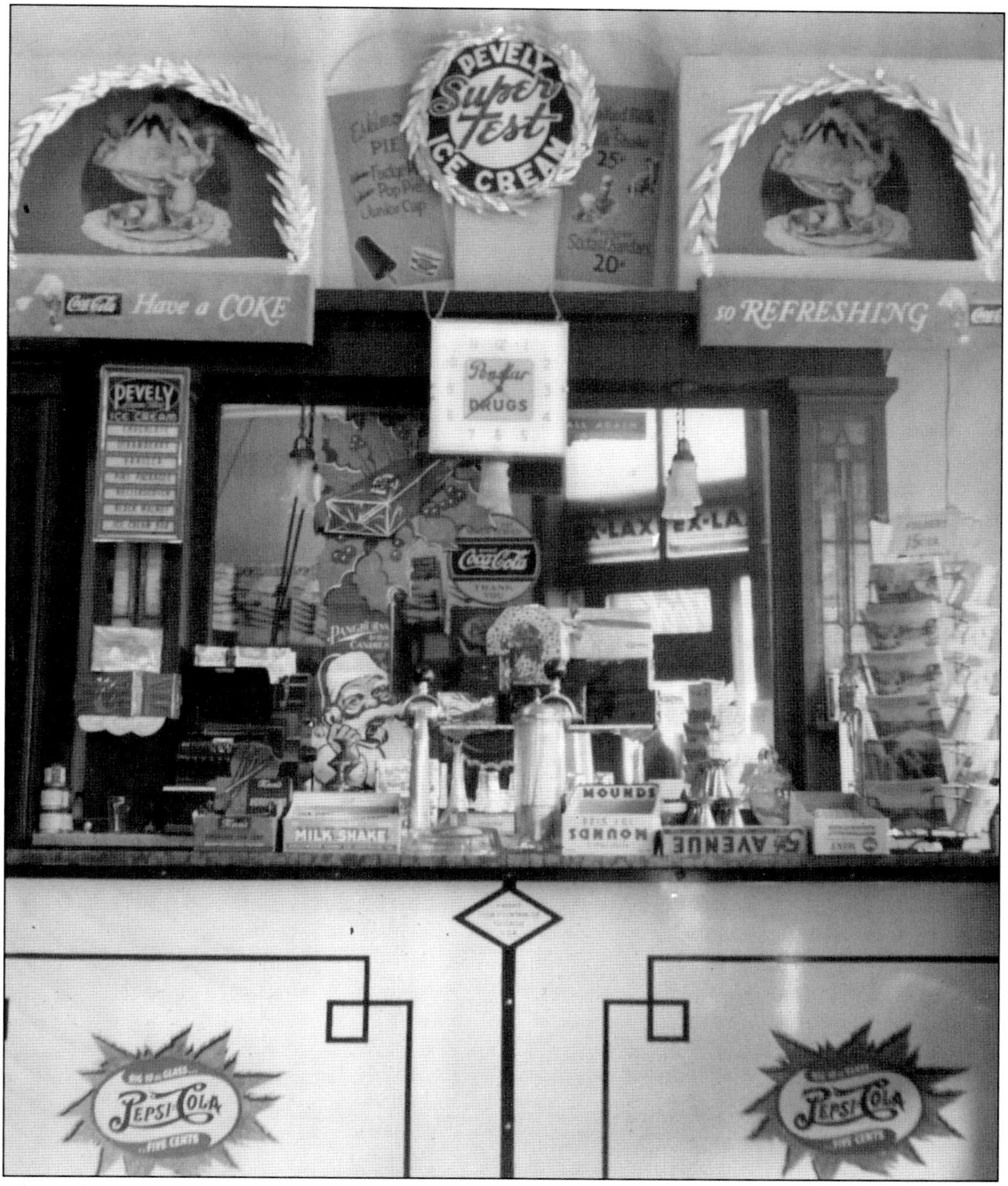

The soda fountain in Rathbun's Drug Store was a draw for many people throughout its existence. March 9, 1922, was the drugstore's opening day, but it was 1931 before it moved to its longtime location in the former Farmers Exchange Bank. Rathbun's Drug Store was open for 47 years until age and health concerns convinced the Rathbuns that it was time to retire in 1969. (Courtesy of Dr. Tommy Macdonnell.)

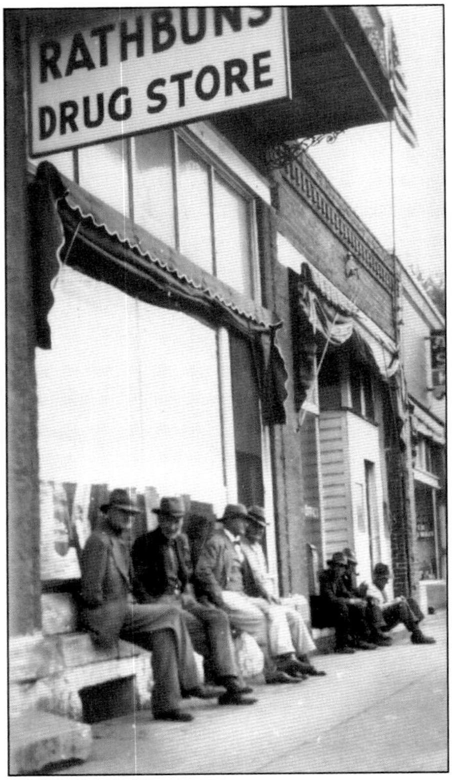

A glance down South Crittenden Street on April 10, 1946, captures several members of the "spit and whittle" club. Perhaps the men were talking about the news that Marshfield was set to get an airport, or who won the city and school elections that were held the week before, or even the New Reynolds Fountain Pen advertised at Rathbun's. (Courtesy of Dr. Tommy Macdonnell.)

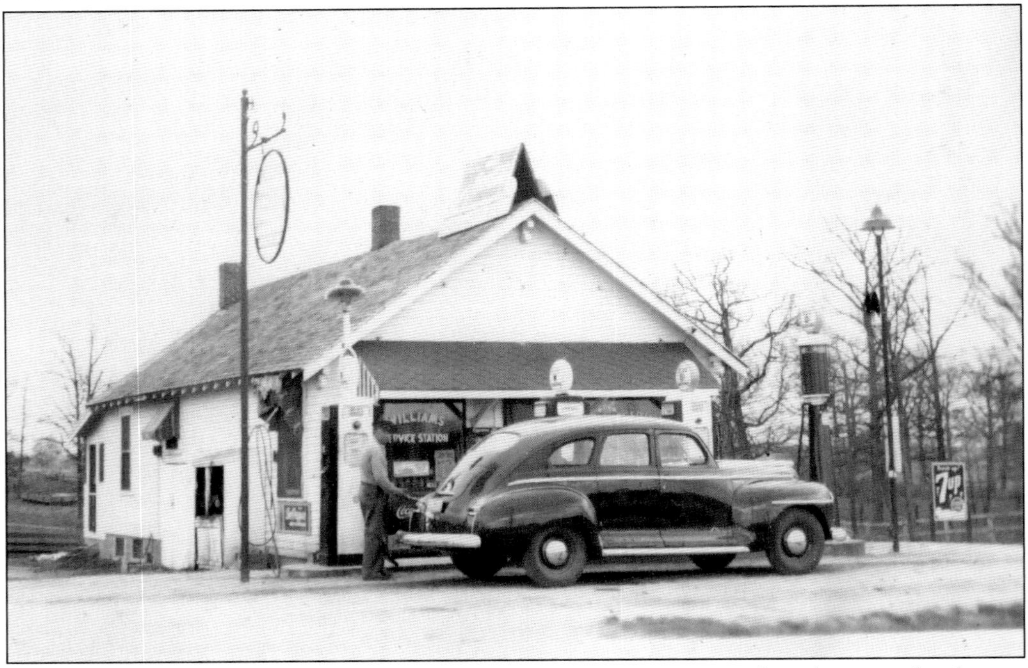

Wint Williams is pictured working at his filling station in 1946. Located on the east side of town, Williams is filling up Dr. C.R. Macdonnell's 1946 Plymouth. Advertisements for soft drinks were not uncommon, evident by the Coca-Cola signs on the roof of the station and 7-Up signs. (Courtesy of Dr. Tommy Macdonnell.)

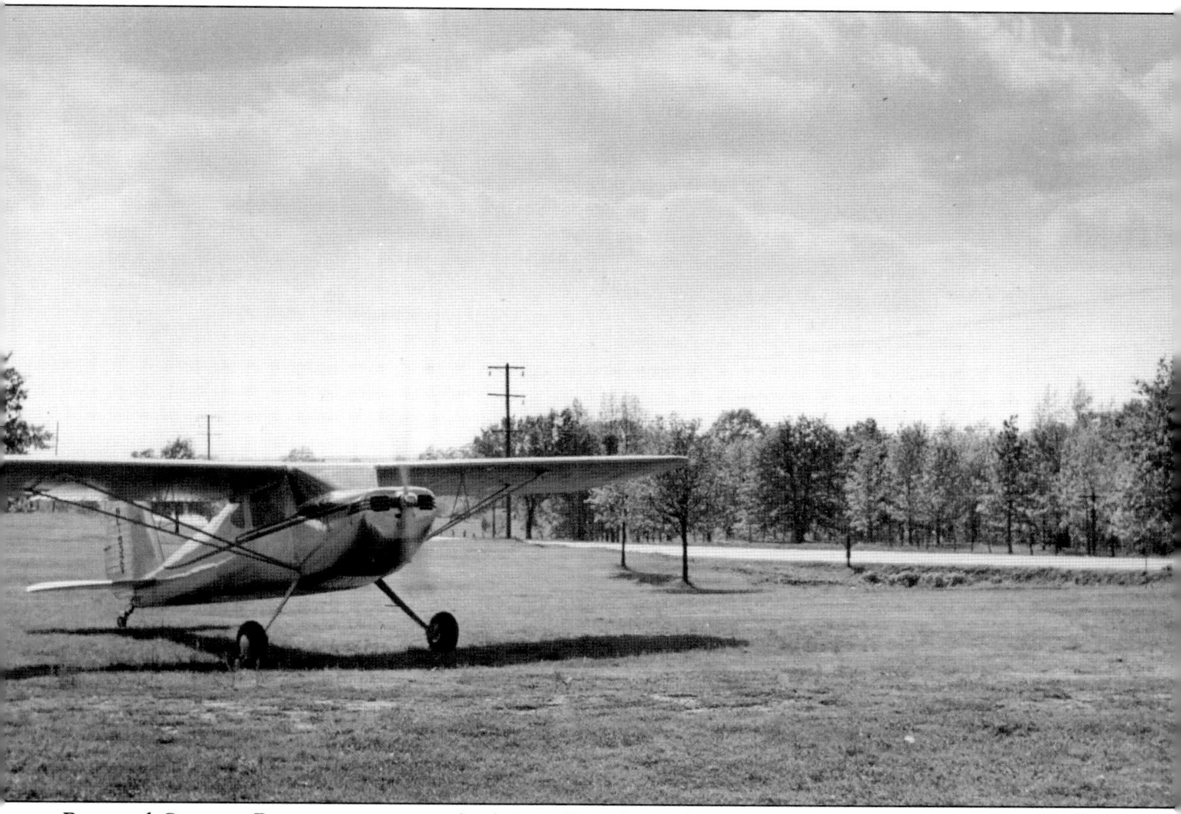

Rex and Carmen Rainey are pictured taking off in their plane at the Marshfield Airport in the late 1940s. The Marshfield Airport, or Marshfield Flying Field, was established in 1930. At the time, the *Marshfield Mail* reported that Marshfield was fortunate to have the airport, because "within a few years it [would have] been necessary for all towns of any importance to have a landing field." (Courtesy of Dr. Tommy Macdonnell.)

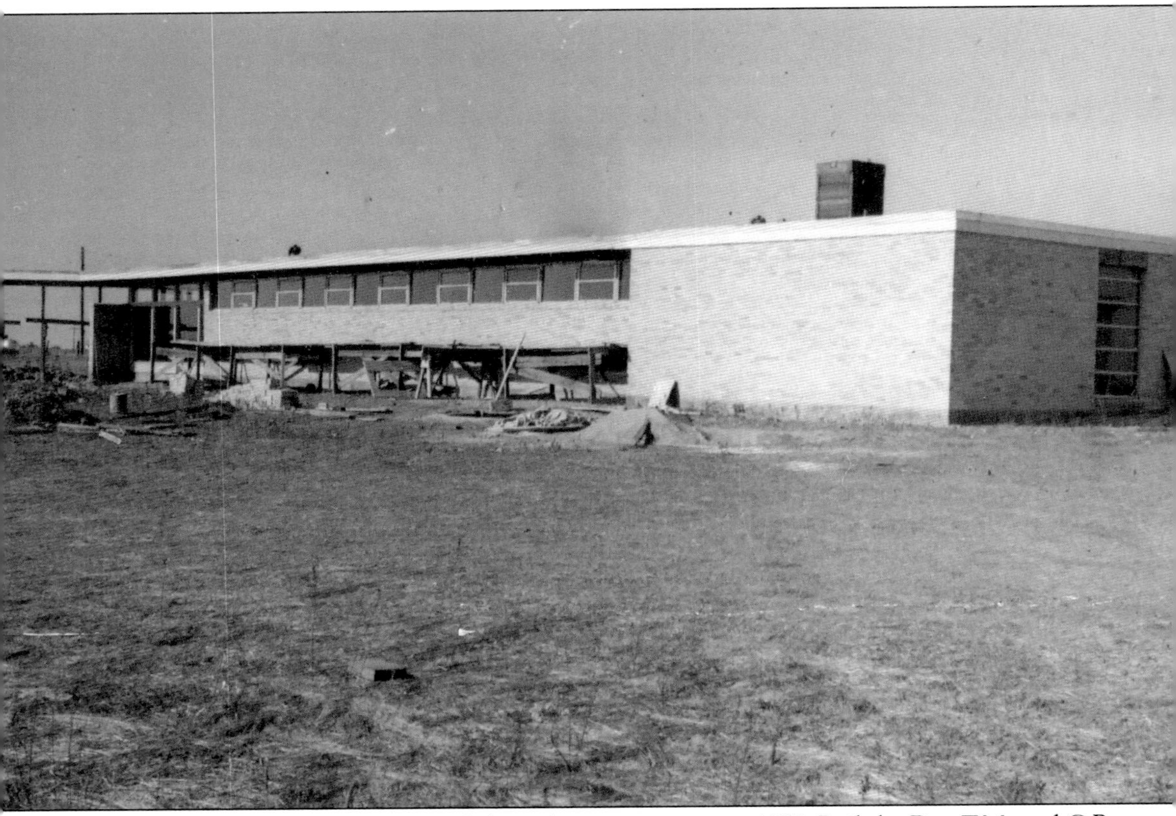

The Marshfield Clinic is shown while under construction in 1953. Built by Drs. T.M. and C.R. Macdonnell, the clinic was located on Spur Drive, where Wal-Mart was later located. Plans for its construction were announced in the *Marshfield Mail* in July; some of its 30 rooms would have labor, delivery, and recovery facilities, a nursery, treatment rooms, space for minor surgeries, and an X-ray room. (Courtesy of Dr. Tommy Macdonnell.)

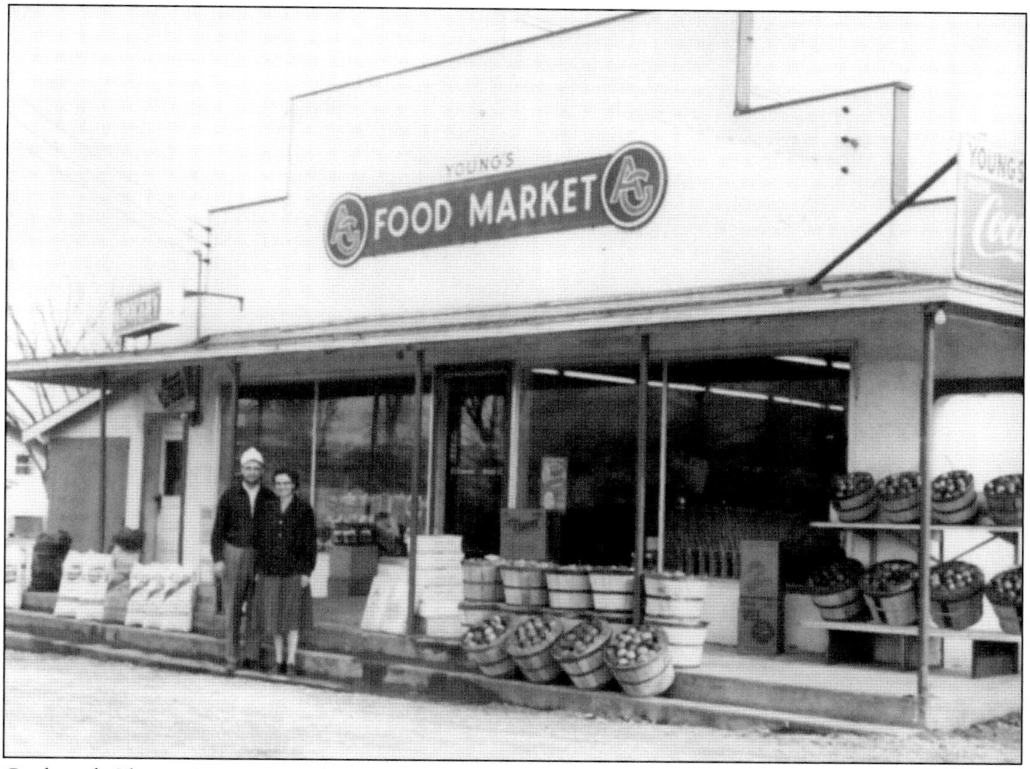

Carl and Glessie Young stand in front of their first Marshfield supermarket in February 1955. Located nearly next door to the future shopping center, the store opened in 1947 with 700 feet of space. Despite a devastating fire in 1950, the couple kept going and expanded the store nearly every three years until the construction of the shopping center in 1970. (Courtesy of the Carl Young collection.)

The Style Shop's window is pictured in the 1950s. Opened in 1950 by Wanda and Paul Beckerdite and Pat Abbott, the shop was a Marshfield go-to for women's clothing for over five decades. In 1984, Pat bought out Wanda's share; she and daughter Susan operated the store until 2005, when Pat decided that it was time to retire and the store was closed. (Courtesy of Dr. Tommy Macdonnell.)

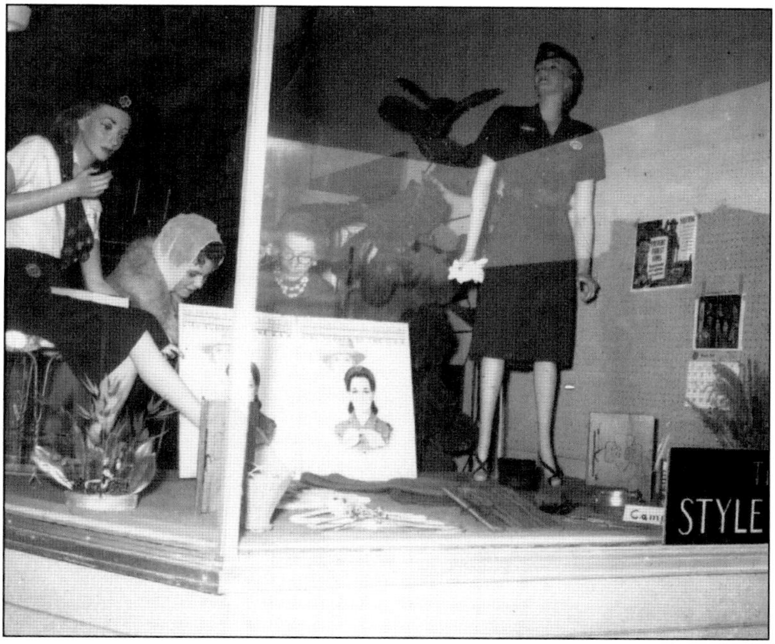

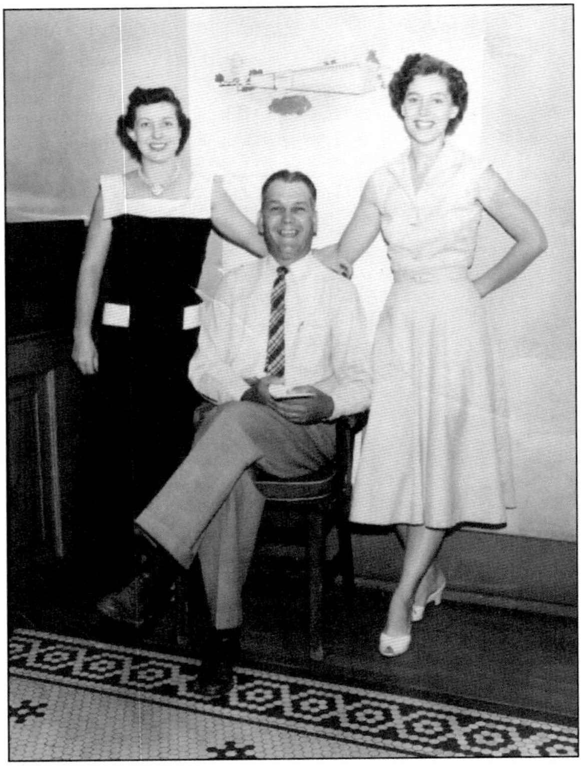

A few Sho-Me Power staff members are pictured in the early 1950s. From left to right are Mary Hobson, Henry Kolmyer, and Bonnie Popejoy Day. Note the rendering in the background of the company's new building, set to be constructed on Jackson Street. Bids for construction on the new facility opened in August 1951; low bidder was Lloyd Bonjour of Springfield with an offer of $239,960. (Courtesy of Jennifer Hartman.)

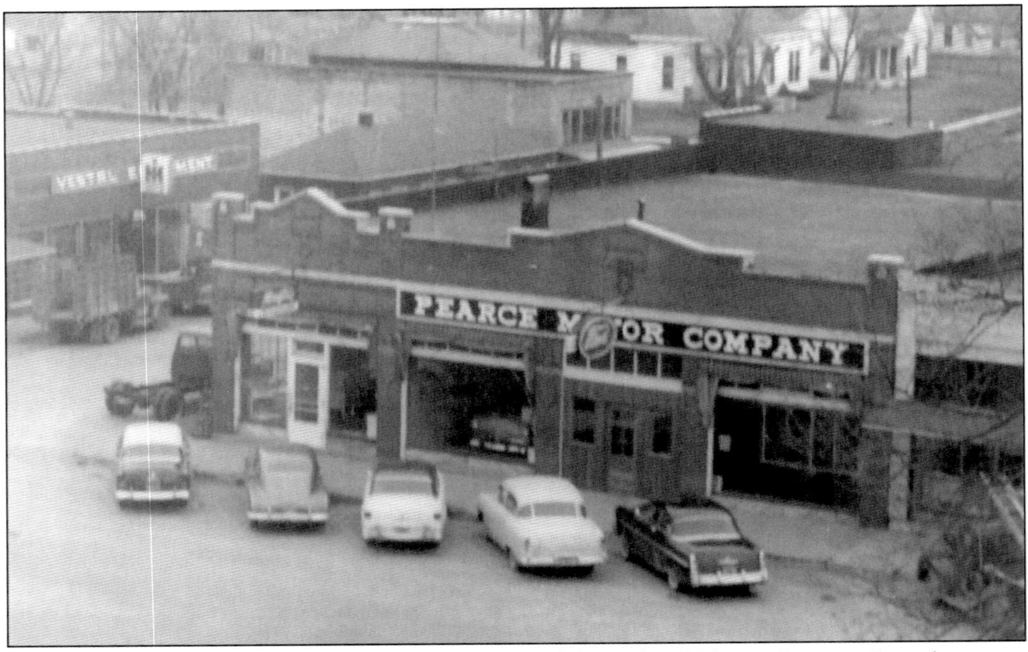

The Pearce Motor Company is shown as it looked from the Webster County Courthouse in 1955. Even though Pearce got into the automobile business by the 1940s, someone else in Marshfield beat him to it. In 1912, the Robertson Motor Company opened in the same location and specialized in Ford and Lincoln cars and Fordson tractors. (Courtesy of the Webster County Historical Museum.)

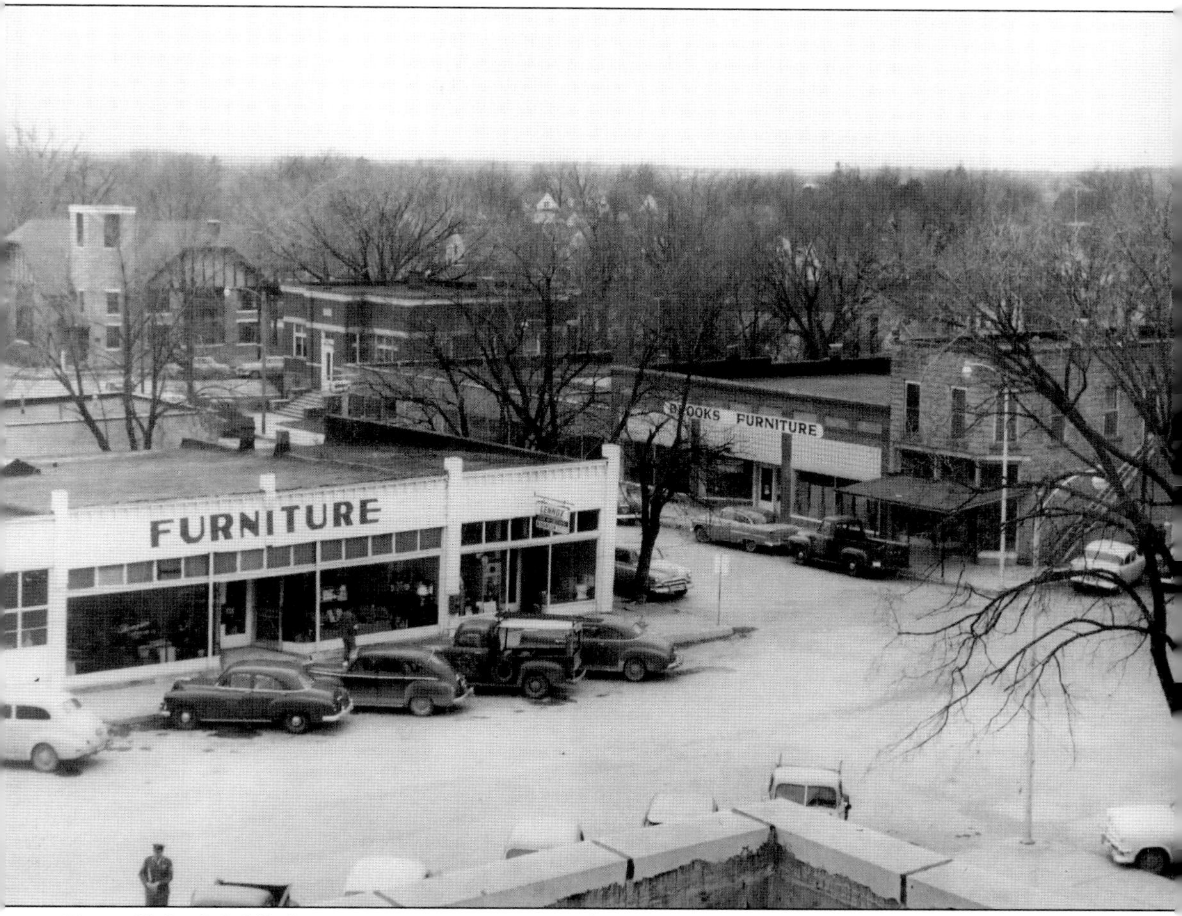

Two of Marshfield's furniture stores are pictured in 1955. Thompson's Furniture Company is shown on the square, while the Brookses owned the store on Clay Street. The store eventually segued into Brooks Gas Company, which was incorporated in 1954, after selling gas for stoves. (Courtesy of the Webster County Historical Museum.)

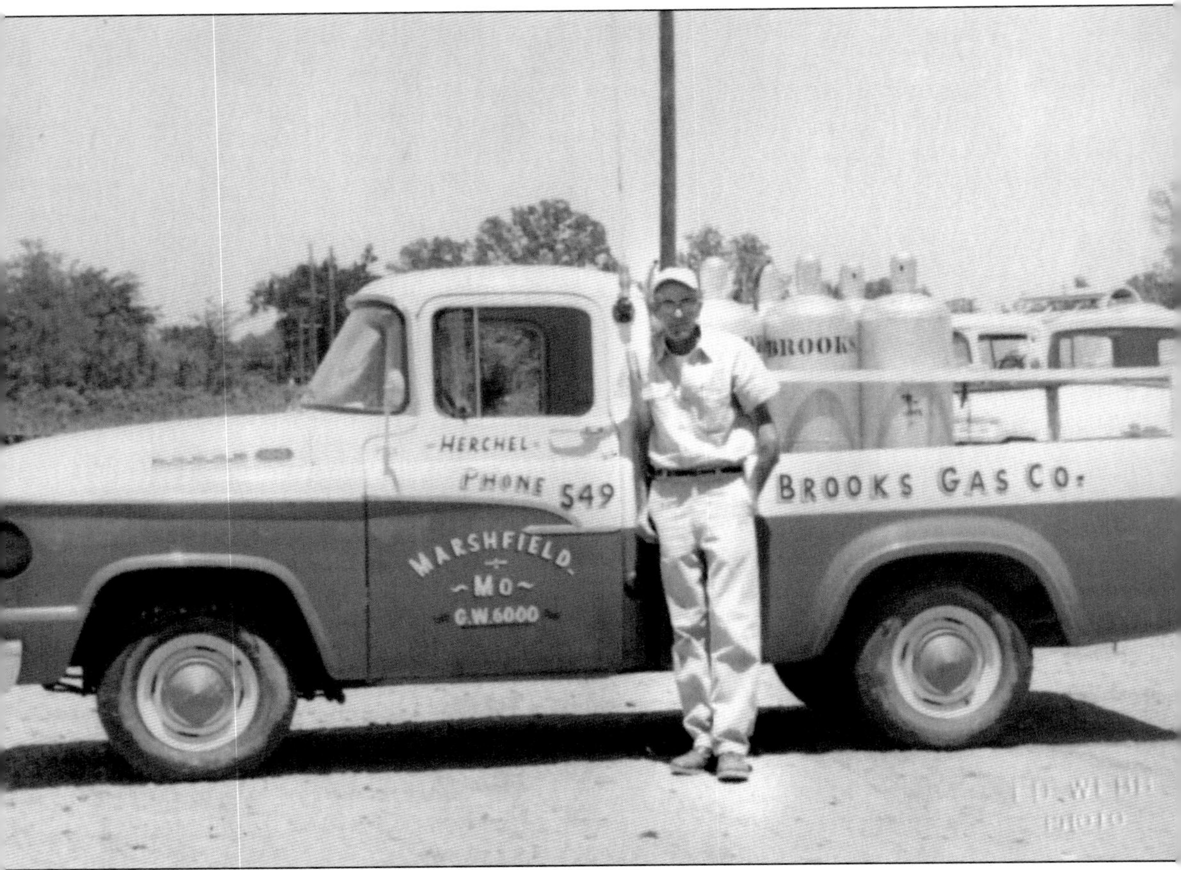

Herchel Tanehill is shown in front of his Brooks Gas Company truck. Incorporated in 1954, the company was originally owned by John William Brooks Sr. and his son Bill. In 1969, the company was transferred over to Bill and Ruth Brooks, and since then it has remained a family-run company and still provides "service you can rely on" from three area locations in Marshfield, Conway, and Seymour. (Courtesy of Ruth Brooks.)

The people of Marshfield were invited to attend the open house for Citizens State Bank on June 19, 1960. The bank's directors are, from left to right, vice president Carl Young, executive vice president Bryan Miller, chairman Herman Pearce, and president Jake Birchfield, along with cashier Bob Lea. The bank was built where the former James Building was located before it was torn down in 1959. (Courtesy of the Carl Young collection.)

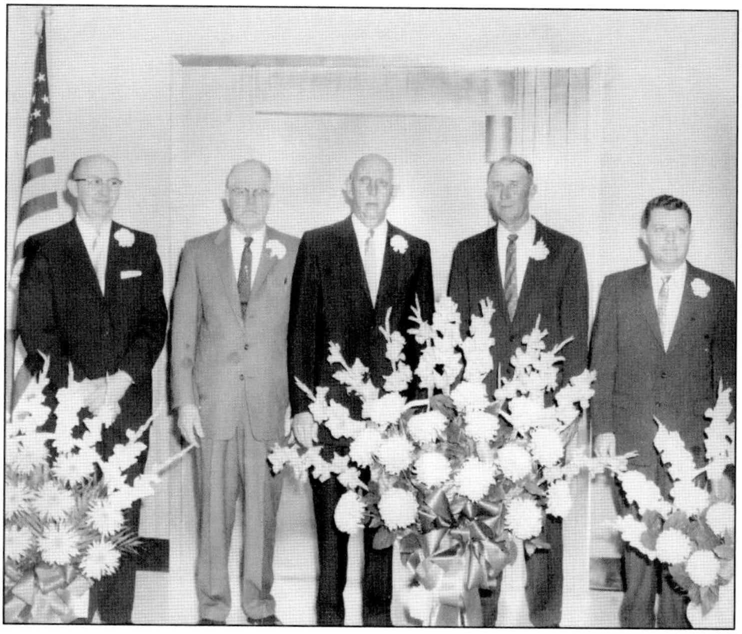

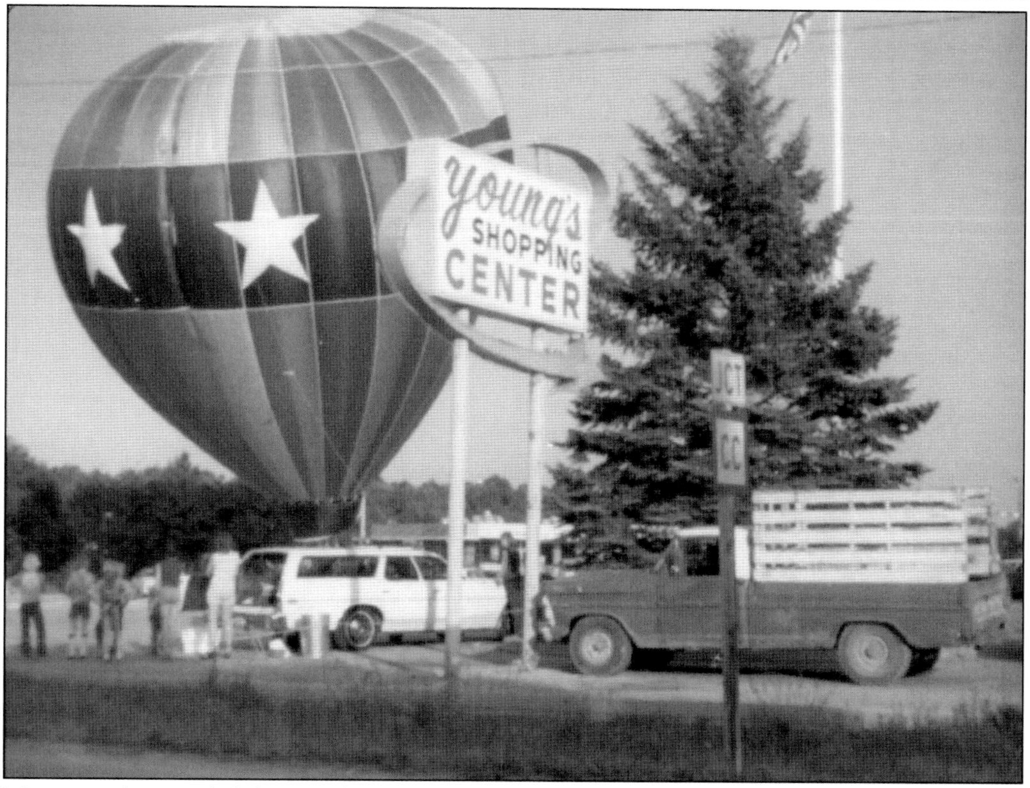

Many people attended the grand opening at Young's Shopping Center in August 1970. Although the celebration marked the opening of the town's Ben Franklin store, the Young's new supermarket did not open until December. Sally Macdonnell, the reigning queen of Webster County, served as the day's official ribbon cutter. One of the daily draws was a hot-air balloon, used to give rides to kids. (Courtesy of the Carl Young collection.)

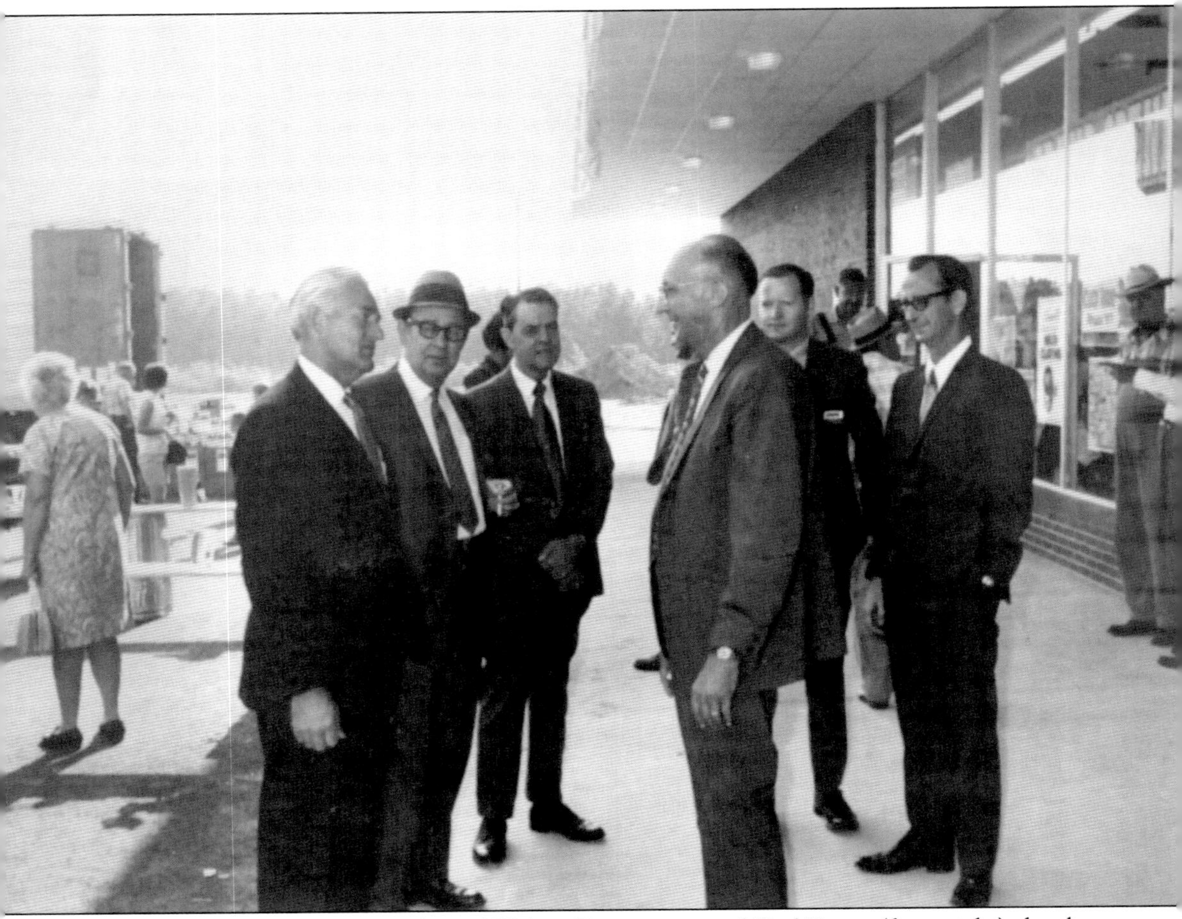

Sam Walton (front left), president of Walton Enterprises, and Carl Young (front right), developer of the Young Shopping Center, talk at the grand opening of Marshfield's Ben Franklin Family Center in August 1970. At the time, Walton Enterprises operated the Ben Franklin stores. The man behind Young in the background is C.R. "Bob" Clark, who would later serve as Marshfield's mayor. (Courtesy of the Carl Young collection.)

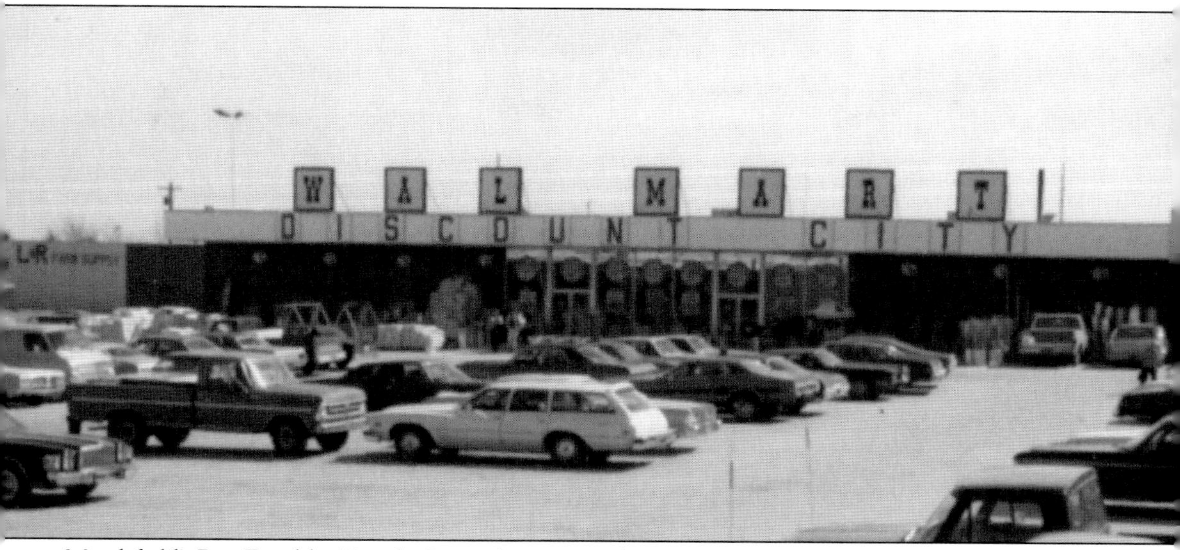

Marshfield's Ben Franklin Family Center became Wal-Mart Discount City in 1973. In preparation for the change, Marshfield's Ben Franklin underwent a major remodeling and expansion, going from 17,000 square feet to 30,000. At the time, Marshfield's Wal-Mart was one of only 68 stores worldwide. It remained in the Young Shopping Center until the late 1980s, when work began on a new store closer to Interstate 44. (Courtesy of the Carl Young collection.)

Andrews Cafe

FEBRUARY 12, 1922 + + FEBRUARY 12, 1978

OUR **56th** YEAR

"It may be a cup of coffee to you, but it's a reputation to us."

JOHN E. ANDREWS MARSHFIELD, MISSOURI

Here is a commemorative card that was passed out in celebration of Andrews Café's 56th birthday. Founded in 1922, the café developed a reputation for great food, which owner Johnny Andrews took seriously. The café was open 24 hours a day, seven days a week, until World War II, when rationed supplies cut hours to six days a week. After 56 years, Andrews closed the café in 1978. (Courtesy of the Webster County Historical Museum.)

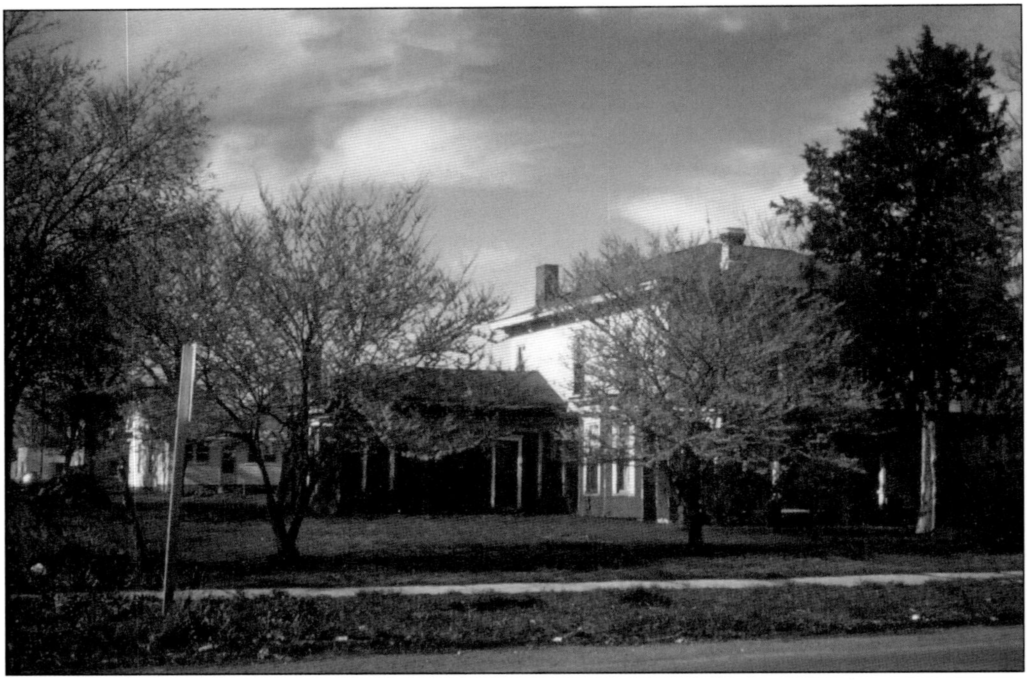

The Ozark Hotel is pictured here in 1969. Opened by R.S. Callaway in 1885, the structure was built in 1881 by N.M. Callaway as his private residence. The building was used as the Frisco Hotel, one of the McMahan Funeral Parlors, and George's Nursing Home. It was also the original site for the Rainey Funeral Home before it was torn down in 1978. (Courtesy of the Webster County Historical Museum.)

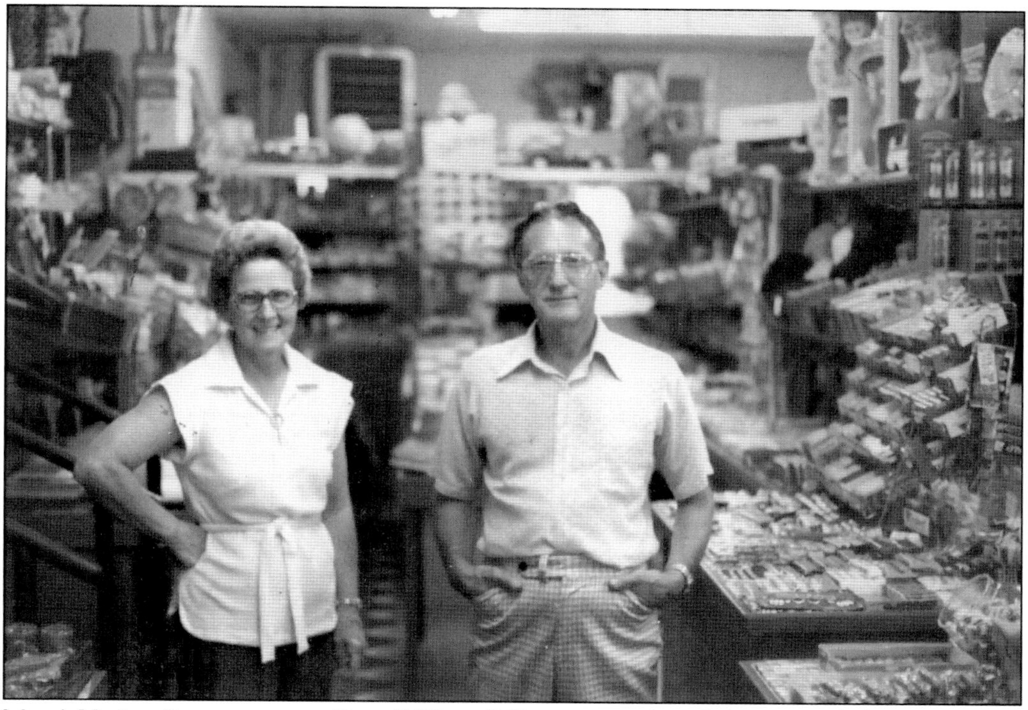

Mary's Variety Store co-owner Carroll "Casey" Gregory stands with longtime clerk Bea Willis in the late 1970s. After it opened around 1935, the store quickly became a popular five-and-dime for local schoolchildren. After a move, expansion, and nearly 80 years, it took health issues to push Mary Gregory, who had owned the store with her husband since 1954, to close. (Courtesy of Mary Gregory.)

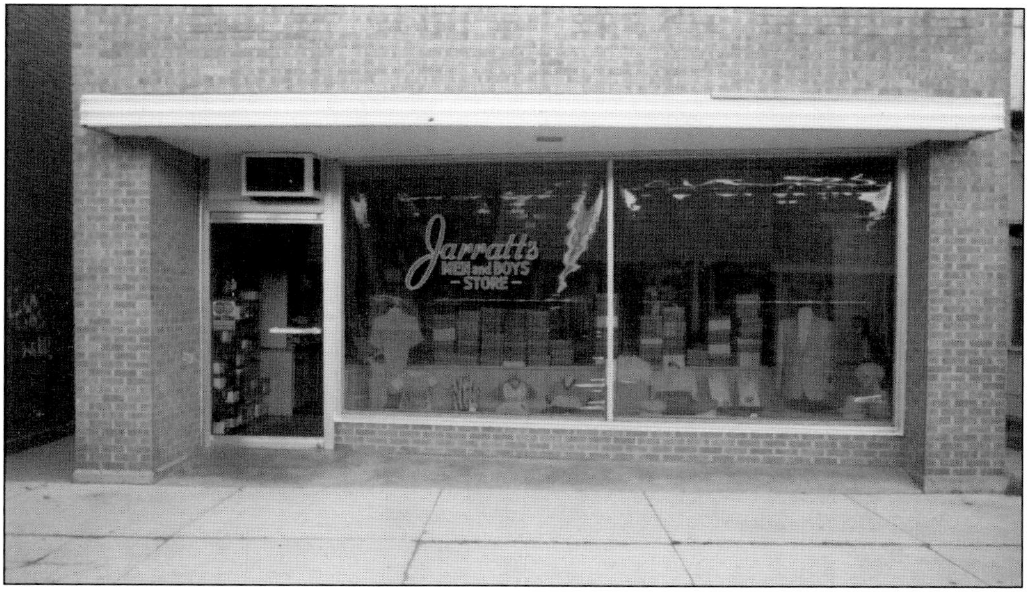

Jarratt's Men and Boys Store is pictured in 1980. Opened in 1952 and located on Crittenden Street, the shop was in operation for 41 years when original co-owner Mildred Jarratt decided it was time to retire in 1993. After it closed, Marshfield's male population was forced to go elsewhere to find clothes for "dad and lad." (Courtesy of the Webster County Historical Museum.)

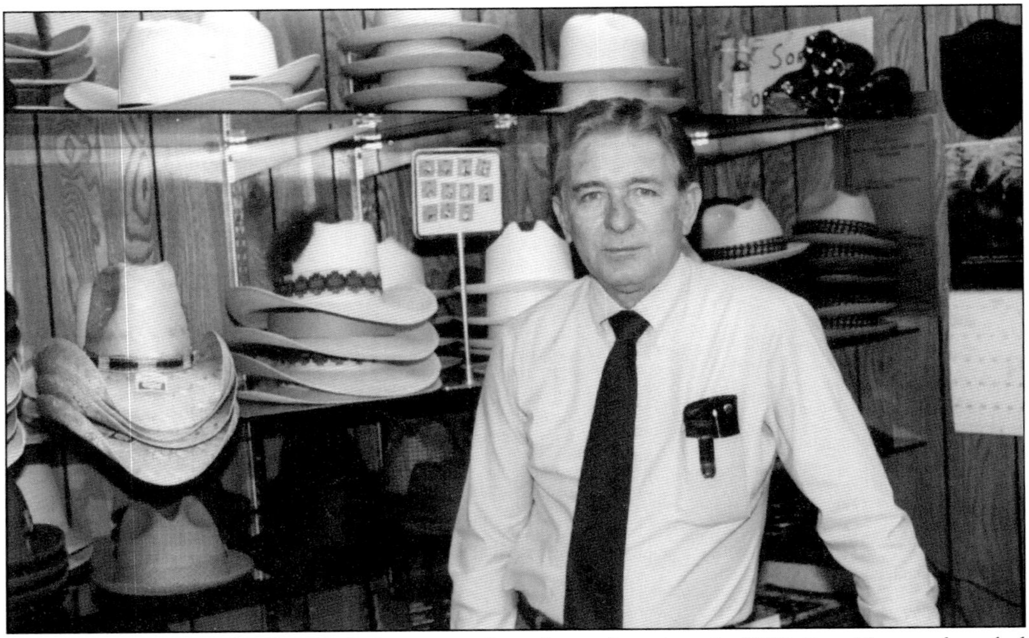

Bob Abbott, owner of Fellin Cash Store, stands at the cash register in 1980. Sam Hoover founded the store around 1923 and sold out to Eugene Pretti and Henry Fellin in the mid-1930s. In 1970, Abbott purchased half of the store from Pretti, and three years later Fellin sold out to Abbott. Abbott continued operation of the store until 2005, when he decided to retire. (Courtesy of the Webster County Historical Museum.)

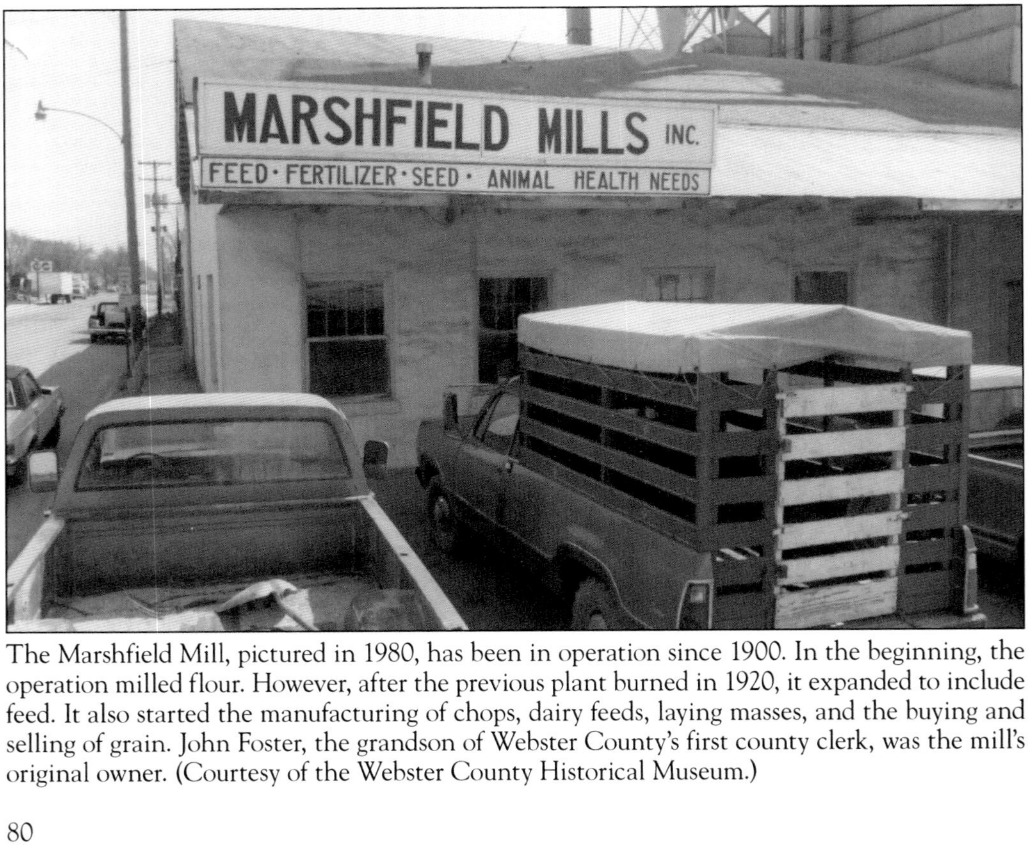

The Marshfield Mill, pictured in 1980, has been in operation since 1900. In the beginning, the operation milled flour. However, after the previous plant burned in 1920, it expanded to include feed. It also started the manufacturing of chops, dairy feeds, laying masses, and the buying and selling of grain. John Foster, the grandson of Webster County's first county clerk, was the mill's original owner. (Courtesy of the Webster County Historical Museum.)

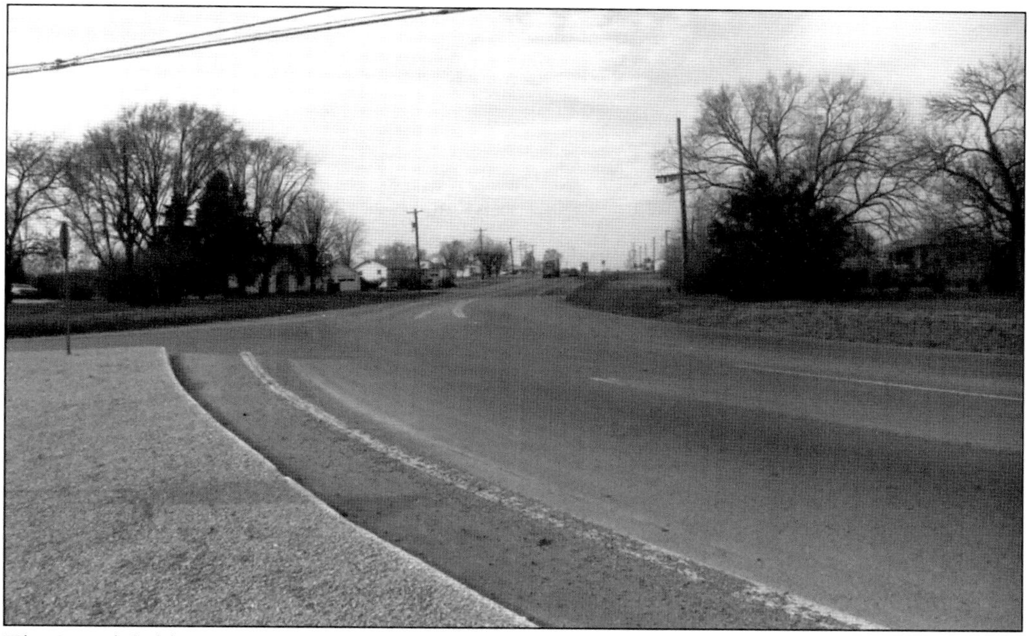

The Marshfield Spur was a much quieter place prior to its development boom in the 1990s. Since then, Kum and Go, Metropolitan Bank, Empire Bank, McDonalds, Wal-Mart, Taco Bell, Dairy Queen, Pizza Hut, Walgreens, Sonic, Antique Mercantile, and numerous other businesses have set up shop, not to mention the addition of several traffic lights and two more traffic lanes. (Courtesy of the Carl Young collection.)

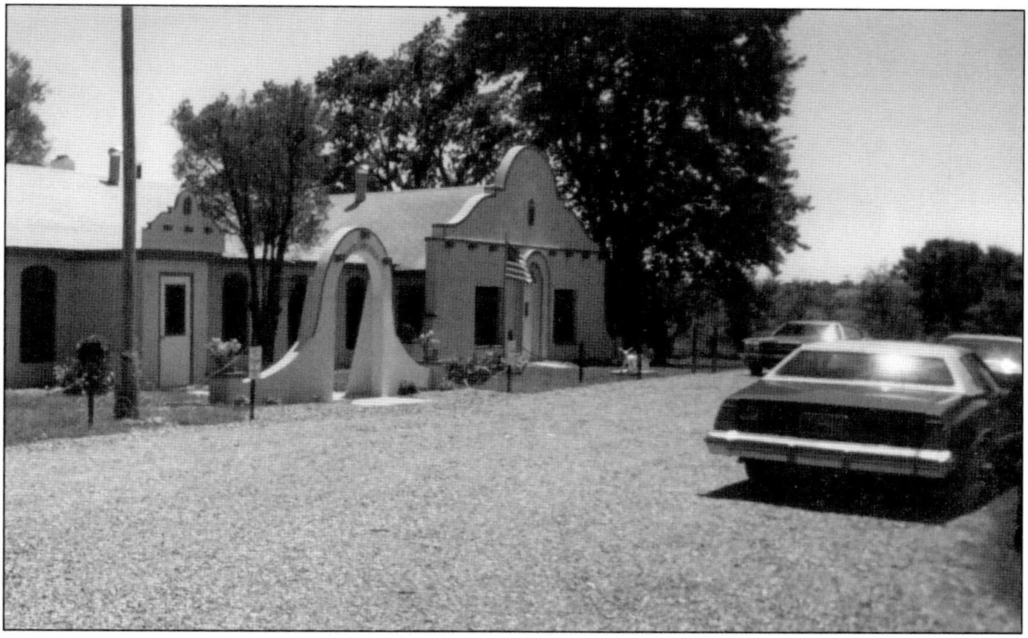

White Oak Villa, formerly known as the Webster County Farm, is pictured in the early 1980s. By the late 1970s, the rising prominence of Medicare was making county homes obsolete, and Webster County was not immune to its effects. Vic and Jackie Perryman purchased the home at auction in 1982 and operated it as a nursing home until 1993, when it was sold and torn down. (Courtesy of Vic Perryman.)

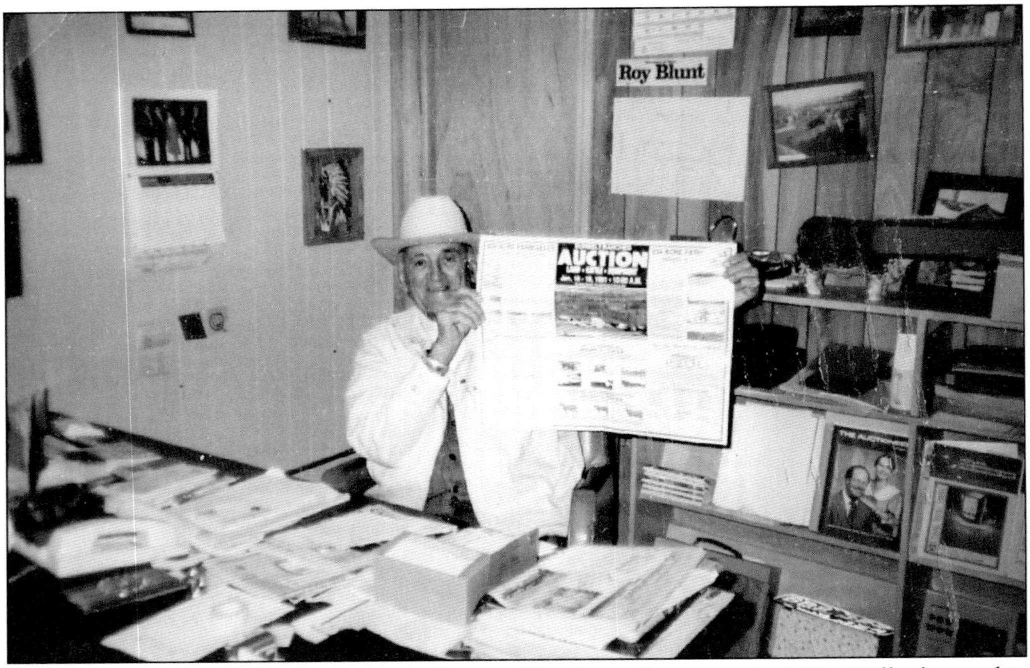

Willis Case is pictured sitting in his office at The Case Company in 1991. Willis began his namesake company on the cusp of World War II, when farmers were selling out to join the service. He already had some training—a week or two of auctioneering school was enough to show him the ropes. The rest of it he learned by 65 years of experience. (Courtesy of Hoover Case.)

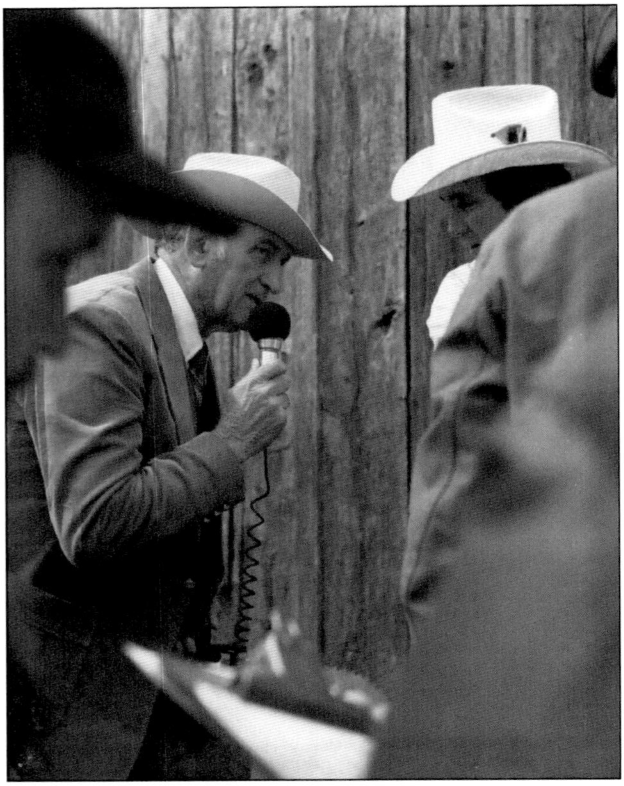

Willis Case and his son Hoover are pictured during an auction. Hoover joined the Case Company in 1969 and has been with the company ever since. While some things have changed over the years, including the expansion of the business to include real estate services, other things such as a friendly, hometown ethic have not. (Courtesy of Hoover Case.)

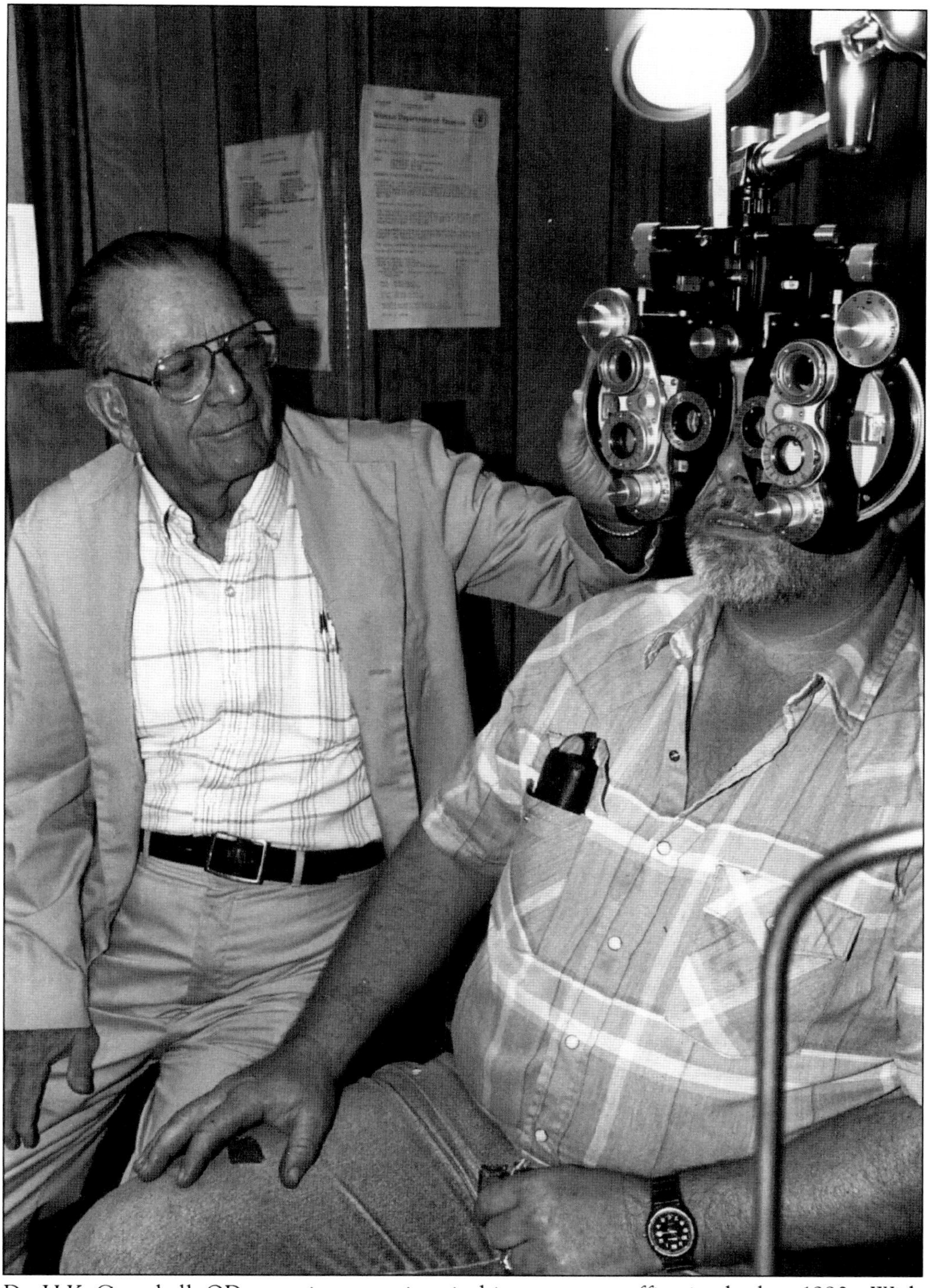

Dr. H.K. Campbell, OD, examines a patient in his optometry office in the late 1990s. With nearly a lifetime in the optometry business, Campbell was a mainstay in Marshfield. Beginning as an apprentice for his father, optometrist John W. Campbell, in 1935, his roots were also close to home. He opened his own practice in 1951, and was there until mere days before his death in 2000. (Courtesy of Diana Hudspeth.)

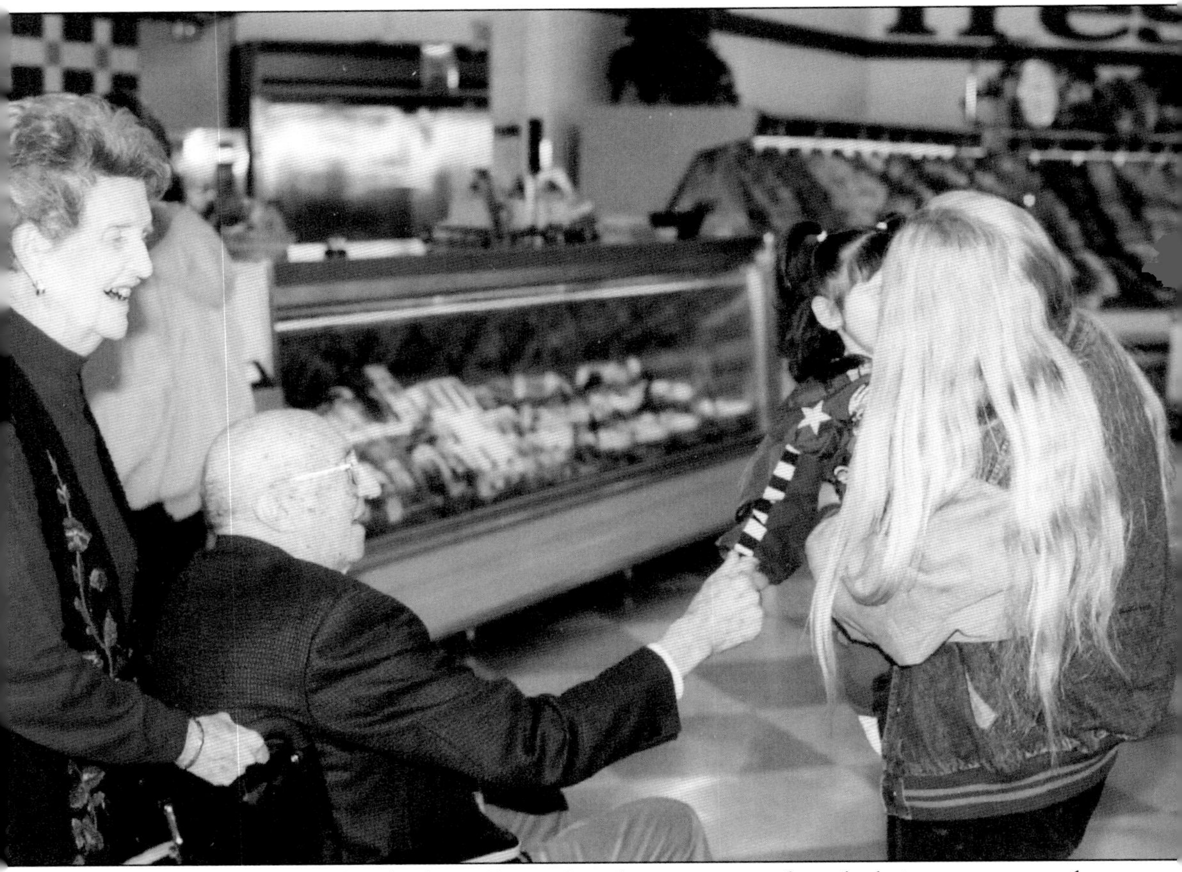

Age did not deter Carl and Glessie Young from keeping in touch with their customers; as long as their health would allow, they were in the store. Their customers were important to them, and they wanted to show it. In 2000, the couple donated 15,000 shares of Wal-Mart stock, worth $1.1 million, to the Marshfield R-I School District for the completion for the high school's auditorium. (Courtesy of the Carl Young collection.)

Three

Learning for Tomorrow

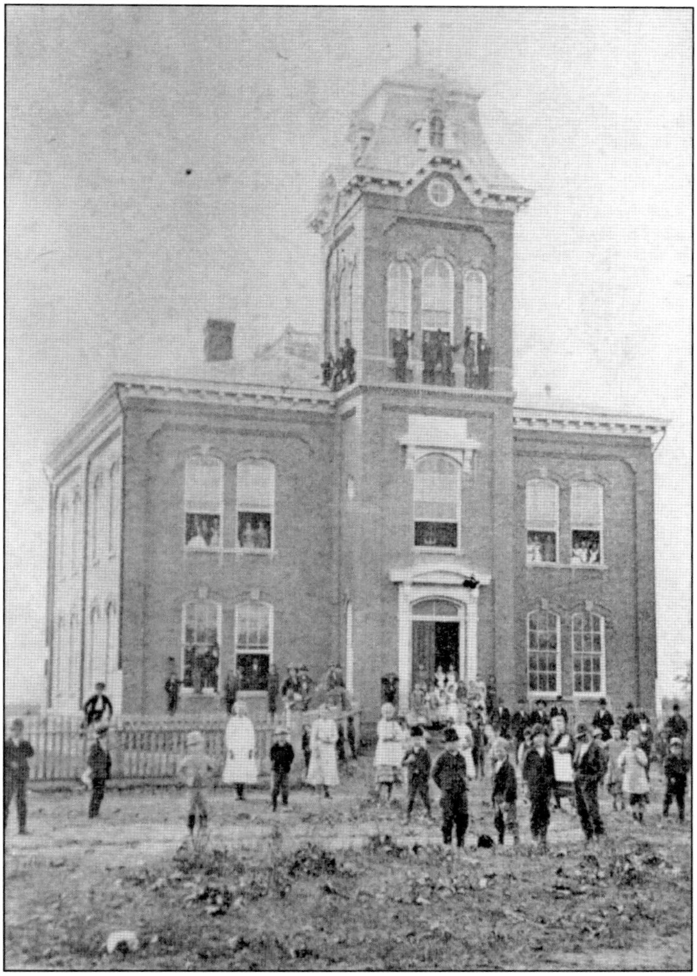

Marshfield Public School and Business Academy is pictured in 1872. Built in 1871, the brick structure replaced the previous school that was located a little north of the square. The new building was constructed three blocks south of the square for $30,000. Eight years later, it was damaged during the 1880 cyclone but not destroyed; instead, it was used as a hospital for the injured. (Courtesy of Randy Clair.)

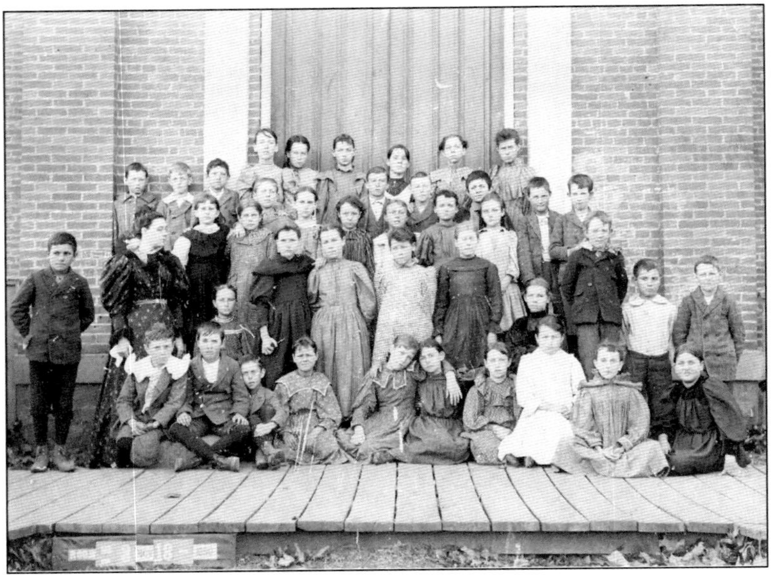

Marshfield students from Room No. 8 pose for a photograph on November 18, 1896. The school housed all ages of students from Marshfield. Rural students, however, attended schools in their local communities until the eighth grade, when those who went on to high school traveled to Marshfield for classes. (Courtesy of Randy Clair.)

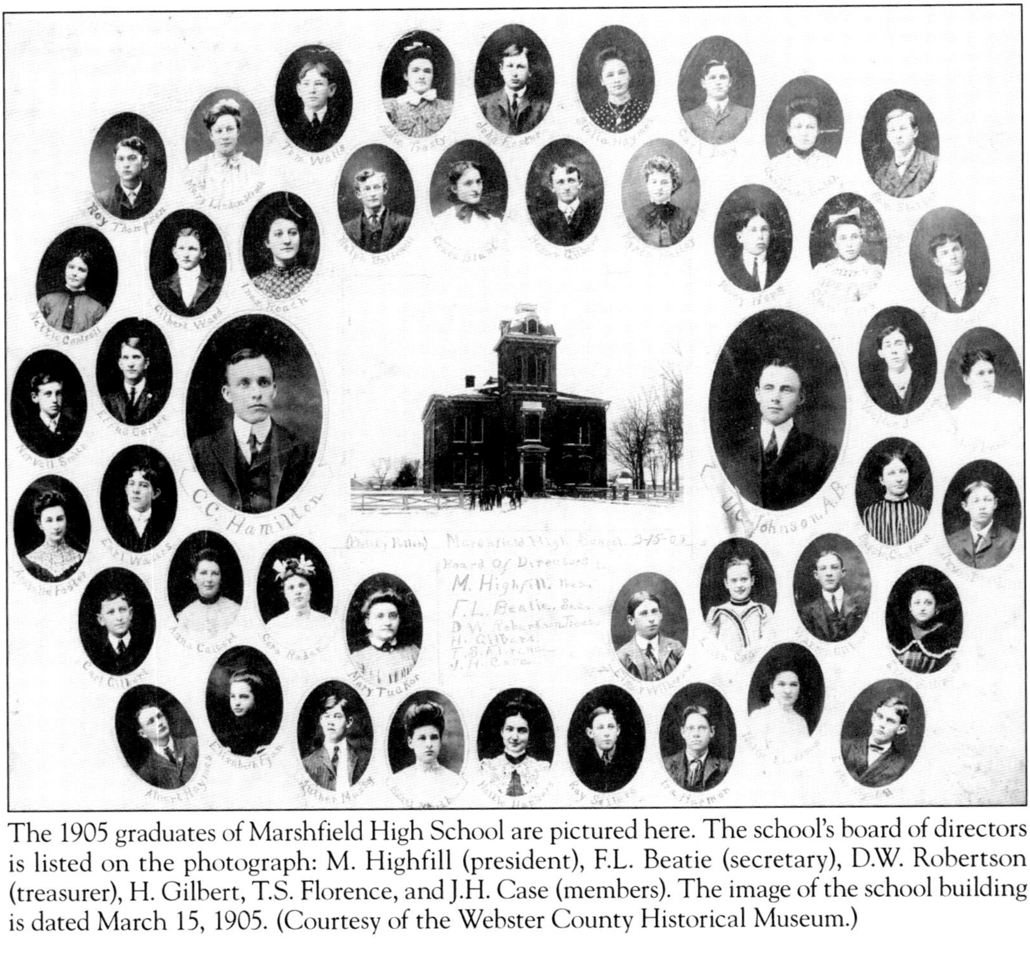

The 1905 graduates of Marshfield High School are pictured here. The school's board of directors is listed on the photograph: M. Highfill (president), F.L. Beatie (secretary), D.W. Robertson (treasurer), H. Gilbert, T.S. Florence, and J.H. Case (members). The image of the school building is dated March 15, 1905. (Courtesy of the Webster County Historical Museum.)

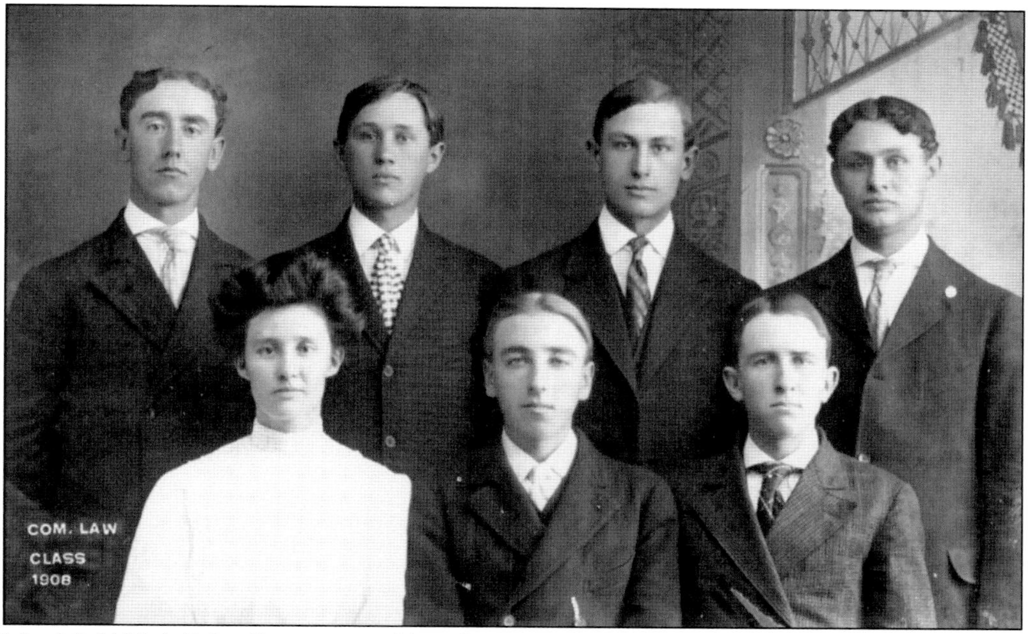

Marshfield High School's commercial law class in 1908 was comprised of five students interested in studying law. The students are, from left to right, (first row) Elza Young Cox, unidentified, and Harry Smith; (second row) Jess Jameson, unidentified, John Foster, and Harry Clair. (Courtesy of the Webster County Historical Museum.)

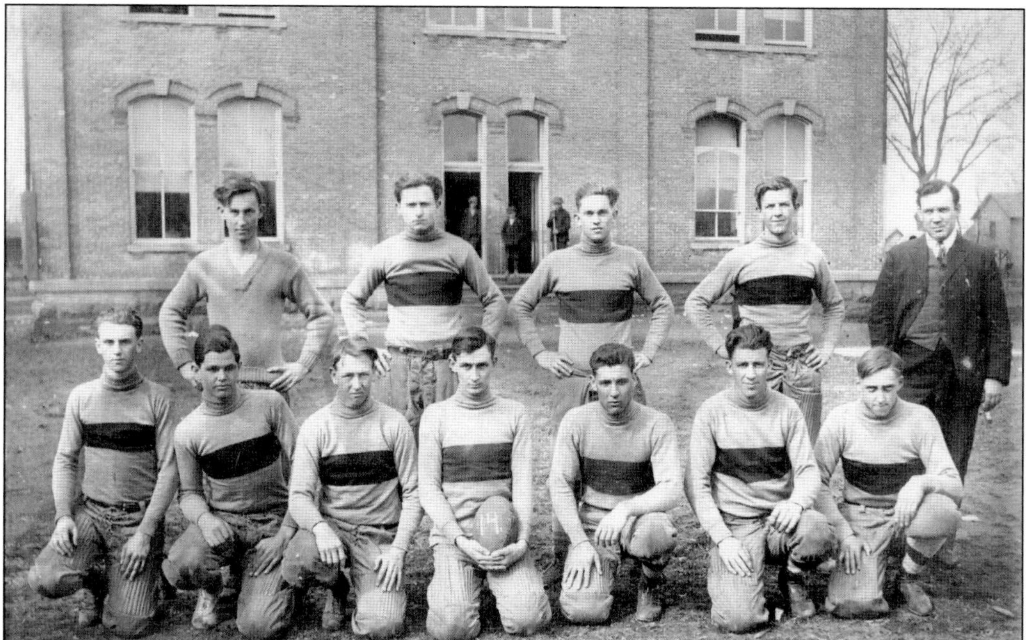

Members of the Marshfield High School football team pose for a photograph around 1910. Murray Thompson, future state representative and owner of Thompson's Furniture Company, is believed to be the player in back to the far right. In the background is the Marshfield School building, which would burn to the ground about six years later. (Courtesy of the Webster County Historical Museum.)

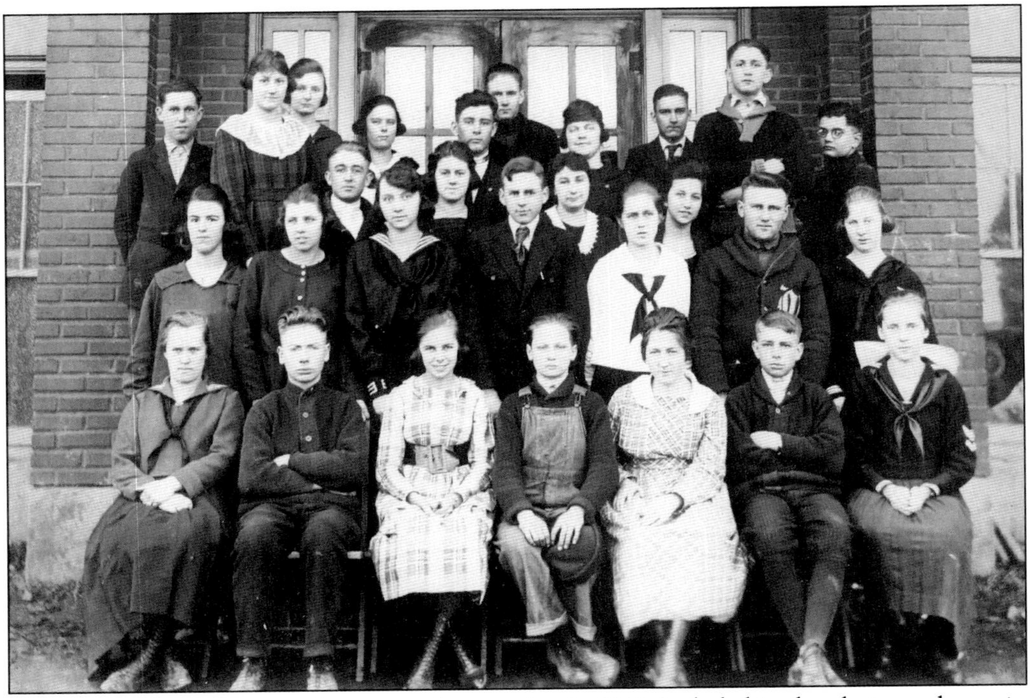

The Marshfield sophomore class is seen here posing in 1919. Included in the photograph are, in no particular order, Agnes Corbett, Albert Elliott, Lucy Mae Smith, Homer Dennis, ? Conrad (Rader), Aubrey Young, Lillian Robertson (Beatie), Opal Watters, Edna Mackey, Ruth Julian, Earl T. Shields, teacher Arabelle Foster, Lena Shook, Lela Wise, Charley Hyde, Jo Hoover (Shields), Thurman Lucas, Etta Stone, Ima Blazer Wright, and Hugh Welch. (Courtesy of Randy Clair.)

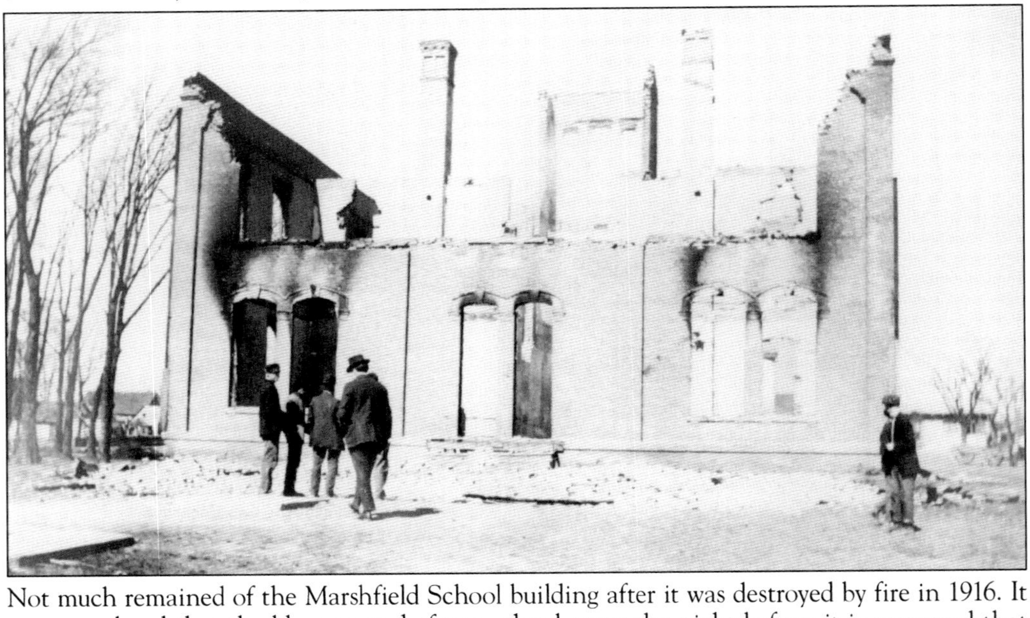

Not much remained of the Marshfield School building after it was destroyed by fire in 1916. It was speculated that the blaze started after a school party the night before; it is presumed that a stove was lit or contained a small fire that may have started the fire. Despite the unexpected events, the 1916 senior class graduated on June 2 in the Marshfield Christian Church. (Courtesy of Randy Clair.)

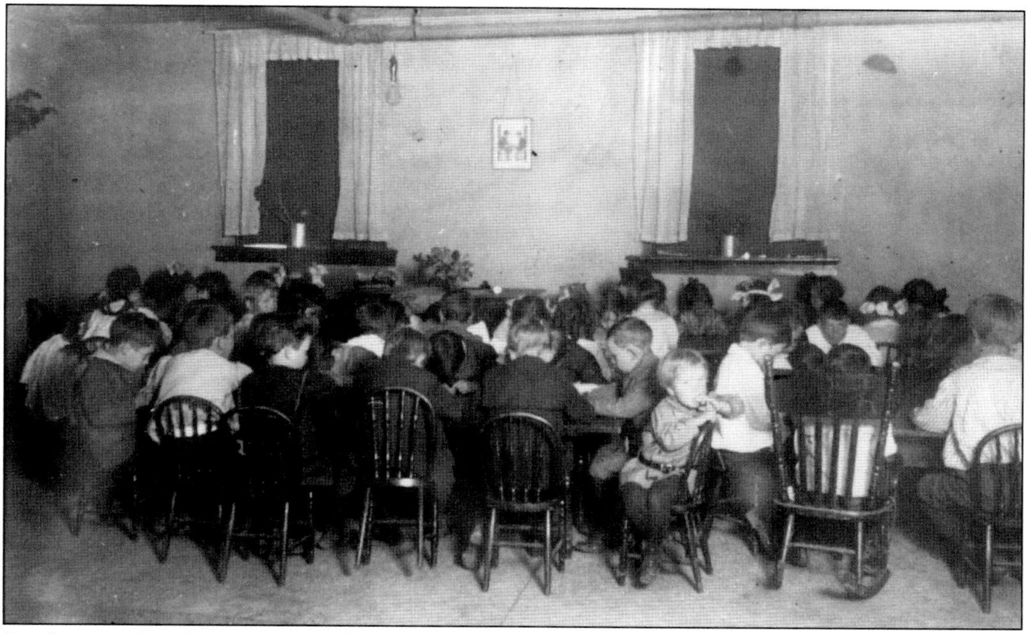

Students are hard at work in the basement of the then Carnegie Library. After Marshfield School burned down in 1916, classes were held many different places around town, including various churches, businesses, and empty buildings until a new structure could be built for future students. Students were once again housed in the library in the 1960s, while there was a private kindergarten housed in the basement. (Courtesy of Randy Clair.)

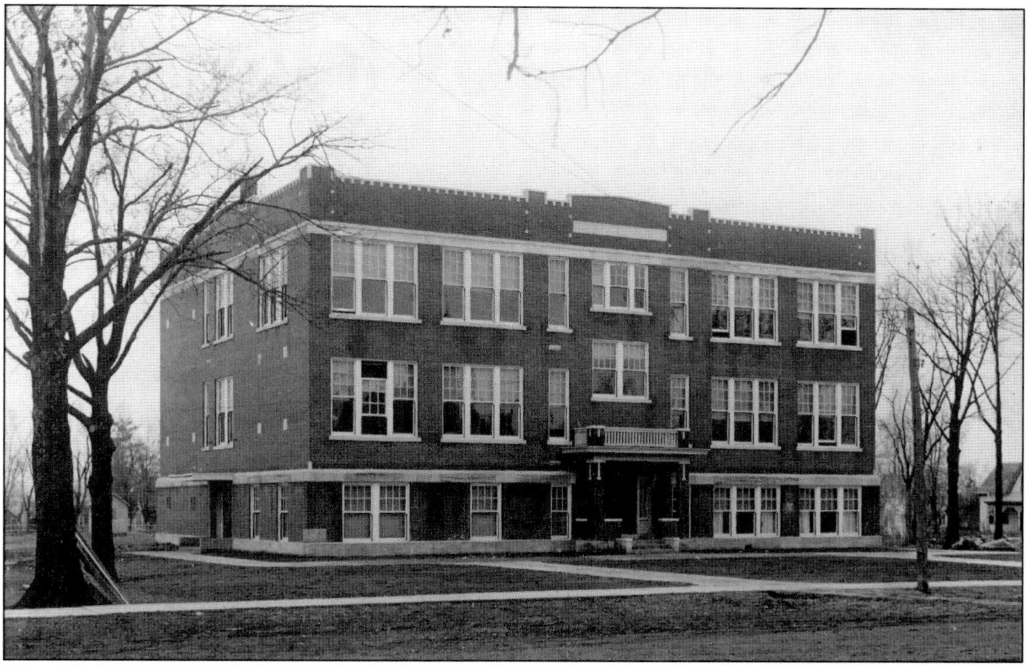

Marshfield's oldest school building in recent memory was constructed between 1916 and 1917 at a cost of $31,000. Many of the bricks used in its construction were recycled from the previous building that was destroyed by fire. Boys were hired to clean the remaining bricks from the burned building and were paid 25¢ per 100 bricks for their work. (Courtesy of Randy Clair.)

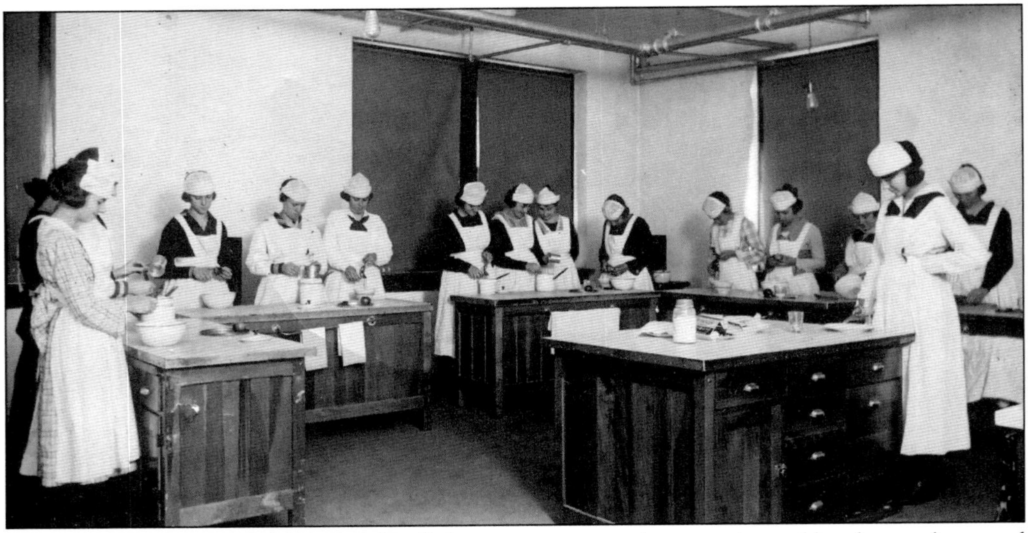

Members of the Marshfield High School's home economics class are pictured hard at work around 1919. Supervised by teacher Arabelle Foster, some of the students include Maggie Mae Robertson, Agnes Corbett, Willie Robertson, Jo Hoover, Hester Haymes, Ruth Julian, and Lucy Mae Smith, who would later serve as Marshfield's home economics teacher. (Courtesy of the Webster County Historical Museum.)

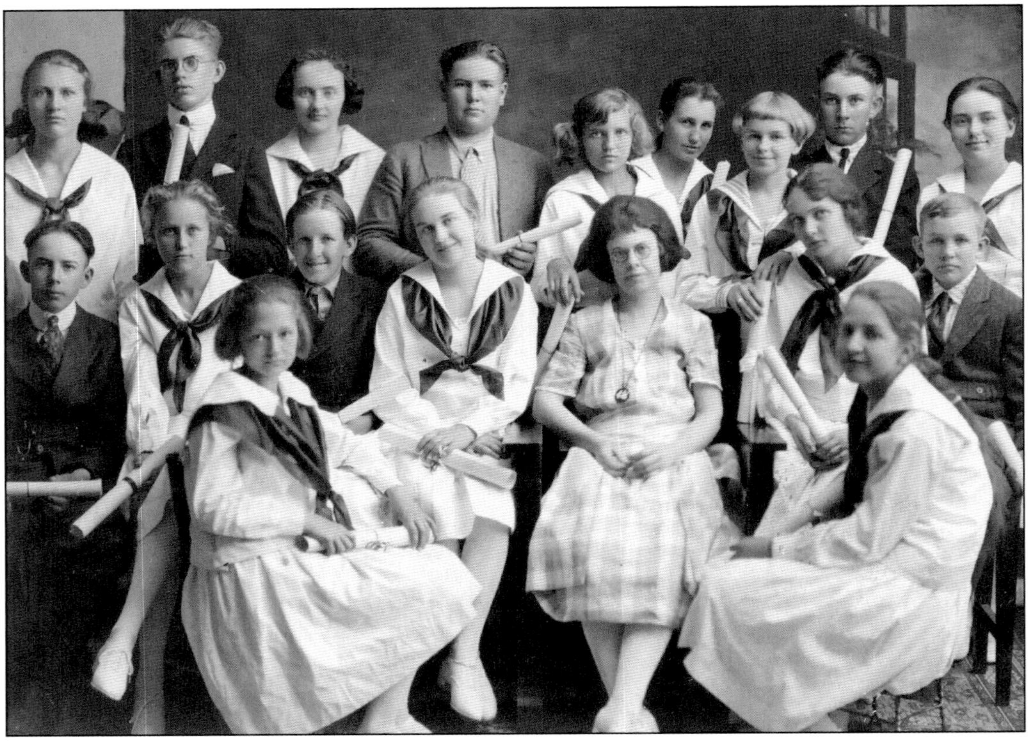

Members of the eighth-grade class at Marshfield pose for a portrait before graduation in 1922. Some of the students identified are Retha Stone, Margaret Thompson, Mildred Koby, Glen Smith, Jewel Banning, Theresa Cantrel, Emil Holmes, Henry Clouse, Thelma Morris, Doris Moore, Frances Haymes, Correy Hedgepath, and Wilma Owens. (Courtesy of the Webster County Historical Museum.)

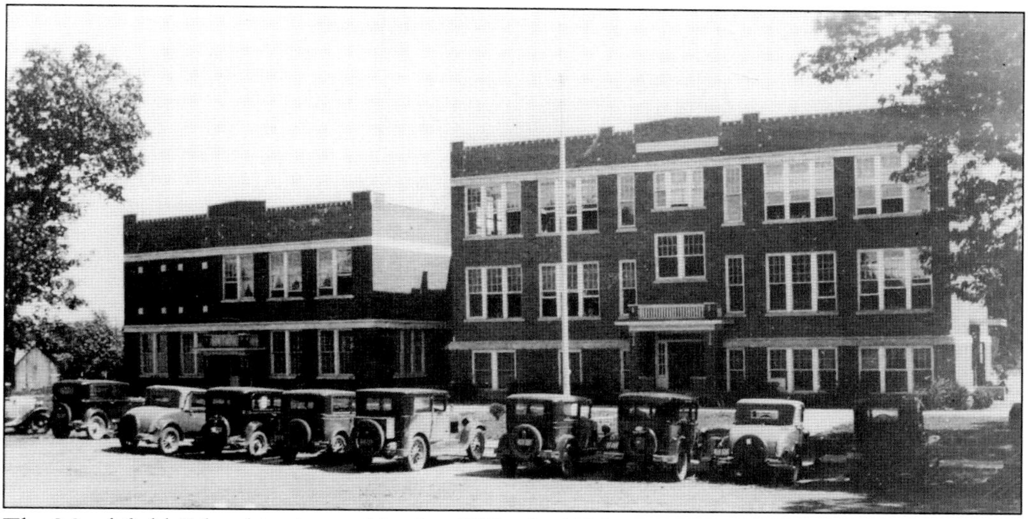

The Marshfield School is pictured in the 1930s. In 1954, a new gymnasium was constructed at a cost of $112,000, and the old gym was converted into classrooms and a library. High school students used the building until 1976, when a new school was constructed across town. Junior high classes were held in the building until the end of the 2001 school year. (Courtesy of the Webster County Historical Museum.)

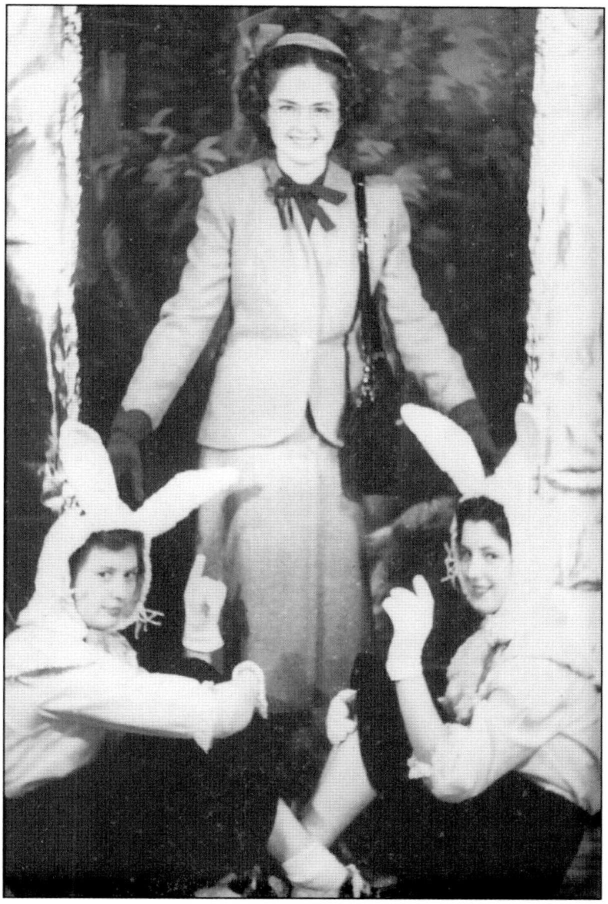

Marshfield High School students Carlene (Young) Williams, Mary (Johnson) McConnell, and Rowena (Young) Wilson model for the school's annual Easter Parade c. 1949. Home economics teacher Lucy May Smith organized the showcase, held in the school gymnasium, as an opportunity for students to show off what they had sewn during their classes. The money raised from the event was used for improvements in the home economics department. (Courtesy of Mary McConnell.)

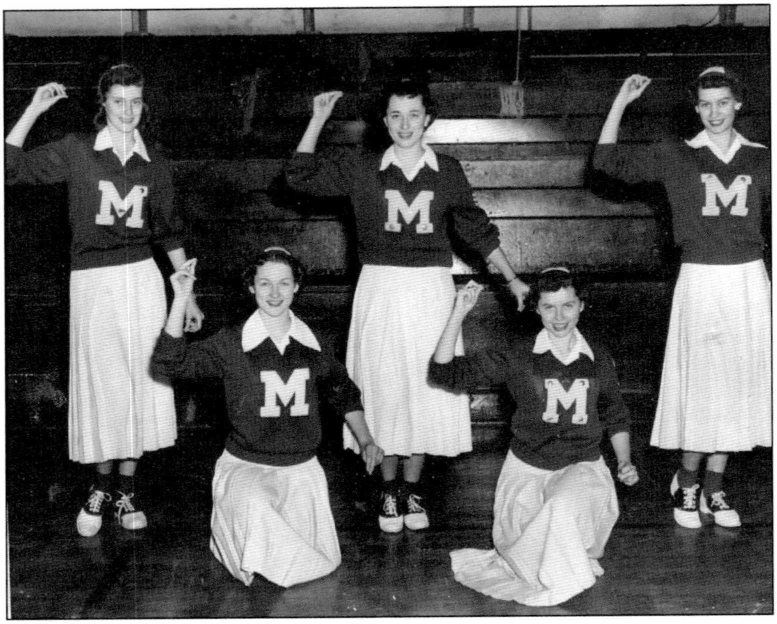

Cheerleaders from the Marshfield High School's "A" team pose for the camera in 1953. Those pictured in no particular order are Jane Beatie, Colleen Glaubitz, Peggy Layman, Conny Layman, and Joyce Renner. The next year, the school added on a new gymnasium to the west side of the school. (Courtesy of the Webster County Historical Museum.)

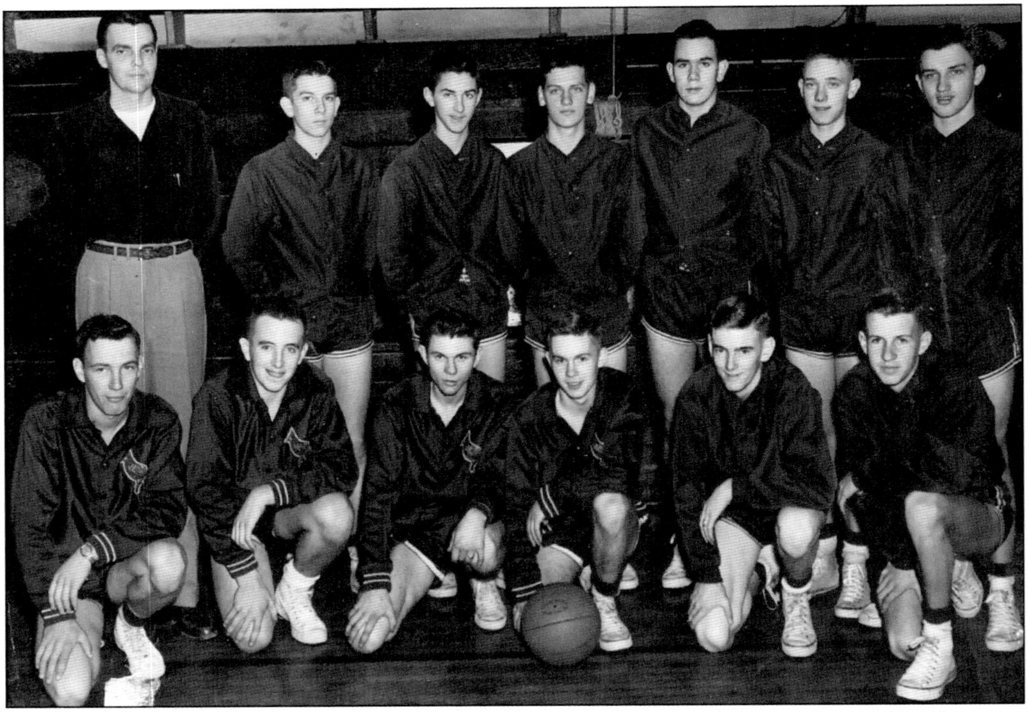

The Marshfield High School "B" basketball team takes time for a photograph in 1953. They are, from left to right, (first row) Larry Day, John Roper, Roy Wilson, Wayne Evans, Mac Case, and Wayne Hurst; (second row) coach Bell, David Gillman, Donnie Rudolph, Terry Lawrence, Bob Bruce, Leon Jones, and Charles Hyde. (Courtesy of the Webster County Historical Museum.)

Wesley Anderson, basketball player John Roper, and Ralph Todd are hanging out in the locker room, apparently checking out basketball jerseys for the 1953 season. The poster on the left explains to players what to do on defense when the opposing team is trying to attempt a shot during a game. (Courtesy of the Webster County Historical Museum.)

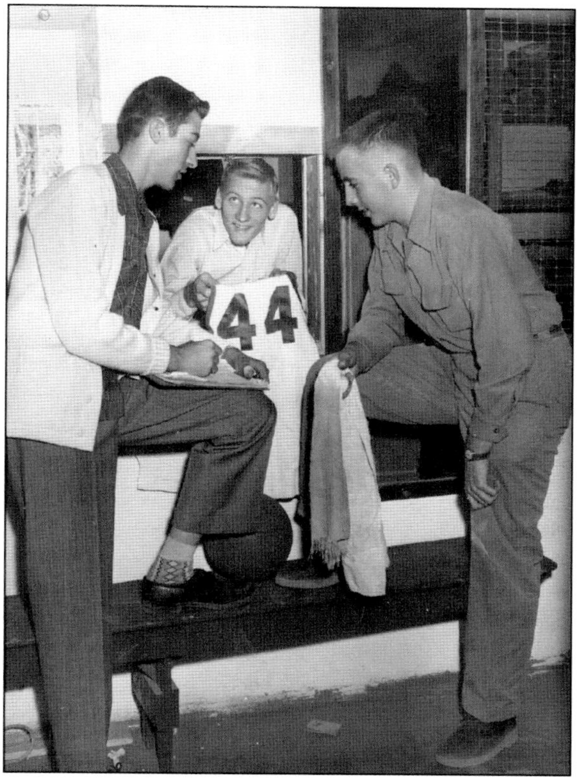

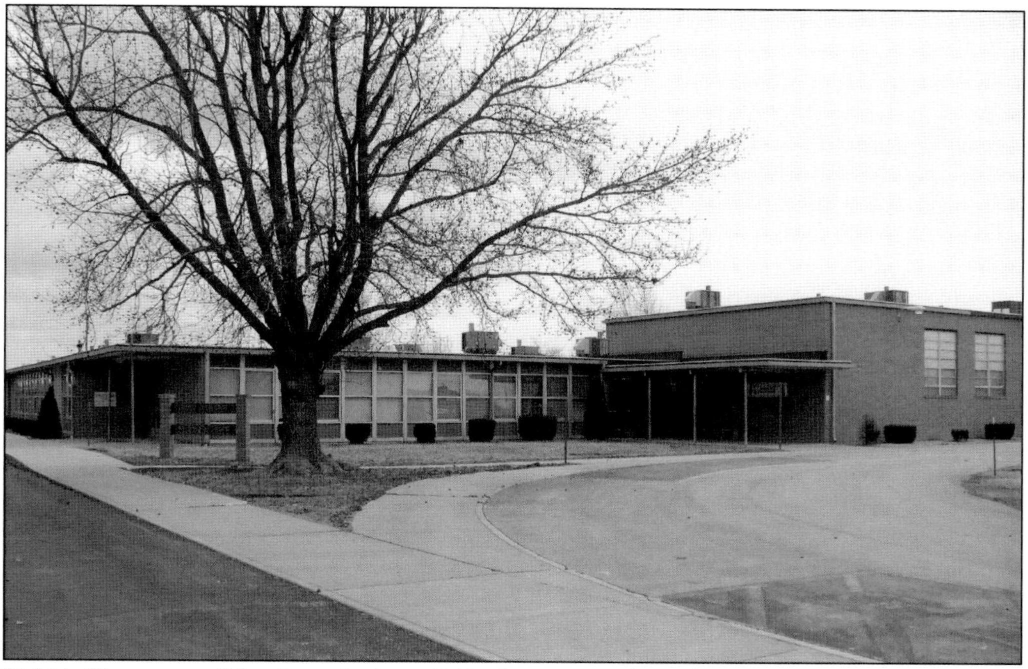

Hubble Elementary School was built in 1960 after increased enrollment in the district prompted the construction of Marshfield's first grade school. The school was joined by another elementary building three years later. In 1965, the two buildings were joined; subsequent additions were also made to the building in 1967, 1969, and 1975. (Courtesy of the Webster County Historical Museum.)

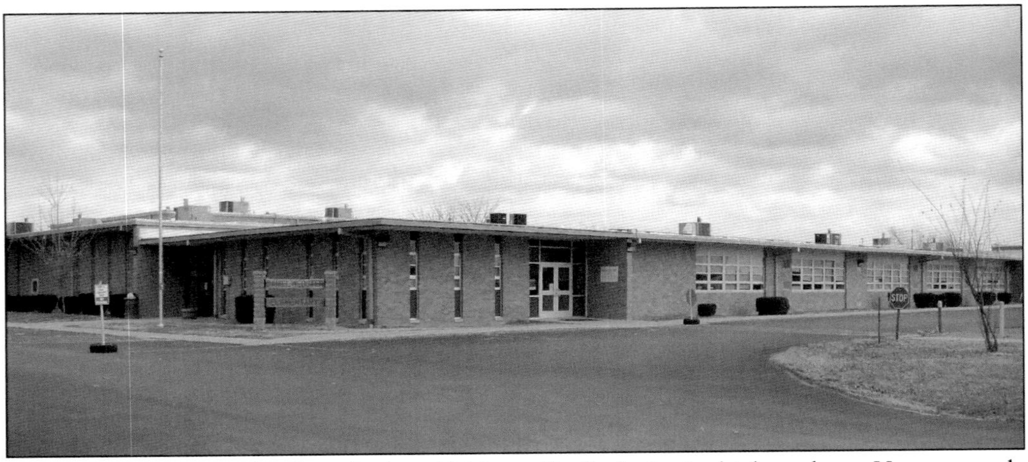

Webster Elementary School was built in 1966 specifically for junior high students. However, only nine years later, crowded conditions prompted plans for the construction of a new high school. After its completion, junior high students went back to the old building on Commercial Street, and the high school occupied both buildings. After several years and numerous campus-wide additions, Webster housed just upper elementary students. (Courtesy of the Webster County Historical Museum.)

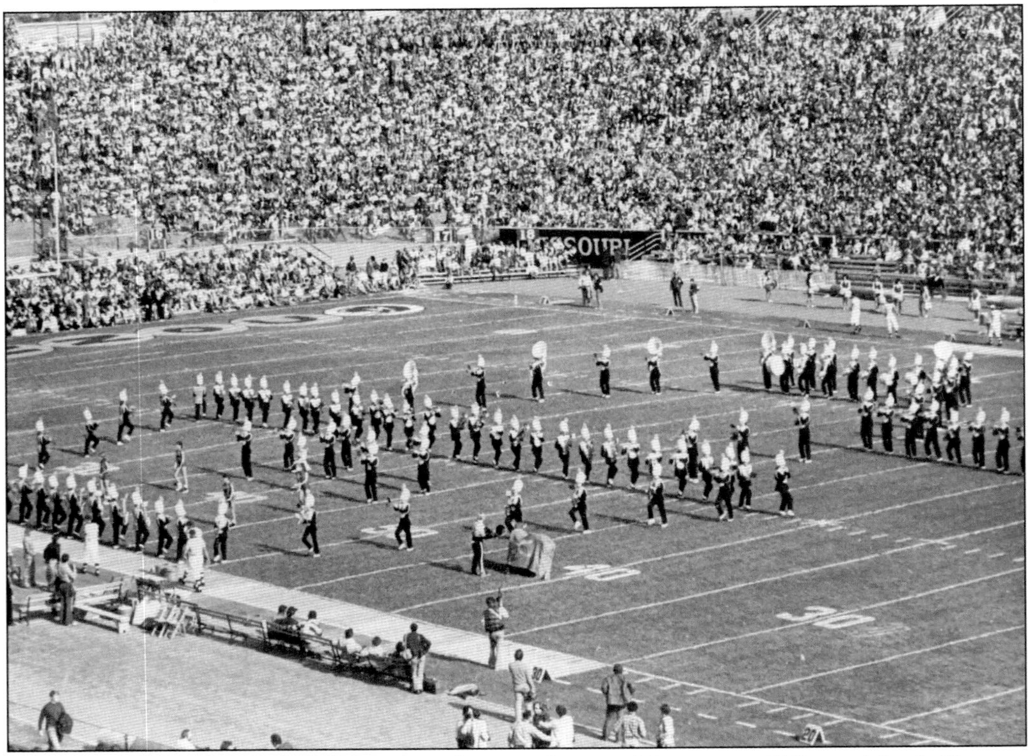

Marshfield High School's band is seen performing during a University of Missouri football game. Marshfield's band program garnered great respect throughout the region over several decades, much due to the hard work and dedication of director F. D. "Dee" Lewis. Under his leadership, the band received nothing but I ratings (the best possible) at district and state contests, along with countless awards for marching and musicality. (Courtesy of the Marshfield High School Band archives.)

Four

Faith of Our Fathers

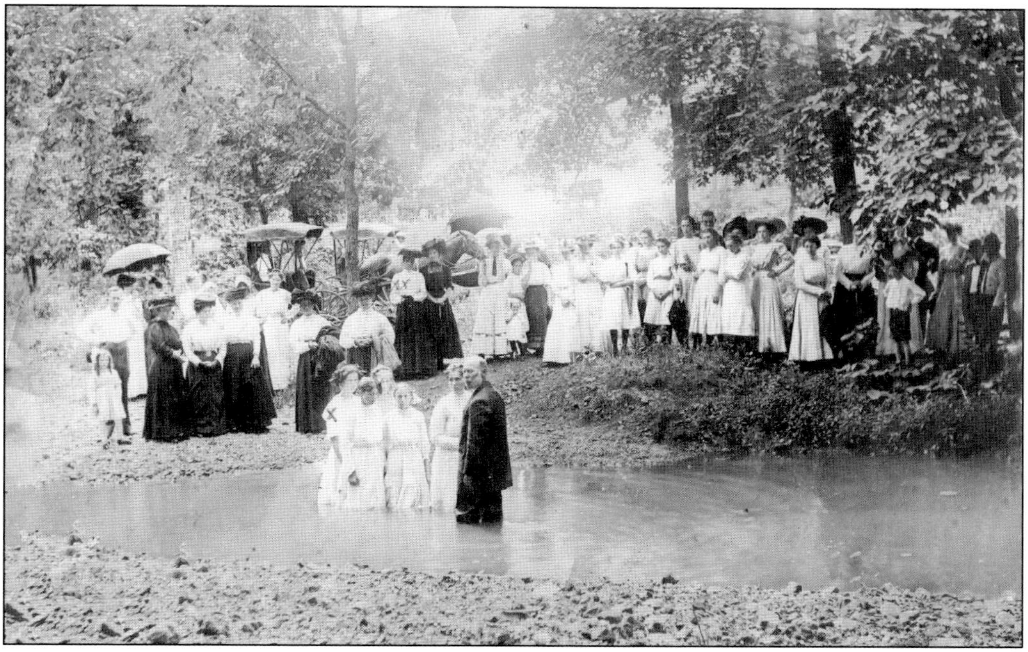

This is a 1910 river baptism being conducted by Marshfield First Baptist Church at Turnbo Creek. Before churches had indoor baptisms, river baptisms were a common occurrence, both throughout the year and during revivals. Those pictured include Reverend Langley, Ruth Popejoy, Ethel Shelton, Clara Letterman, Mrs. W.M. Popejoy, and Ola "Ollie" Popejoy. (Courtesy of Jennifer Hartman.)

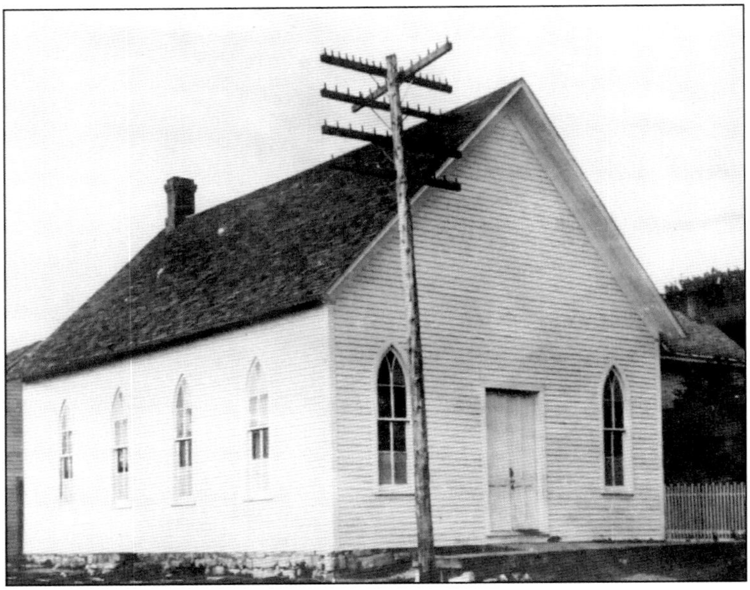

Work on the Marshfield Christian Church's first building began in December 1881, two years after the church was organized. The white frame building, which cost $1,170 to construct, was used by the congregation for nearly 30 years until a new building was constructed at the corner of Clay and Jackson Streets. (Courtesy of the Webster County Historical Museum.)

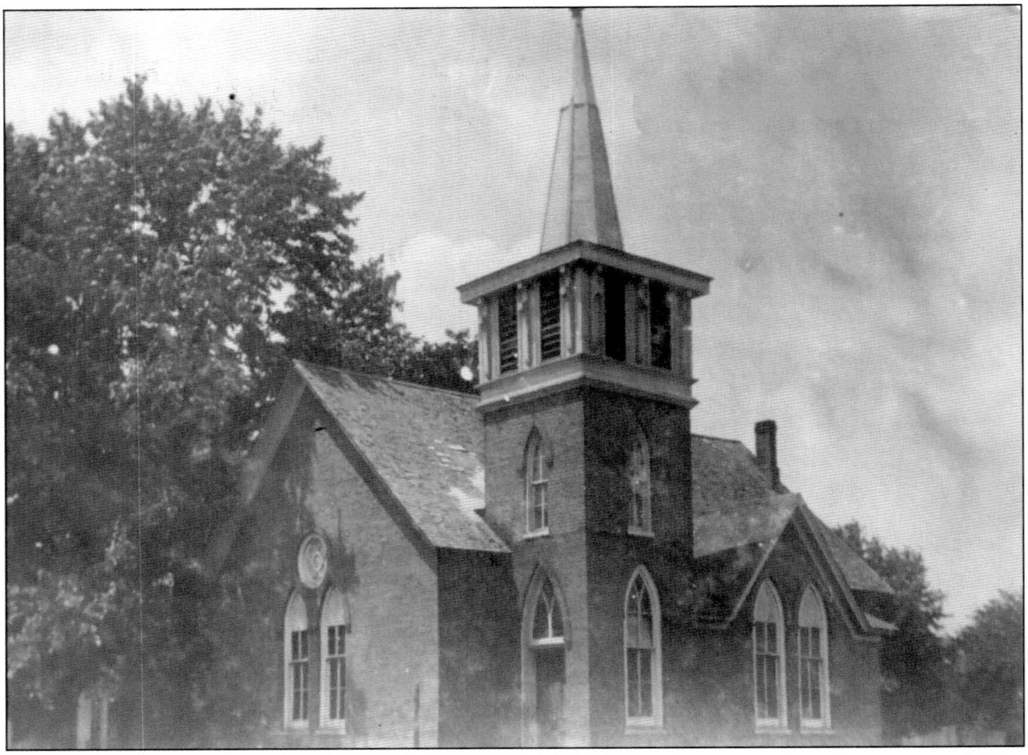

The Methodist Episcopal Church is pictured in the early 1900s. Located at the corner of Clay and Jackson Streets, the building was constructed after the 1880 cyclone destroyed the previous church. It was renamed the Condo Church after the congregation's minister, Rev. E.E. Condo, who was killed in the tornado. (Courtesy of the Webster County Historical Museum.)

The Methodist Episcopal Church, South, is pictured sometime between 1880 and 1909. The structure was built after the previous church was destroyed in the 1880 cyclone. The building itself was destroyed in a windstorm in 1909 and was replaced by a brick building that housed Methodist services until 1986. (Courtesy of the Webster County Historical Museum.)

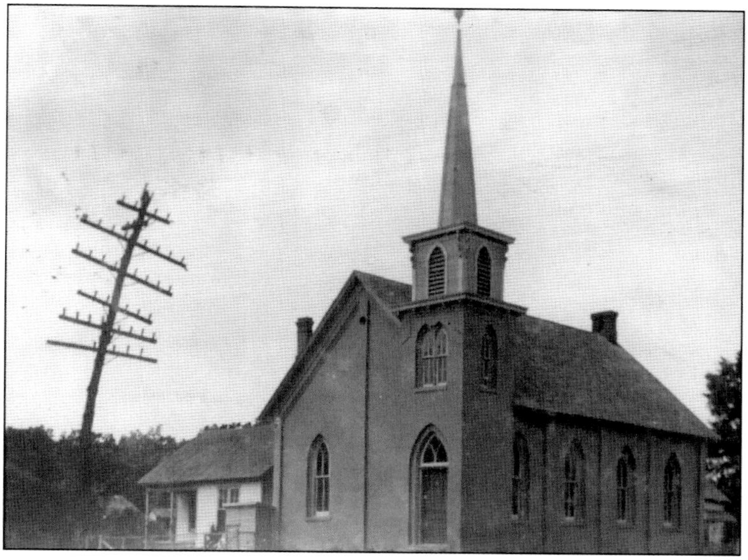

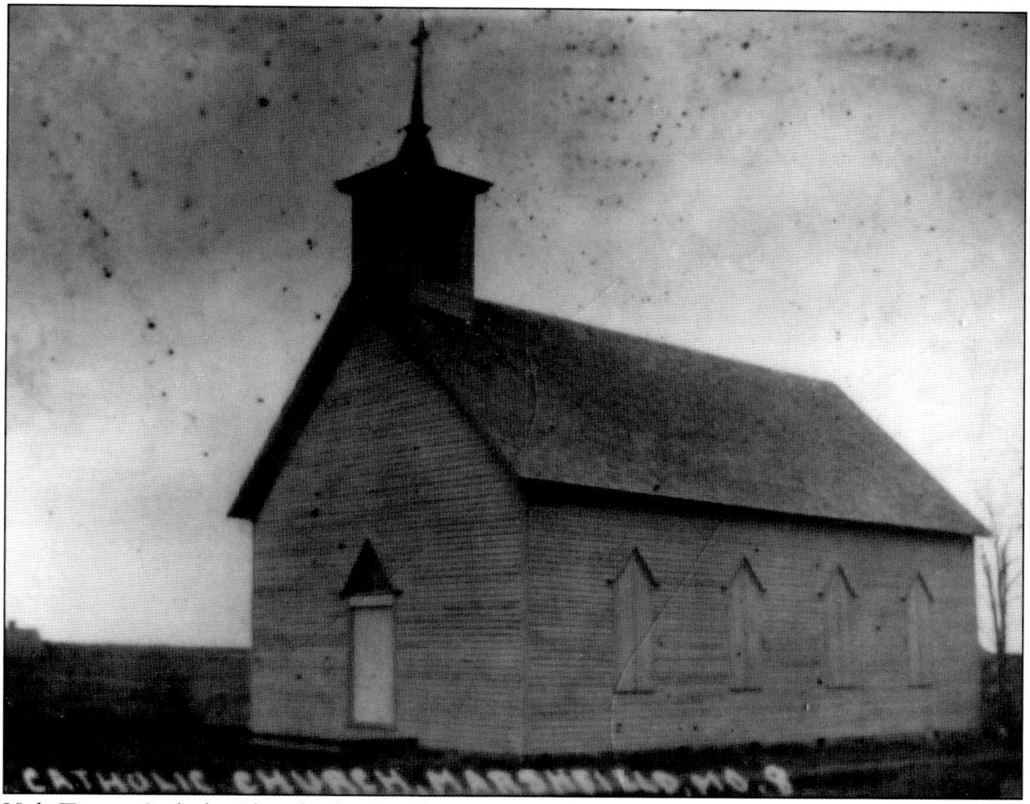

Holy Trinity Catholic Church's first building is pictured in the early 1900s. The parish's initial Mass was held in the Calahan family home. In 1890, services were held on the second floor of what was to become Rathbun's Drug Store. Construction on a building began in 1892, and the first Mass in the new church was held the following year. (Courtesy of Holy Trinity Catholic Church.)

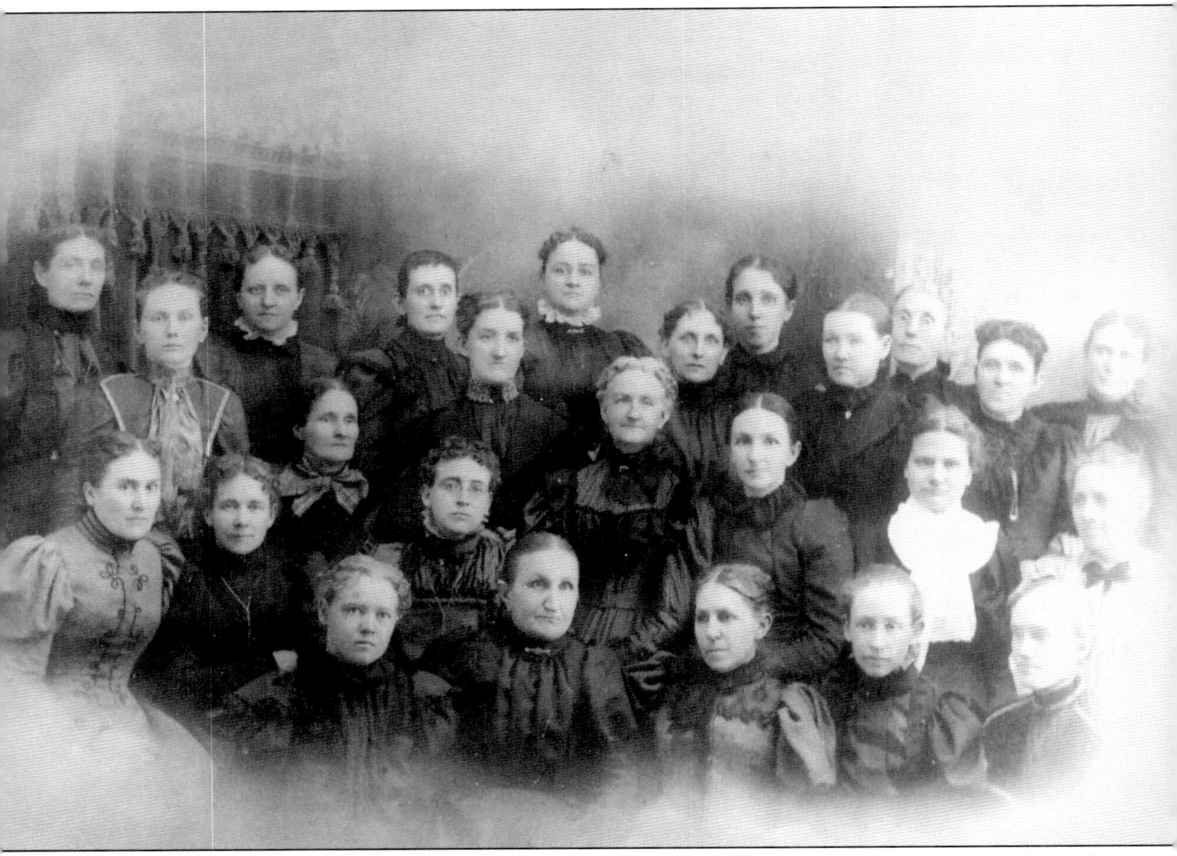

Members of the Condo Methodist Ladies' Aid are pictured around 1905. In no particular order in this photograph are Ida Case, Ida Brooks, Lottie Long, Jessie Gilbert, Maggie Jackson, Laura Winslow, Hattie Hyde, Mrs. W.S. Thompson, Ollie Prater, Annie Richardson, Mrs. Malone, Kate Bodenhammer, Jenny Humphrey, Mrs. Edmonds, Louis Yarbrough, Hannah Nelson, Josephine Gilbert, Nannie Gilbert, Mrs. Jones, Mollie Gilbert, Fannie Evans, Ida Derrick, Mrs. Hill, Mamie Watters, and Judy Barnes. (Courtesy of the Marshfield United Methodist Church.)

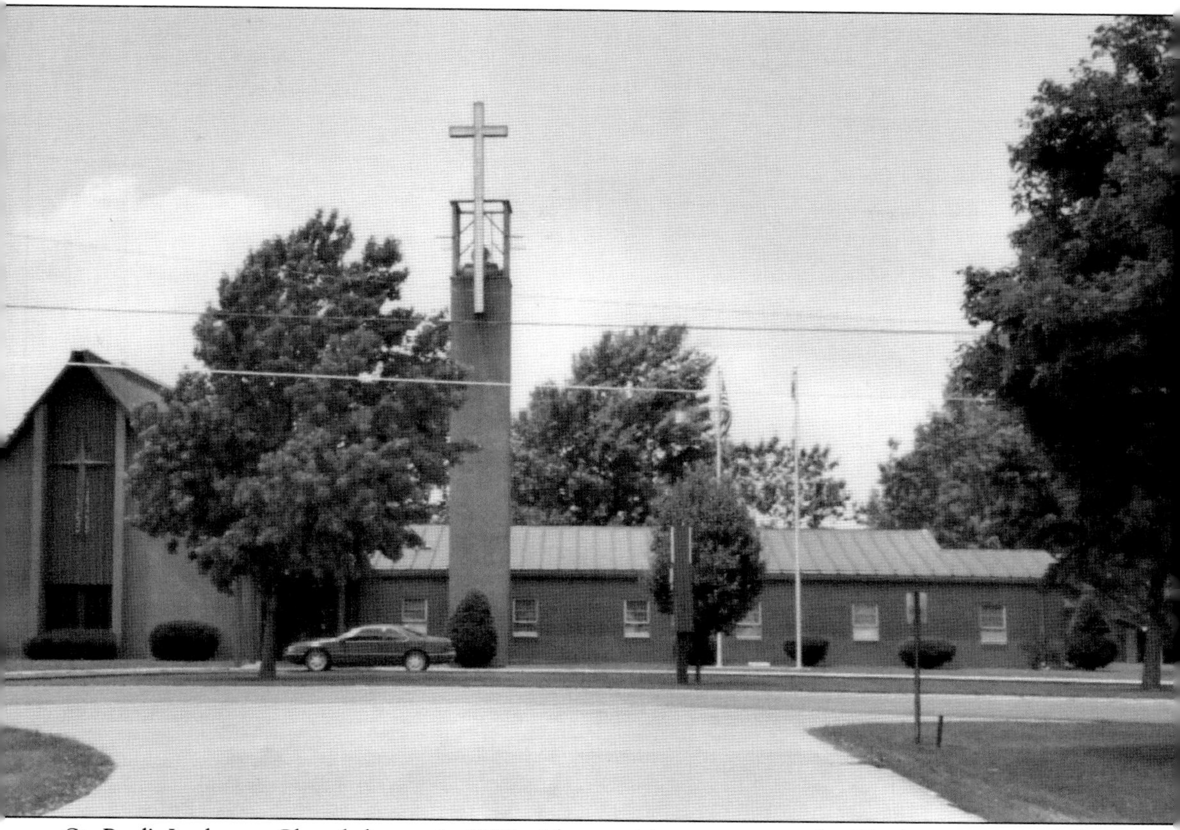

St. Paul's Lutheran Church began in 1875 with monthly meetings in the Plank community led by Rev. Andrew Rader. The first church was destroyed in the 1880 cyclone; the congregation moved to Marshfield and built a small basement chapel in 1923. After forming a joint parish in 1938 with Zion Lutheran Church, and under the direction of a regular pastor, the church grew exponentially. (Courtesy of the Webster County Historical Museum.)

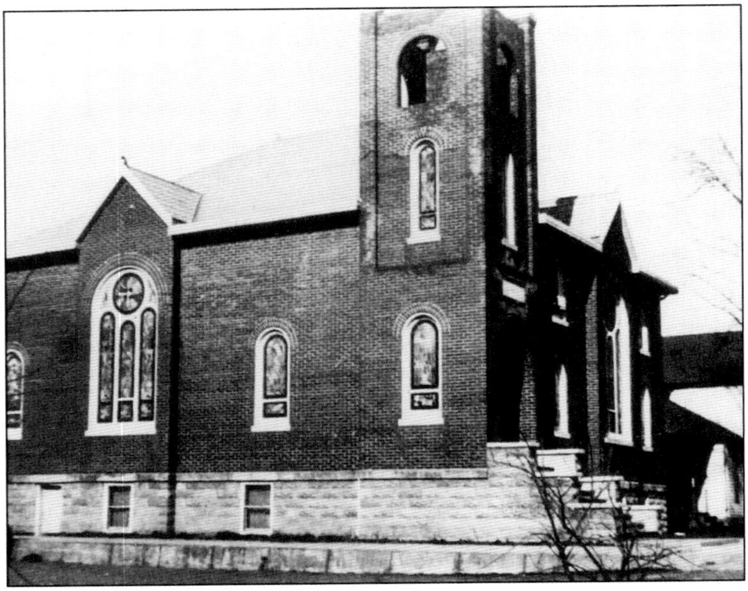

The Marshfield Christian Church is shown after construction of the church's second building. Constructed in 1912, the redbrick facility was used until the dedication of a new building in April 1993. During those eight decades, the church became famous for its chicken potpie dinners that occurred from the 1920s through the 1950s. (Courtesy of the Webster County Historical Museum.)

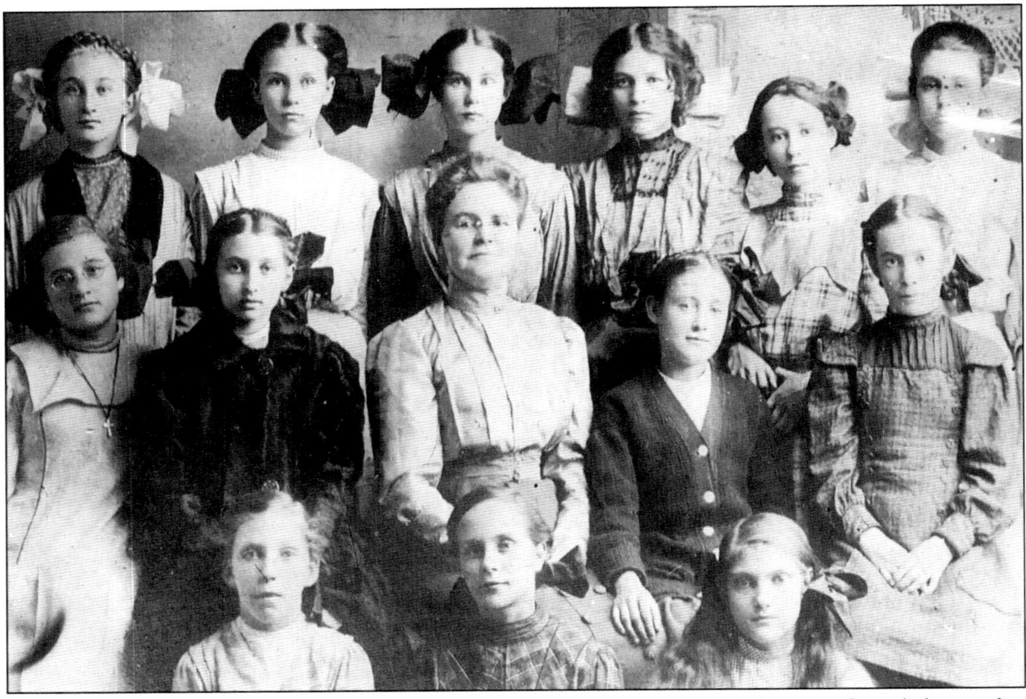

A Marshfield First Baptist Church Sunday School class poses in 1912. They are, from left to right, (first row) unidentified, unidentified, and Lucile Olivant; (second row) Letha Wallace, Gladys Anderson, Mrs. Langley (the teacher and pastor's wife), Maybelle Jameson, and unidentified; (third row) Ethel Shelton, unidentified, Mary Hamilton, Ruth (Popejoy) Greer Carter, Sadie Vanpool, and Clara Letterman. (Courtesy of Jennifer Hartman.)

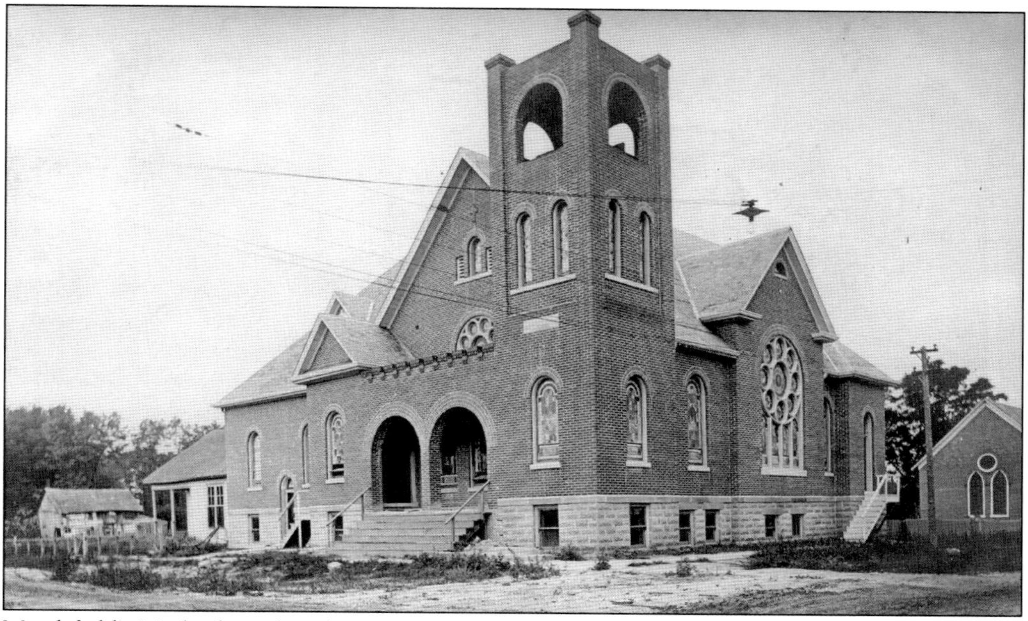

Marshfield's Methodist Church, South, built the St. John's Church for $30,000 in 1909 after a windstorm destroyed the previous facility. The building solely housed the Southern Methodist Congregation until 1939, when northern and southern Methodists united. The Marshfield congregation became the Marshfield Methodist Church, which used the building until the completion of a new facility in 1986. (Courtesy of the Webster County Historical Museum.)

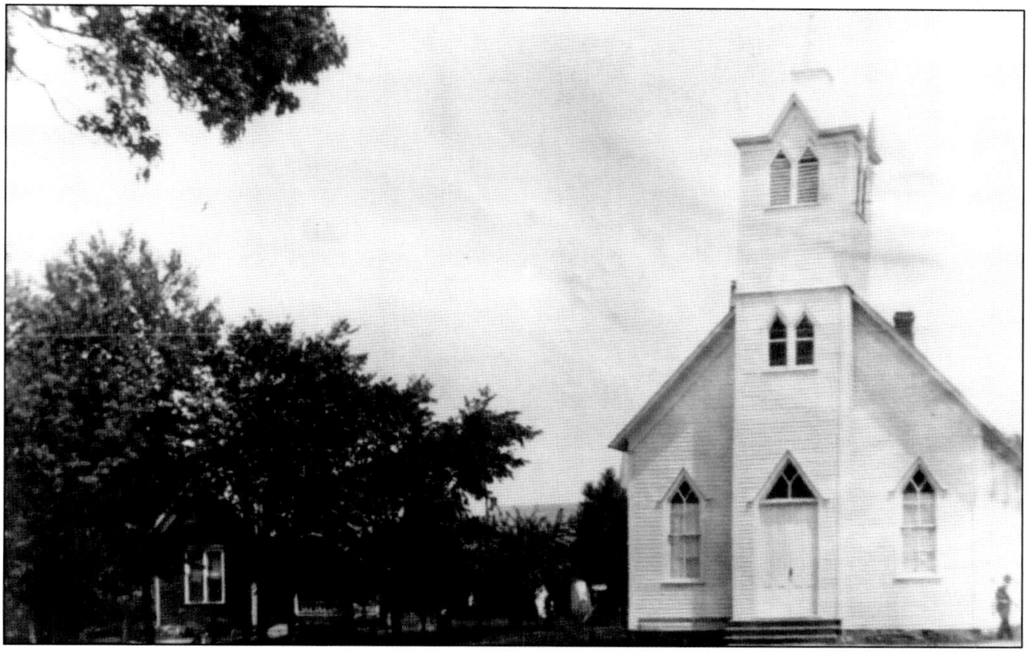

One of Marshfield First Baptist Church's first buildings is pictured in the early 1900s. Construction on the white frame building was completed in 1891 after the church's previous building was destroyed by fire. It housed the congregation until 1924, when a new brick building was constructed and the old structure was moved to face Crittenden Street and was later removed. (Courtesy of the Webster County Historical Museum.)

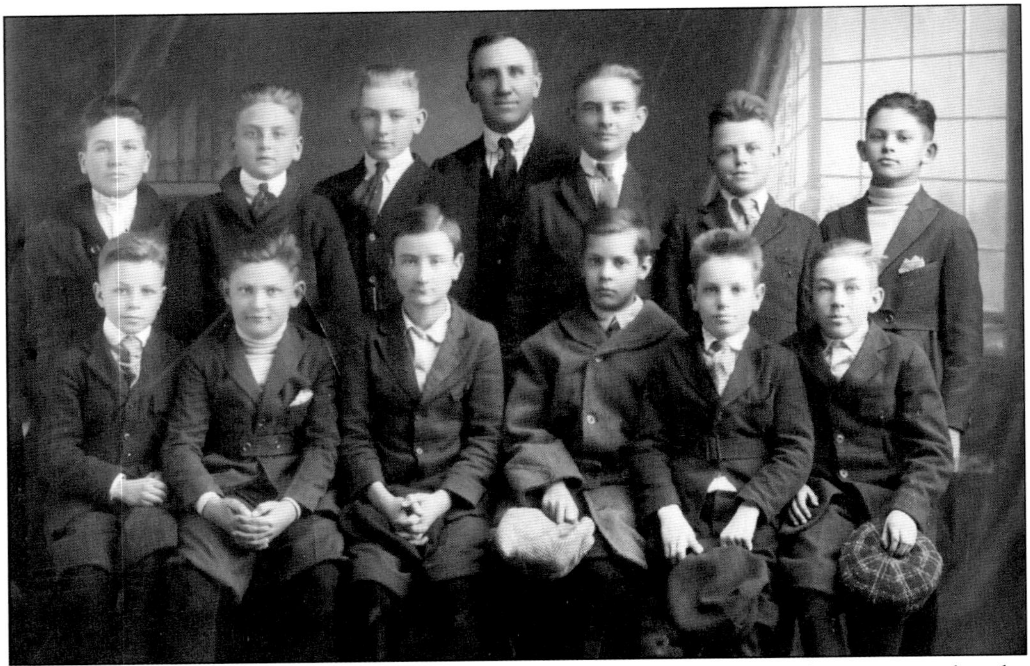

Members of a Sunday school class at the Methodist Episcopal Church, South, are pictured in the early 1900s. Included in no particular order are (first row) Chs. Brooks, Robert Highfill, ? Young, and Noel Conrad; (second row) Mark Cantrell, Charlie Warren, Charles Mitchell, E.W. Brooks, Fred ? , John Brooks, and Paul Highfill. (Courtesy of Ruth Brooks.)

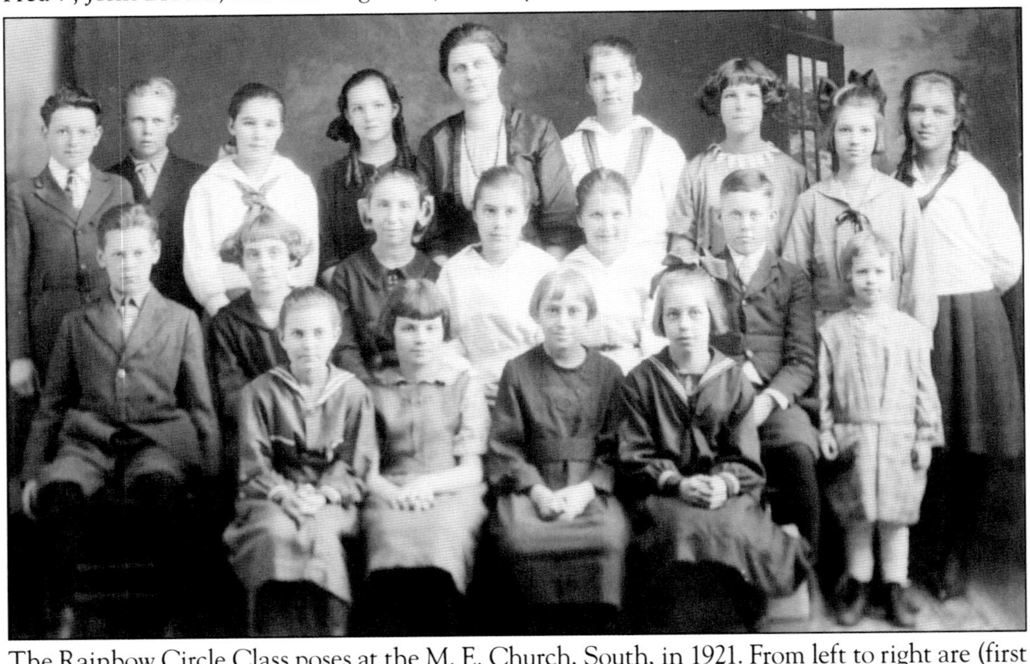

The Rainbow Circle Class poses at the M. E. Church, South, in 1921. From left to right are (first row) Frances Daily, Kathryn Ellett, Louise Conrad, and Margaret Shanks; (second row) Earl Moore, Evelyn Robertson, Lucille Leidsky, Faye Mosier, Helen Wright, Cecil Robertson, and Dorothy Swing; (third row) Russel Stigal, Joe Brooks, Irene Daily, Content Wise, teacher Minnie Brooks, Naomi Wright, Martha Hewett, Margaret Swing, and Clara Hewett. (Courtesy of Mary McConnell.)

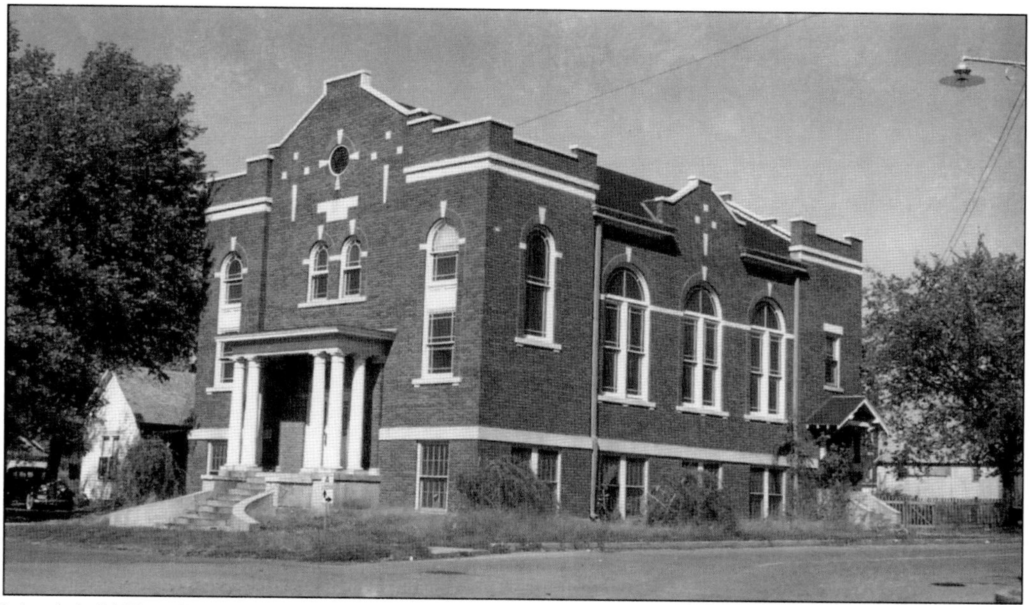

Marshfield First Baptist's next building was completed in 1924. The brick structure housed the church's services until 1978, when extreme growth led the congregation to break ground on a new facility. The new building was dedicated on April 22, 1979. After First Baptist vacated the building, it was purchased by Rosalee Perryman and became home to the Jubilee Theater. (Courtesy of the Webster County Historical Museum.)

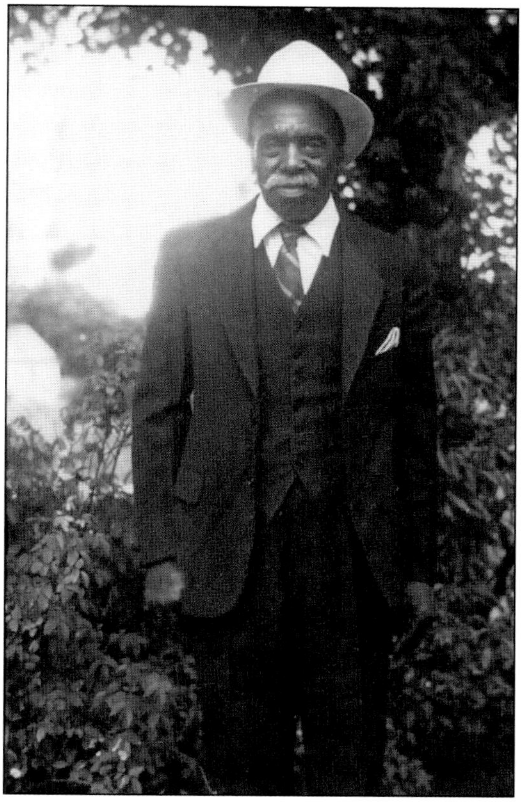

Emanuel Burford is pictured in Marshfield in the late 1930s. At one time, Marshfield had two churches for its African American residents: the African Presbyterian Church, which was in existence from 1887 to the early 1900s; and the M.E. Church, Colored, which began in 1892 and sat just off the square on North Marshall Street. Burford was the sole surviving executor of the church when it disbanded around 1940. (Courtesy of the Webster County Historical Museum.)

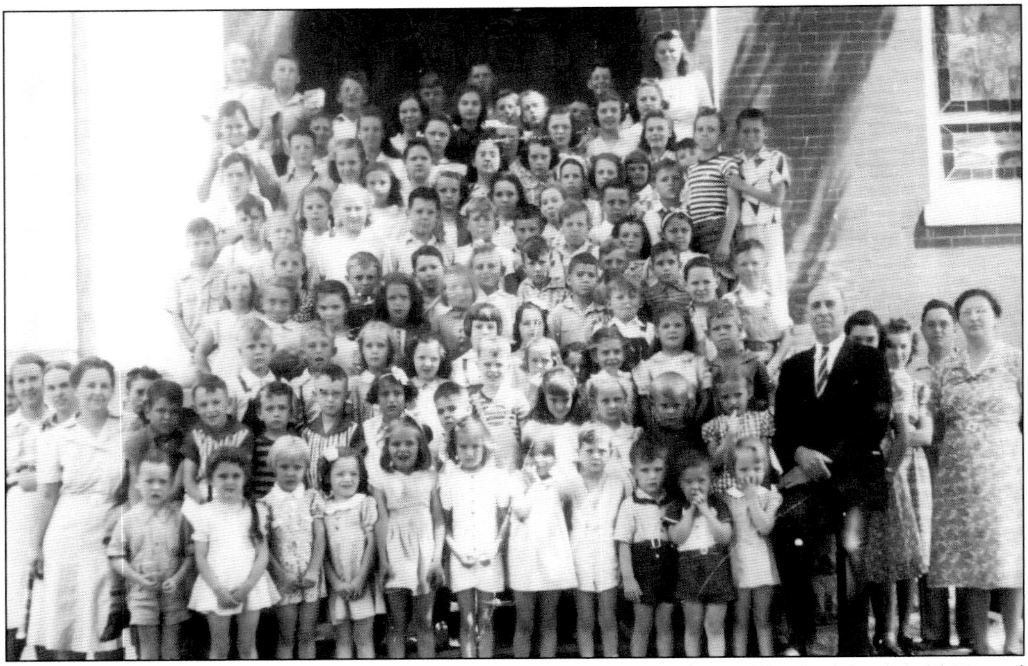

Many students gathered for the joint Union Bible School sessions hosted by the Marshfield United Methodist Church and the Marshfield Christian Church during the 1940s. An annual group picture also accompanied each session, taken either in front of one of the churches or even by the nearby Carnegie Library. (Courtesy of the Marshfield United Methodist Church.)

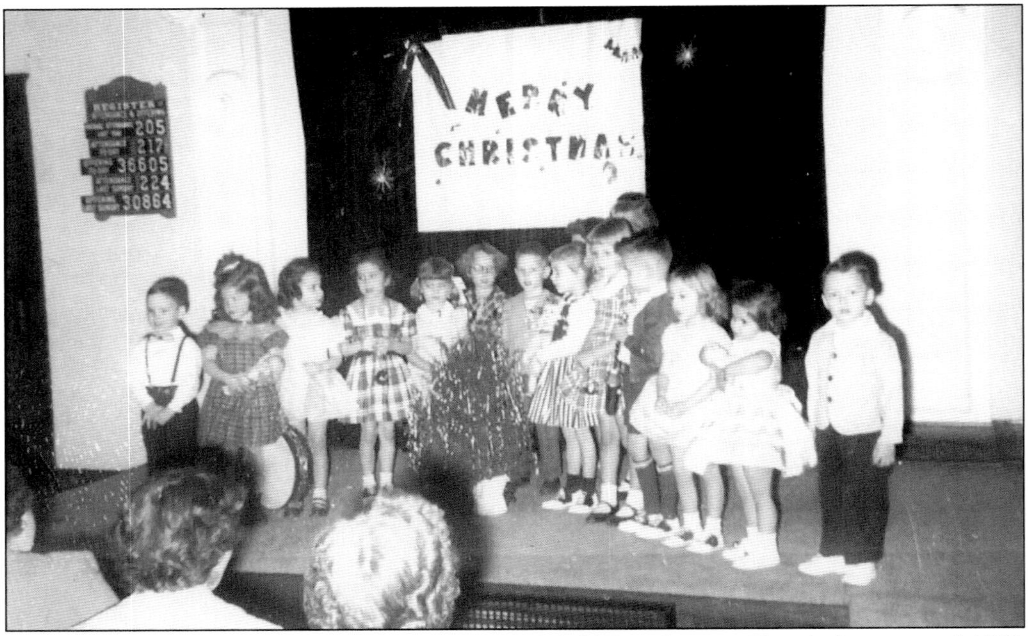

This is a snapshot of a Christmas pageant at Marshfield First Baptist Church from around 1955. Some of the members of this group are Jennifer Day (fifth from the left), Roger Todd, Leanna Webb, Eddie Hood, and Deanna Rust. The photograph was taken while the congregation was meeting in the church located at the corner of Commercial and Crittenden Streets. (Courtesy of Jennifer Hartman.)

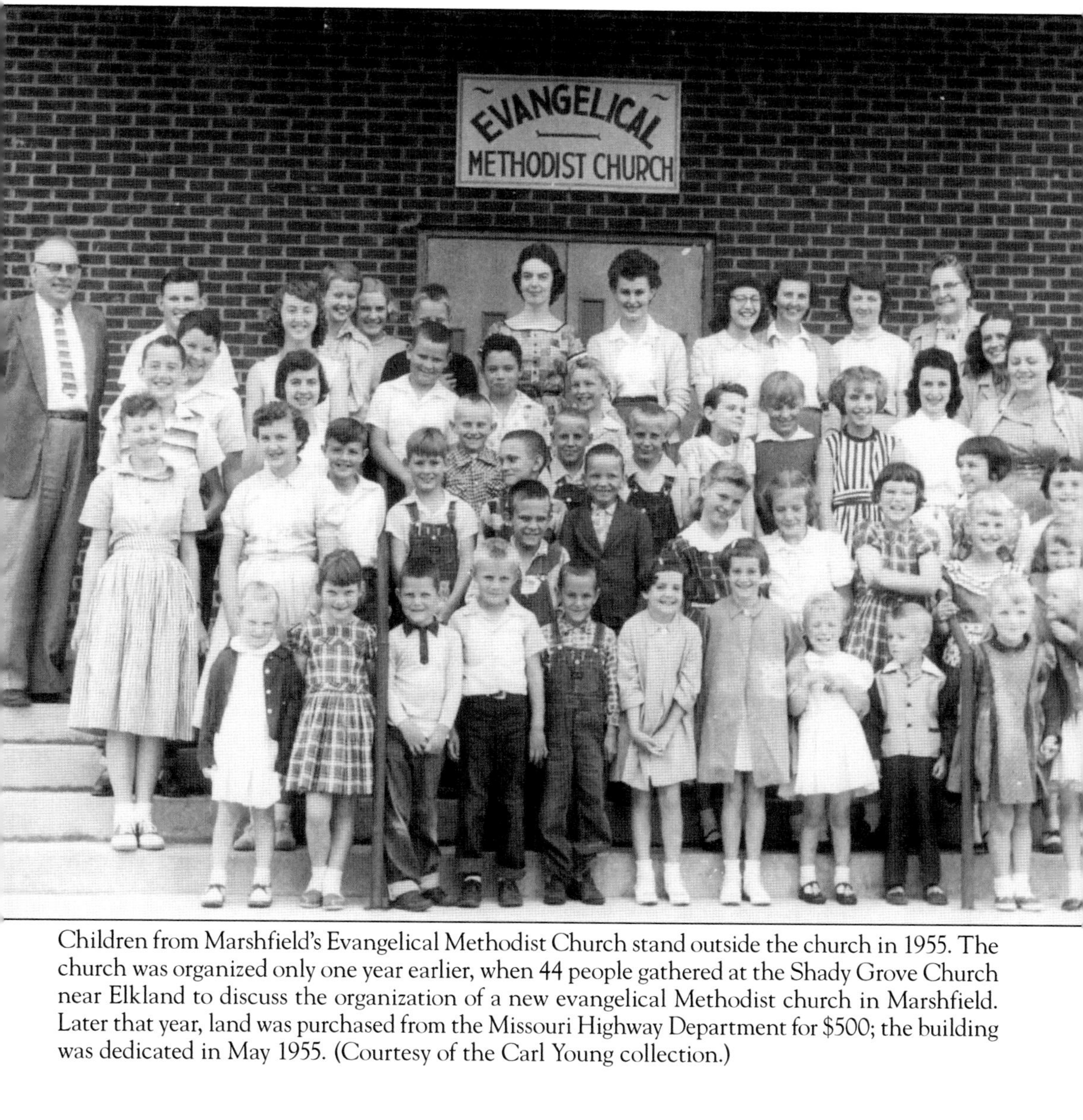

Children from Marshfield's Evangelical Methodist Church stand outside the church in 1955. The church was organized only one year earlier, when 44 people gathered at the Shady Grove Church near Elkland to discuss the organization of a new evangelical Methodist church in Marshfield. Later that year, land was purchased from the Missouri Highway Department for $500; the building was dedicated in May 1955. (Courtesy of the Carl Young collection.)

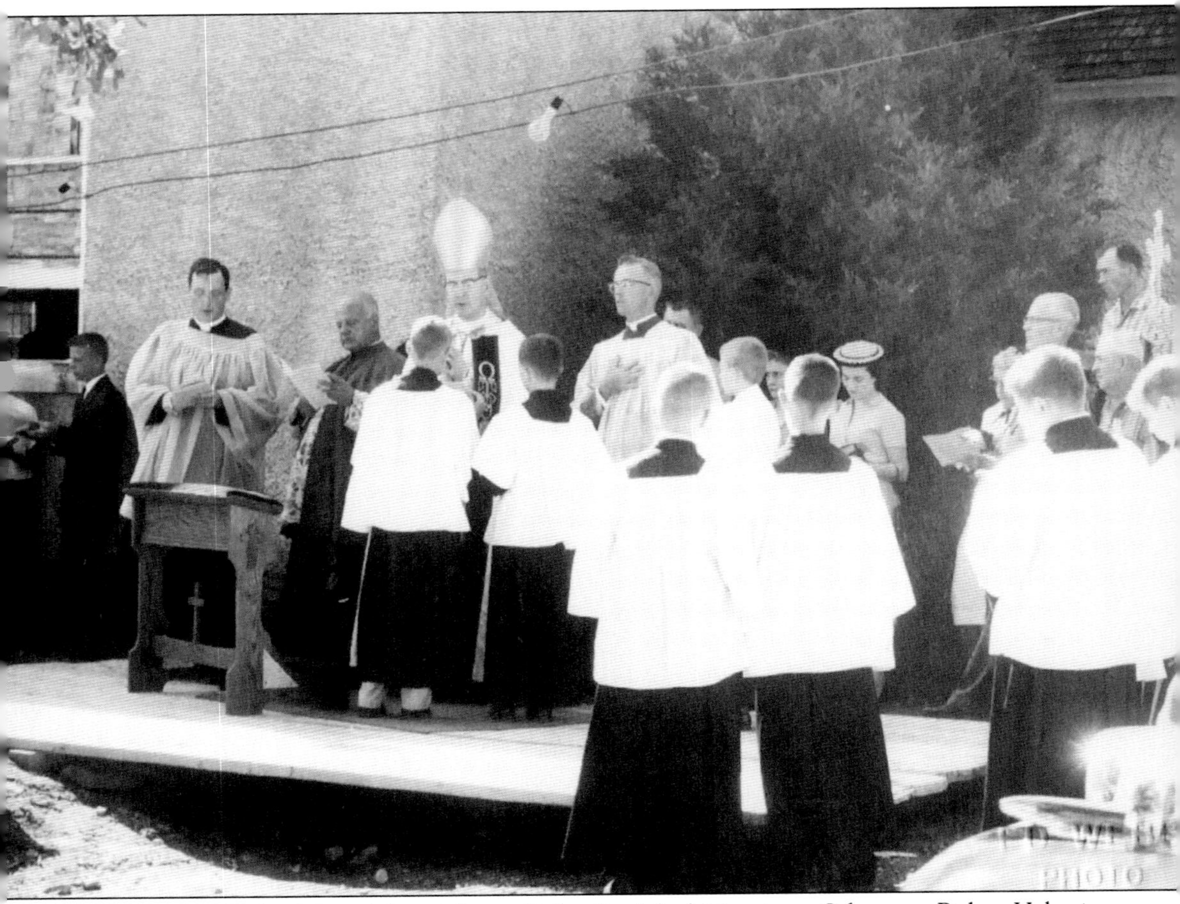

Pictured in the back from left to right are Father Rochford, Monsignor Schroeger, Bishop Helmsing, and Monsignor Westhues at Holy Trinity Catholic Church for its cornerstone laying on September 6, 1959. The parish decided to construct a new building after it was evident that extensive repairs would be needed to save the original structure. The new church seated approximately 200 people and was designed with air-conditioning. (Courtesy of the Holy Trinity Catholic Church.)

Five

Days of Celebration and Leisure

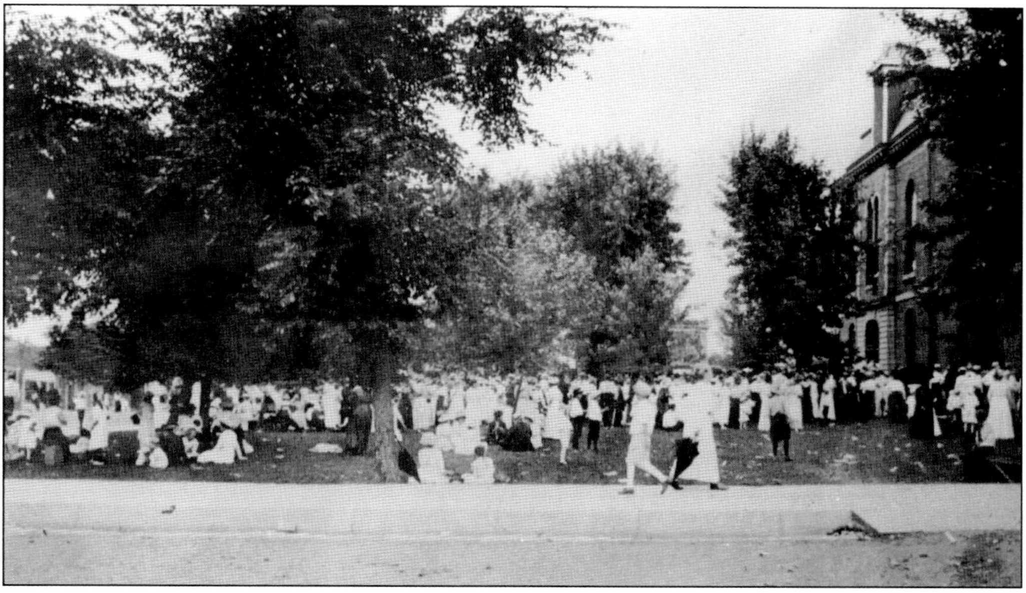

Years ago, it was tradition to eat dinner on the courthouse grounds on Independence Day. It was also a tradition to end the celebration with a band concert from 7:30 p.m. to midnight, cake and ice cream, bushels of confetti, and fireworks shot from the courthouse's roof. According to *The History of Webster County*, the festivities "altogether it simulated a miniature Mardi Gras." (Courtesy of Randy Clair.)

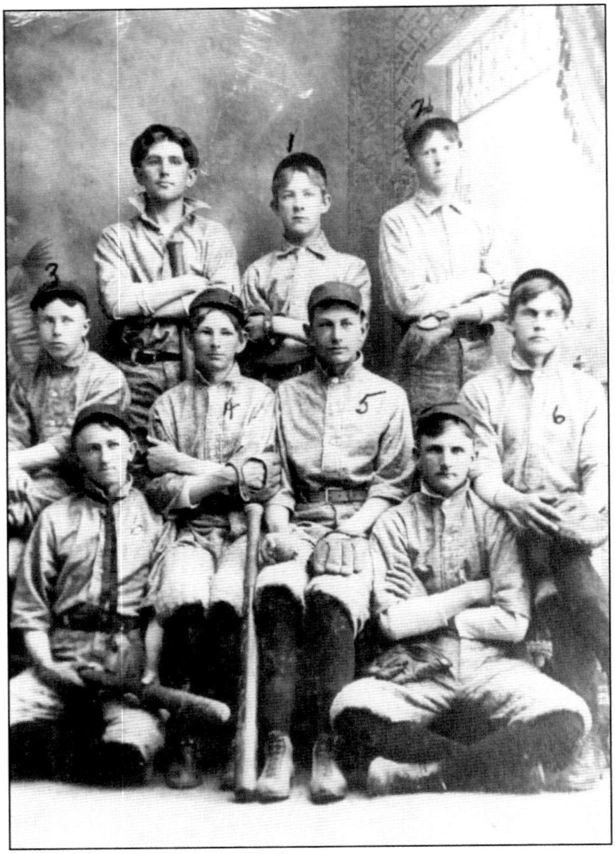

Marshfield baseball team members pose in 1906. Those pictured include Peck Gilbert, Harv Evans, Percy Hope, Dan Wells, John Foster, and Jack Robertson. Marshfield has had a long interest in baseball and even organized a club in March 1879, with members George F. Gilbert, W.H. Smith, James Wallis, Charles Rush, John Chitty, J.L. Ward, W.L. Smith, Alfred Smith, and H.A. Smith. (Courtesy of Randy Clair.)

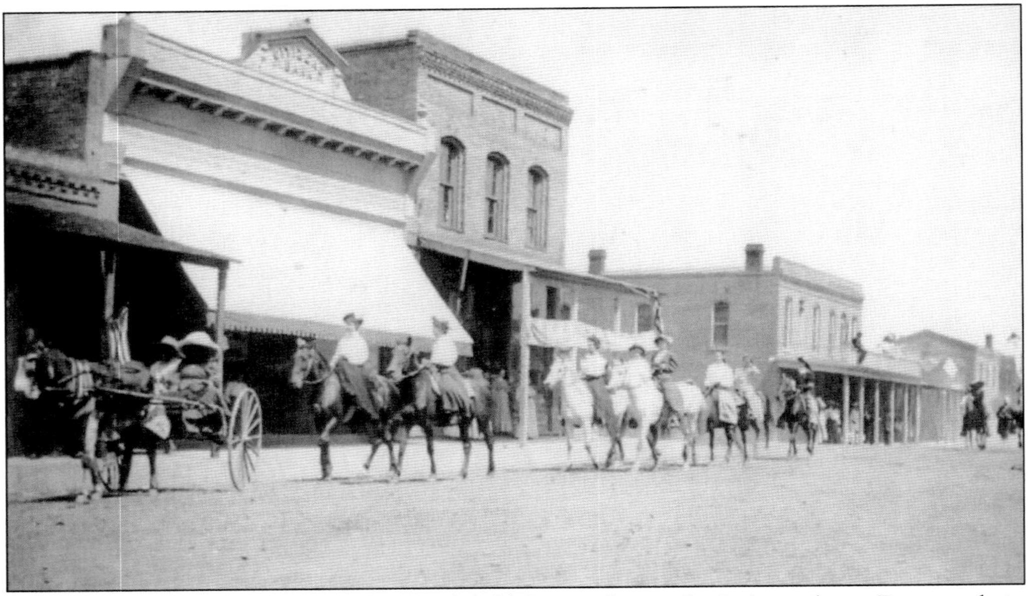

Here is a view of the west side of the Marshfield Square during the Independence Day parade in 1910. In addition to the parade, the day contained a lineup of other activities. According to the *Marshfield Mail*, "It was a pleasant day, and convinced all present that 'a safe and sane' celebration was possible, as there were no explosives of any kind in evidence." (Courtesy of Randy Clair.)

In 1910, a feature of the Independence Day celebration was a hot-air balloon. According to the *Marshfield Mail*, "At 4 p.m., Professor Horn made a fine ascension in his mammoth balloon, returning to earth from about 3,000 feet in height in a parachute." Horn landed in the Marshfield Cemetery after jumping from the balloon, which was found three miles from town the next day. (Courtesy of Randy Clair.)

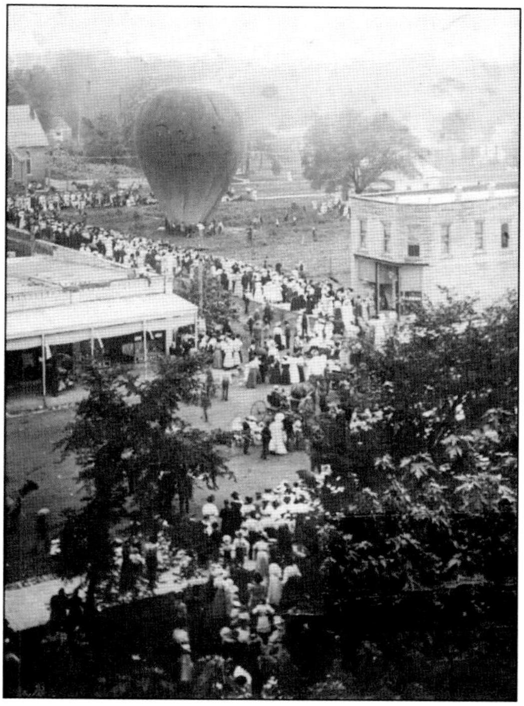

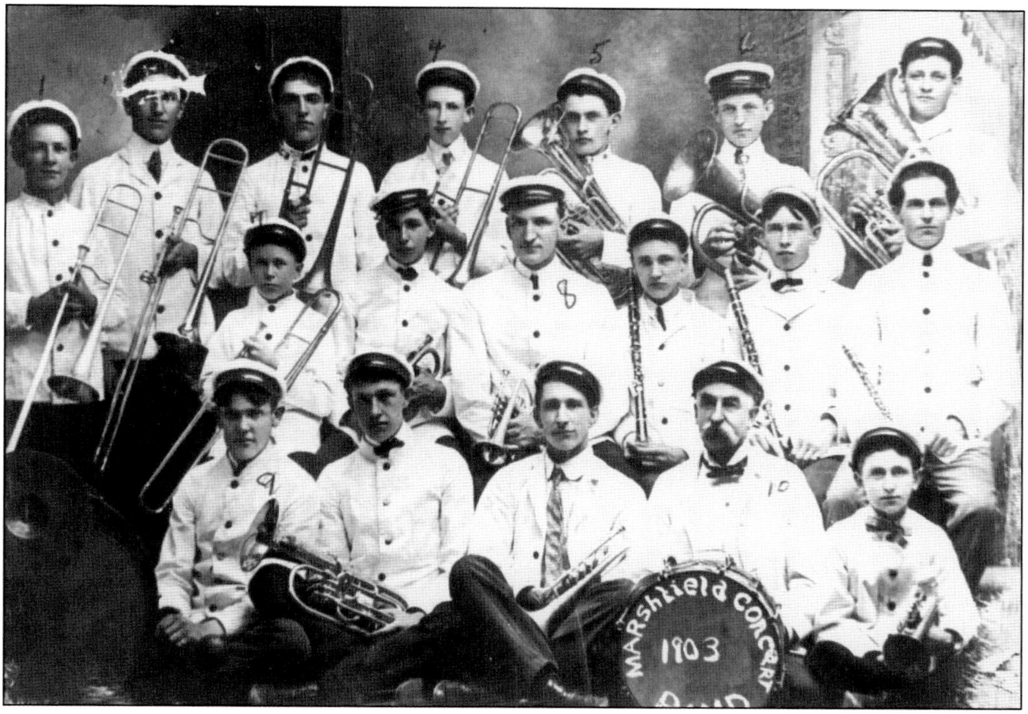

The Marshfield Concert Band poses in 1903. Originally known as the Marshfield Cornet Band, and then as the Marshfield Cyclone Band, it rehearsed weekly and performed at many community events. It disbanded in 1928 upon the death of leader Theron H. Watters, pictured second from the right in the first row. As a memorial to Watters, the group erected a memorial to him at the cemetery. (Courtesy of Randy Clair.)

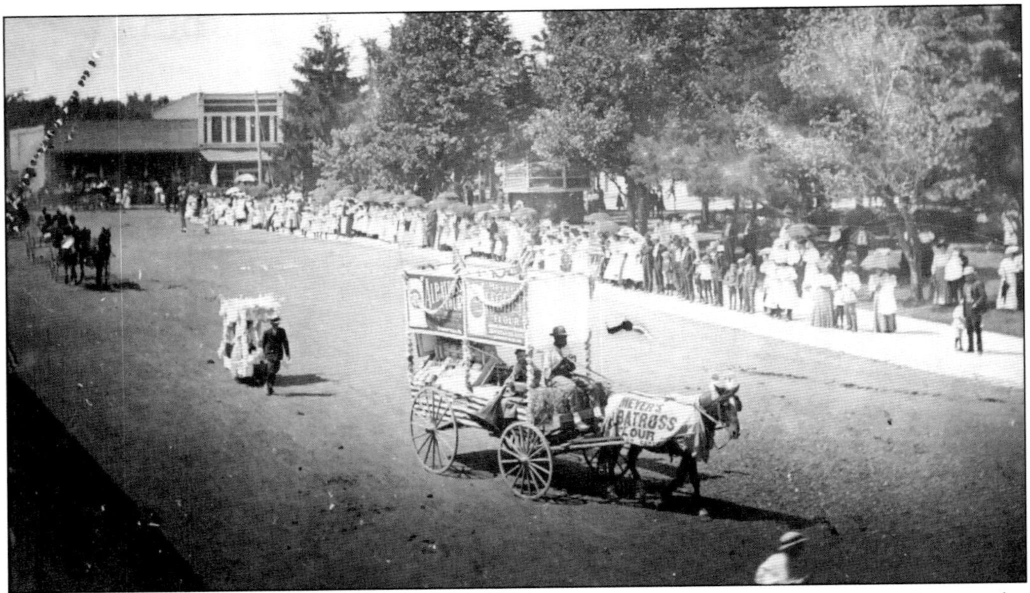

This is a bird's-eye view of the Marshfield Fourth of July Parade around 1910. The float in the foreground is advertising flour. Notice the parasols in use by many of the women watching the parade, presumably to keep out of the sun. Another noticeable element of the photograph is the town gazebo, located on the courthouse lawn. (Courtesy of Randy Clair.)

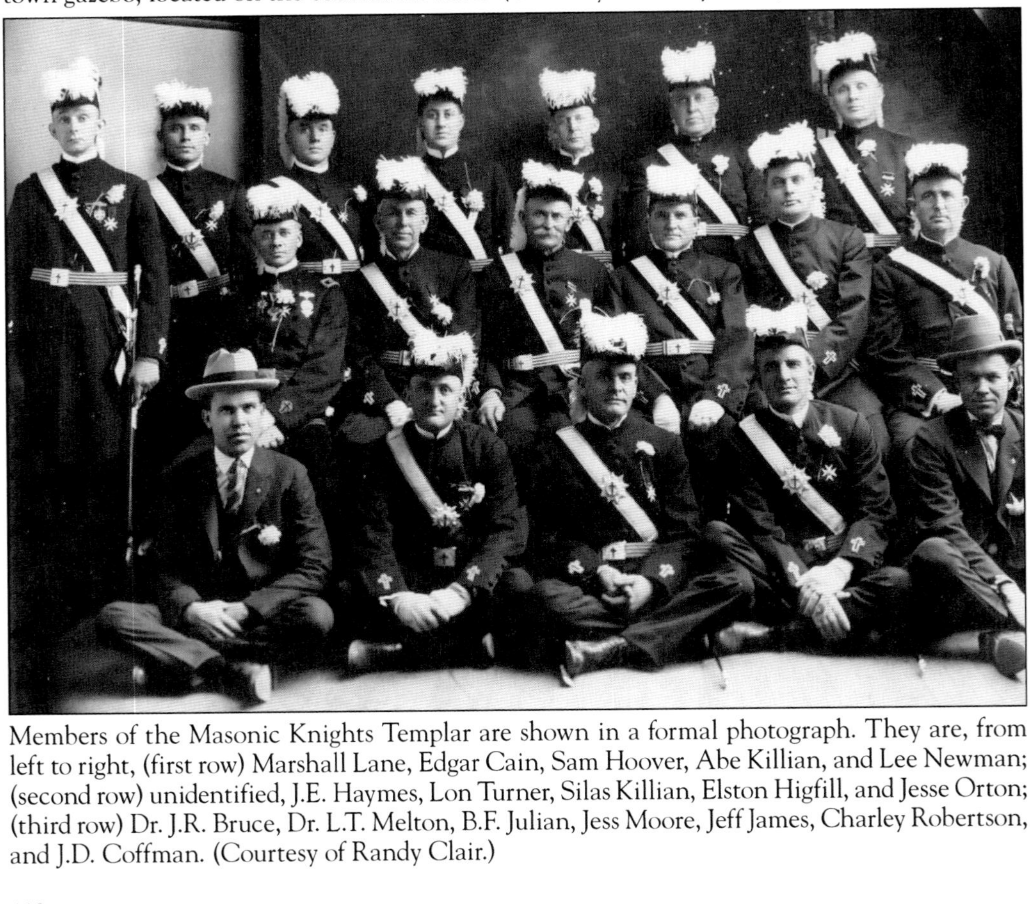

Members of the Masonic Knights Templar are shown in a formal photograph. They are, from left to right, (first row) Marshall Lane, Edgar Cain, Sam Hoover, Abe Killian, and Lee Newman; (second row) unidentified, J.E. Haymes, Lon Turner, Silas Killian, Elston Higfill, and Jesse Orton; (third row) Dr. J.R. Bruce, Dr. L.T. Melton, B.F. Julian, Jess Moore, Jeff James, Charley Robertson, and J.D. Coffman. (Courtesy of Randy Clair.)

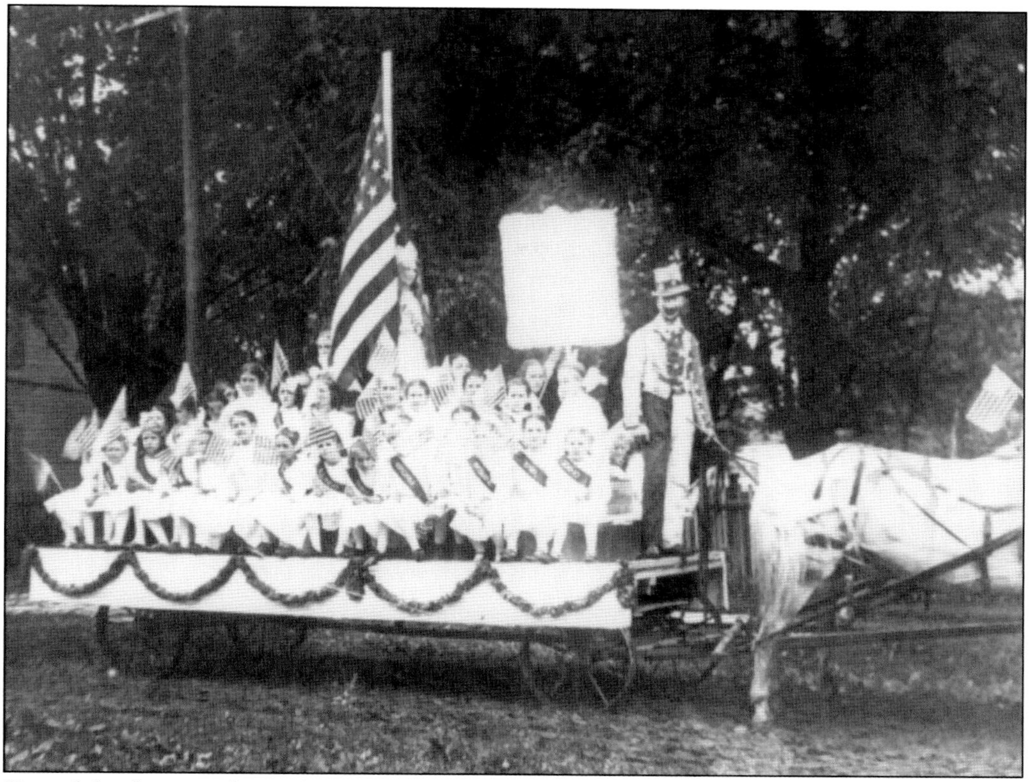

One of the floats in the 1917 Fourth of July parade was a moving advertisement in support of Prohibition. Several individuals wore red sashes representing dry states, while the white were wet states. Even after Prohibition was repealed, Webster County maintained a chapter of the Women's Christian Temperance Union, an organization supporting the abolition of alcohol, for several more decades. (Courtesy of Randy Clair.)

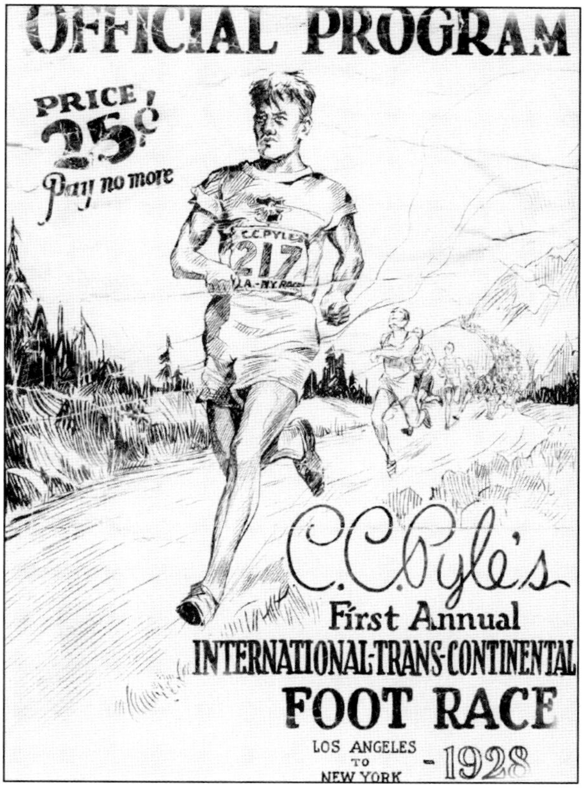

Pictured is a 1928 program from the C.C. Pyle's first annual International-Trans-Continental Foot Race, otherwise known as the "Bunion Derby." Starting out in Los Angeles, 199 male runners from around the world were challenged to run nearly 60 miles a day to New York City along Route 66 for a chance at $25,000. Nearly half of the runners had already dropped out before they reached Marshfield the next month. (Courtesy of the Carl Young collection.)

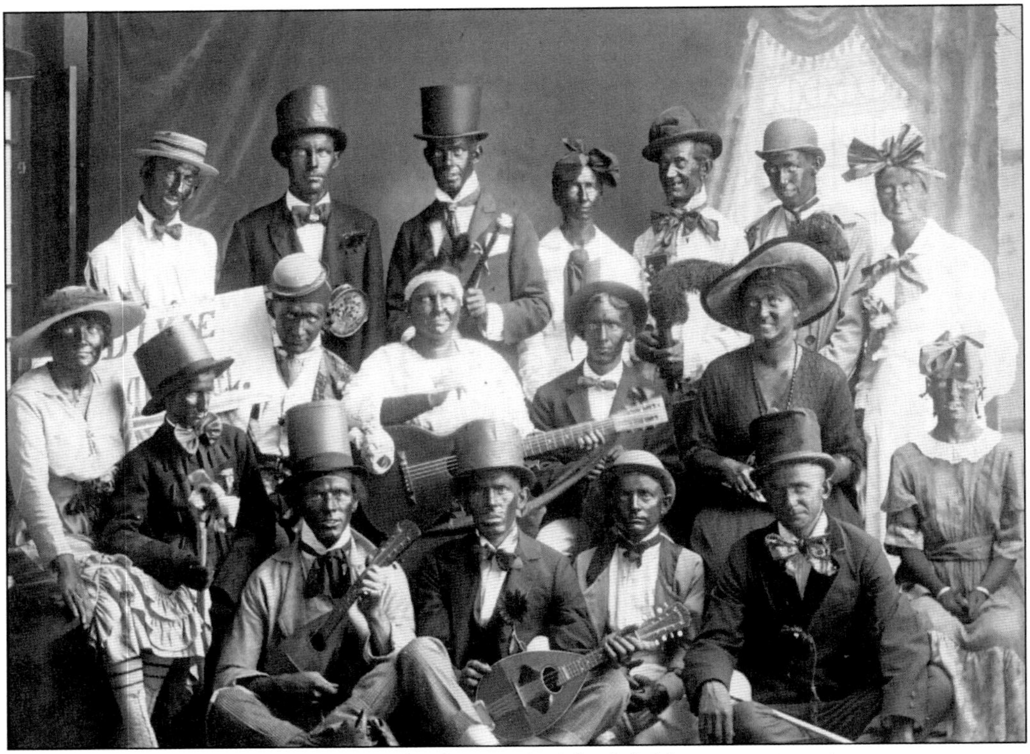

Dixie minstrel shows were common fundraisers for Marshfield organizations in years past, even for groups such as the school PTA. Pictured from left to right are (first row) Gilbert Clarence Hyde, Arthur Muzzy, Bess Evans, Harve Evans, Morton X, and Minnie Brooks; (second row) Mrs. Arthur Muzzy, Mutt Fellin, Daisy Morris, Byron, Fross, and Lena Bollinger; (third row) Wilma Gilbert, Pearl Killiam, John Barkley, Stanley Cox, Henry Fellin, and Hester Haymes Jackson. (Courtesy of Randy Clair.)

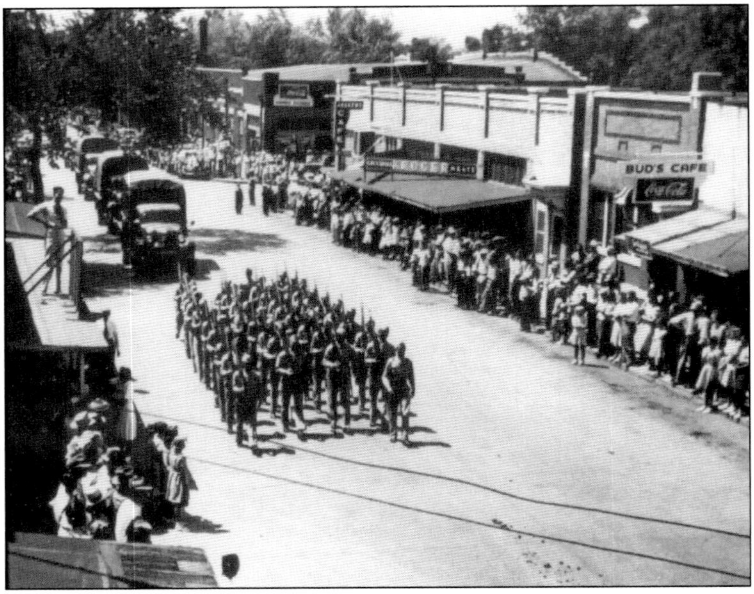

Soldiers from the 63rd Infantry at Fort Wood march in the 1941 Independence Day parade. In the midst of World War II, the men traveled to Marshfield to take part in the festivities and were fed a picnic lunch at noon. According to the *Marshfield Mail*, "The soldiers seemed to appreciate the home atmosphere which they miss so much in army life at camp." (Courtesy of Randy Clair.)

Local attorney Elsworth Haymes plays golf at the Marshfield Country Club in the late 1940s. The golf course was incorporated as the Marshfield Country Club in 1933. At the time, it was a nine-hole sand green course, but in the 1950s it changed to a grass green course. Adjacent to the club was the Marshfield Flying Field, where several Marshfield schools were later constructed. (Courtesy of Dr. Tommy Macdonnell.)

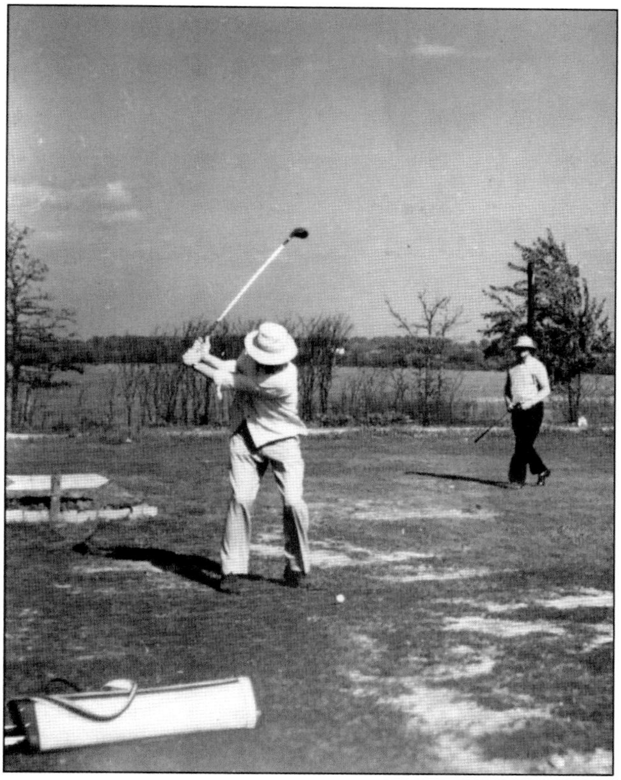

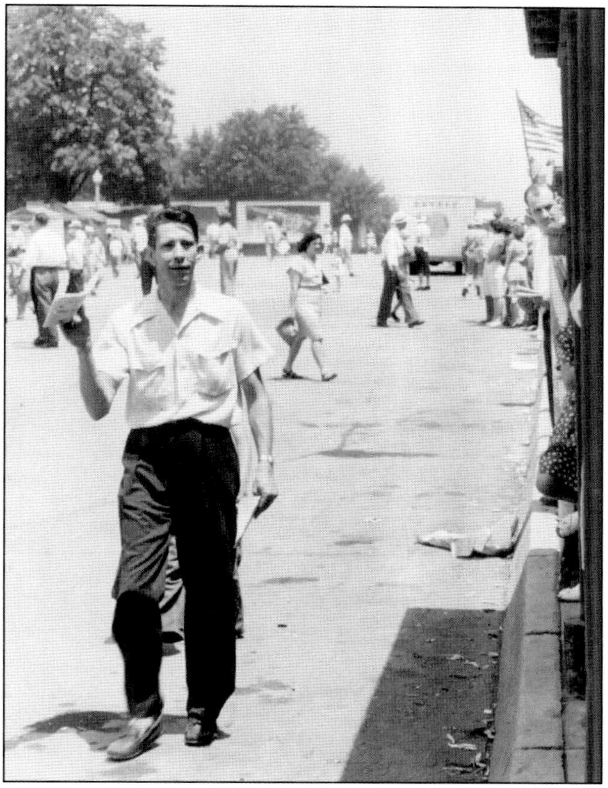

Paul Watters walks down Crittenden Street as he passes out copies of the "Peerade Xtra" in July 1947. Published by the *Marshfield Mail*, the satirical news bulletin had a humorous take on community life, such as slightly mixing up names of citizens and including mild jokes. The annual publication began distribution around 1921 and continued for decades. (Courtesy of Dr. Tommy Macdonnell.)

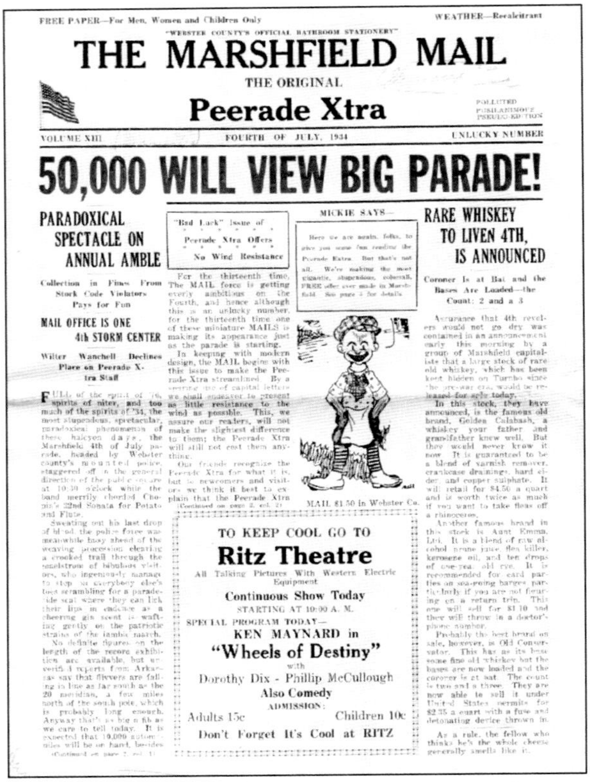

FREE PAPER—For Men, Women and Children Only

"WEBSTER COUNTY'S OFFICIAL BATHROOM STATIONERY"

WEATHER—Recalcitrant

THE MARSHFIELD MAIL

THE ORIGINAL

Peerade Xtra

POLLUTED
PSEUDO-EDITION

VOLUME XIII — FOURTH OF JULY, 1934 — UNLUCKY NUMBER

50,000 WILL VIEW BIG PARADE!

PARADOXICAL SPECTACLE ON ANNUAL AMBLE

Collection in Fines From Stork Code Violators Pays for Fun

MAIL OFFICE IS ONE 4th STORM CENTER

Wilter Wanchell Declines Place on Peerade Xtra Staff

FULL of the spirit of '76, spirits of niter, and too much of the spirits of '34, the most stupendous, spectacular, paradoxical phenomenon of these halcyon days, the Marshfield 4th of July parade, headed by Webster county's mounted police, staggered off in the general direction of the public square at 10:30 o'clock while the band merrily chorded Chopin's 22nd Sonata for Potato and Flute.

Sweating out his last drop of blood, the police force was meanwhile busy ahead of the weaving procession clearing a crooked trail through the maelstrom of bibulous visitors, who ingeniously manage to step on everybody else's toes scrambling for a parade-side seat where they can lick their lips in cadence as a cheering gin scent is wafting gently on the patriotic strains of the iambic march.

No definite figures on the length of the record exhibition are available, but unverified reports from Arkansas say that flivvers are falling in line as far south as the 20 meridian, a few miles north of the south pole, which is probably long enough. Anyway that's as big a fib as we care to tell today. It is expected that 10,000 automobiles will be on hand, besides

(Continued on page 2, col. 1)

"Bad Luck" Issue of Peerade Xtra Offers No Wind Resistance

For the thirteenth time, The MAIL force is getting overly ambitious on the Fourth, and hence although this is an unlucky number, for the thirteenth time one of these miniature MAILS is making its appearance just as the parade is starting.

In keeping with modern design, the MAIL begins with this issue to make the Peerade Xtra streamlined. By a sparing use of capital letters we shall endeavor to present as little resistance to the wind as possible. This, we assure our readers, will not make the slightest difference to them; the Peerade Xtra will still not cost them anything.

Our friends recognize the Peerade Xtra for what it is, but to newcomers and visitors we think it best to explain that the Peerade Xtra

(Continued on page 2, col. 2)

MICKIE SAYS—

Here we are again, folks, to give you some fun reading the Peerade Extra. But that's not all. We're making the most gigantic, stupendous, [illegible] FREE offer ever made in Marshfield. See page 4 for details.

MAIL $1.50 in Webster Co.

RARE WHISKEY TO LIVEN 4TH, IS ANNOUNCED

Coroner Is at Bat and the Bases Are Loaded—the Count: 2 and a 3

Assurance that 4th revelers would not go dry was contained in an announcement early this morning by a group of Marshfield capitalists that a large stock of rare old whiskey, which has been kept hidden on Turnbo since the pre-war era, would be released for sale today.

In this stock, they have announced, is the famous old brand, Golden Calabash, a whiskey your father and grandfather knew well. But they would never know it now. It is guaranteed to be a blend of varnish remover, crankcase drainings, hard cider, and copper sulphate. It will retail for $4.50 a quart and is worth twice as much if you want to take fleas off a rhinoceros.

Another famous brand in this stock is Aunt Emma, Ltd. It is a blend of raw alcohol, prune juice, flea killer, kerosene oil, and ten drops of one-year old rye. It is recommended for card parties on sea-going barges, particularly if you are not figuring on a return trip. This one will sell for $1.10 and they will throw in a doctor's phone number.

Probably the best brand on sale, however, is Old Conservator. This has as its base some fine old whiskey but the bases are now loaded and the coroner is at bat. The count is two and a three. They are now able to sell it under United States permits for $2.35 a quart with a fuse and detonating device thrown in.

As a rule, the fellow who thinks he's the whole cheese generally smells like it.

A copy of the 1934 "Peerade Xtra" rings with amusing headlines, including "Rare Whiskey to Liven 4th, is Announced," "Walter Wanchell Declines Place on Peerade Xtra staff," and the paper's tagline, "Webster County's Official Bathroom Stationery." Despite the publication's reach for humor, real advertisements were also included, obvious by the ad placed by the Ritz Theatre for a special showing. (Courtesy of Randy Clair.)

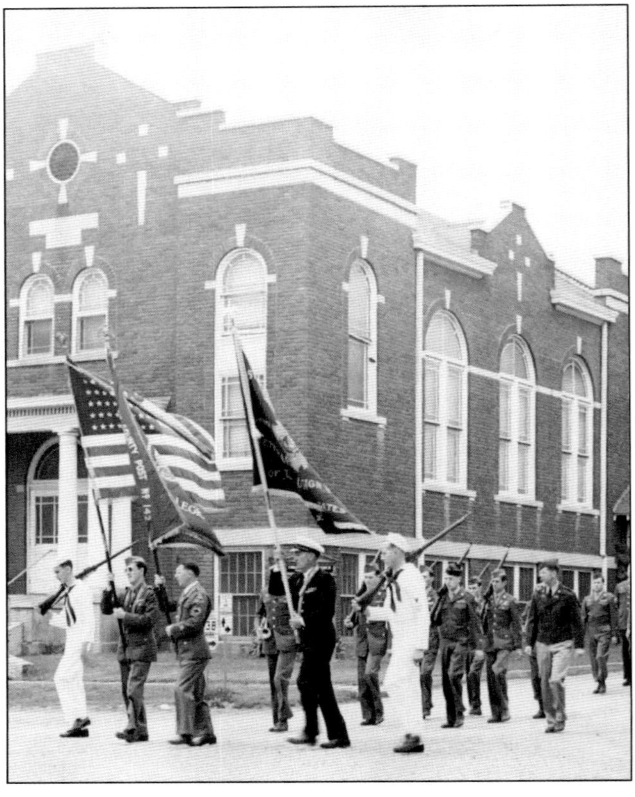

About 300 people attended Marshfield's Memorial Day parade in 1948, led by military personnel from Webster County Post No. 4101, Veterans of Foreign Wars, and Webster County Post 142 of the American Legion. The parade began at the town square and marched to the town cemetery, where it cumulated with a program for attendees. (Courtesy of Dr. Tommy Macdonnell.)

Marjorie Smith Breech chats with a friend at the Marshfield Cemetery after the Memorial Day ceremonies finished in 1948. After the parade reached the cemetery, attorney Elsworth Haymes delivered a short address, Warren Johnson gave a prayer, Stan Dawson played "Taps," and John Cox performed an echo to "Taps." (Courtesy of Dr. Tommy Macdonnell.)

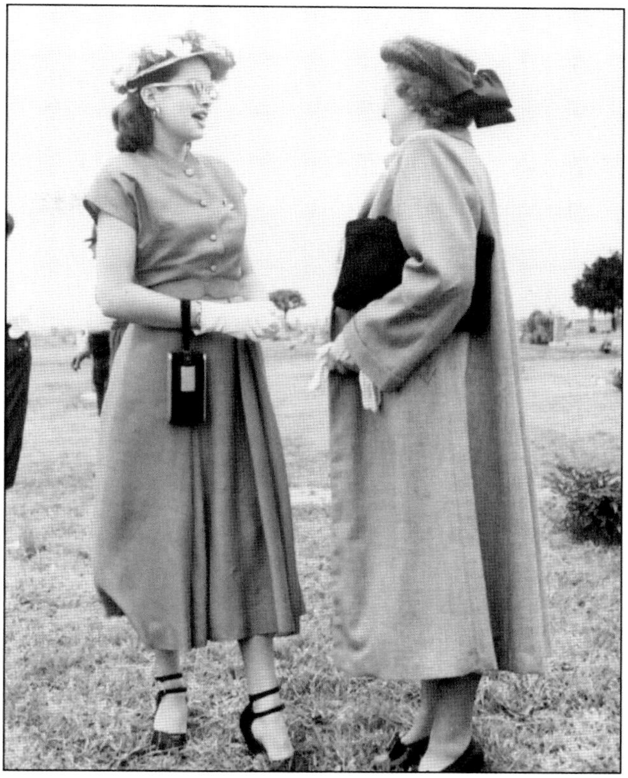

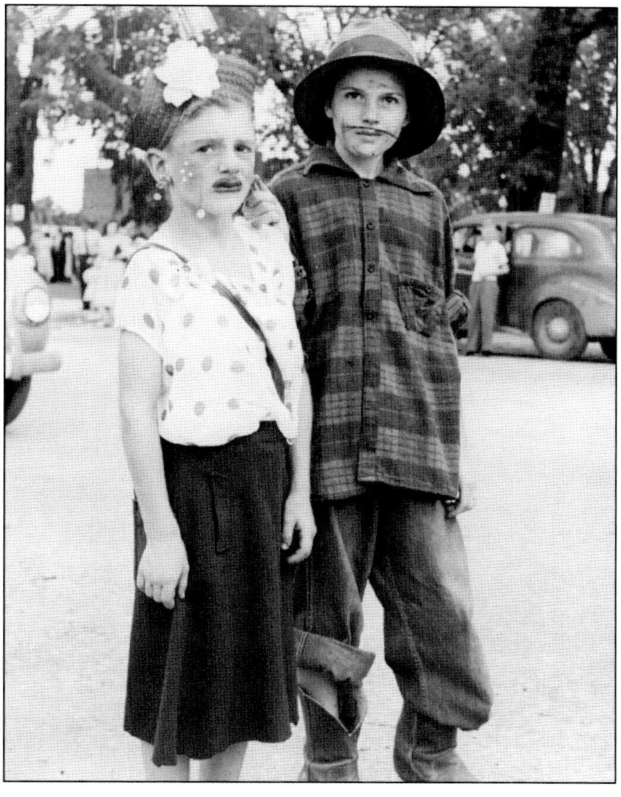

Junior and Mary (Lee) Haymes decided to dress up for Marshfield's Independence Day parade in the late 1940s. That afternoon, Marshfield school superintendent Harry Talbot gave an address; although meaningful, it was not fully appreciated. The *Marshfield Mail* reported, "As usual not too many gave attention to his address. It seemed that people were more interested in visiting with each other than in the program." (Courtesy of Dr. Tommy Macdonnell.)

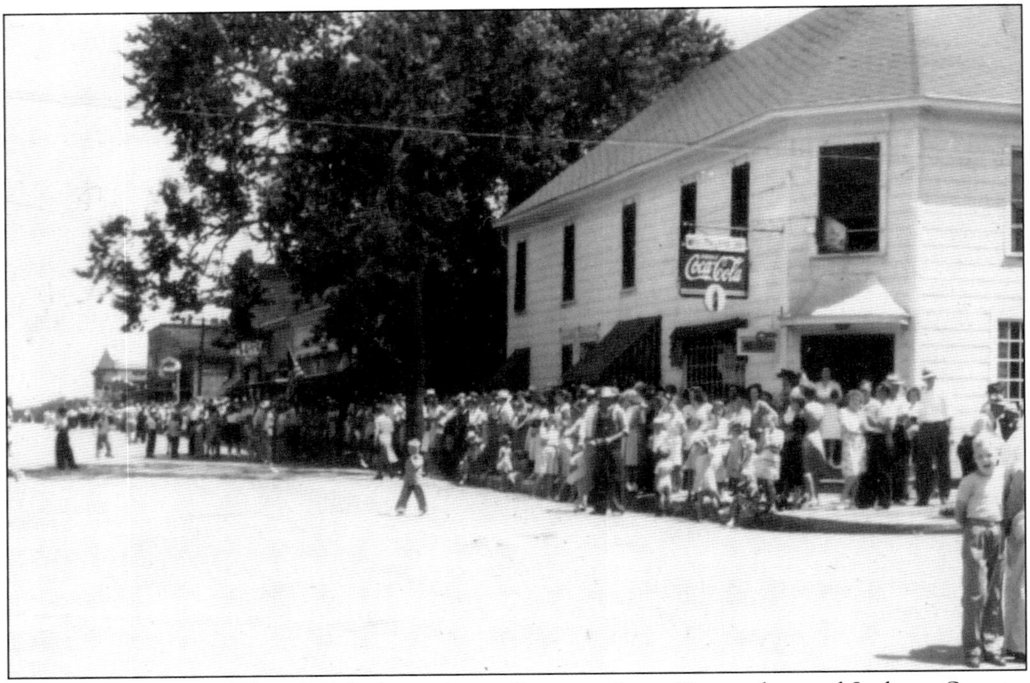

Pictured is a view of the 1948 Independence Day parade at Crittenden and Jackson Streets. According to the *Marshfield Mail*, preparations for the event began in early June, when Willis Case was elected chairman of the executive committee. Nine subcommittees were also established: parade, program, arrangements, finance, sports, fireworks, concessions, and publicity and advertising. (Courtesy of Dr. Tommy Macdonnell.)

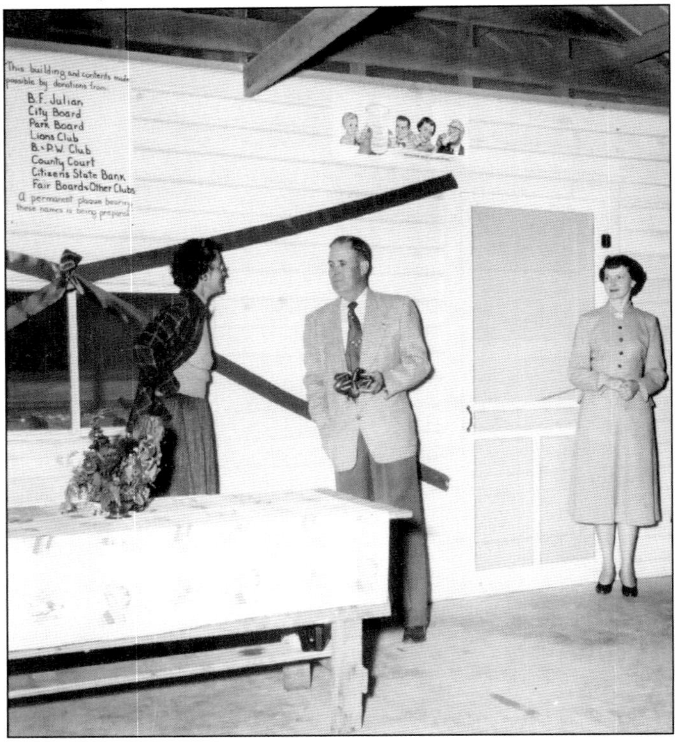

Members of Marshfield's Business and Professional Women's Club are pictured at the dedication of the fairground's new kitchen in November 1953. They are, from left to right, Mrs. Hartley (president), Ellis Jackson (secretary of the Webster County Fair board), and Sylvia Patterson (vice president). The women's club helped fund various kitchen equipment for the pavilion. (Courtesy of the Webster County Historical Museum.)

Sheriff Isam Cunningham, Gary W. Hyde, and Susan Brooks ride in the Webster County centennial parade in 1955. Sheriff Cunningham's time in office from 1945 to 1955 is surrounded by a great deal of what would seem to be urban legend—but not Cunningham's entire larger-than-life legacy is false. (Courtesy of the Webster County Historical Museum.)

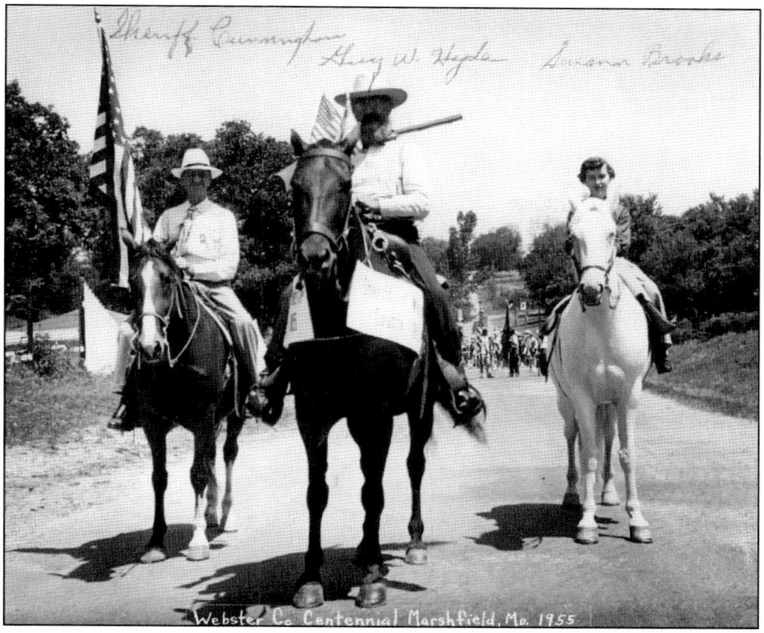

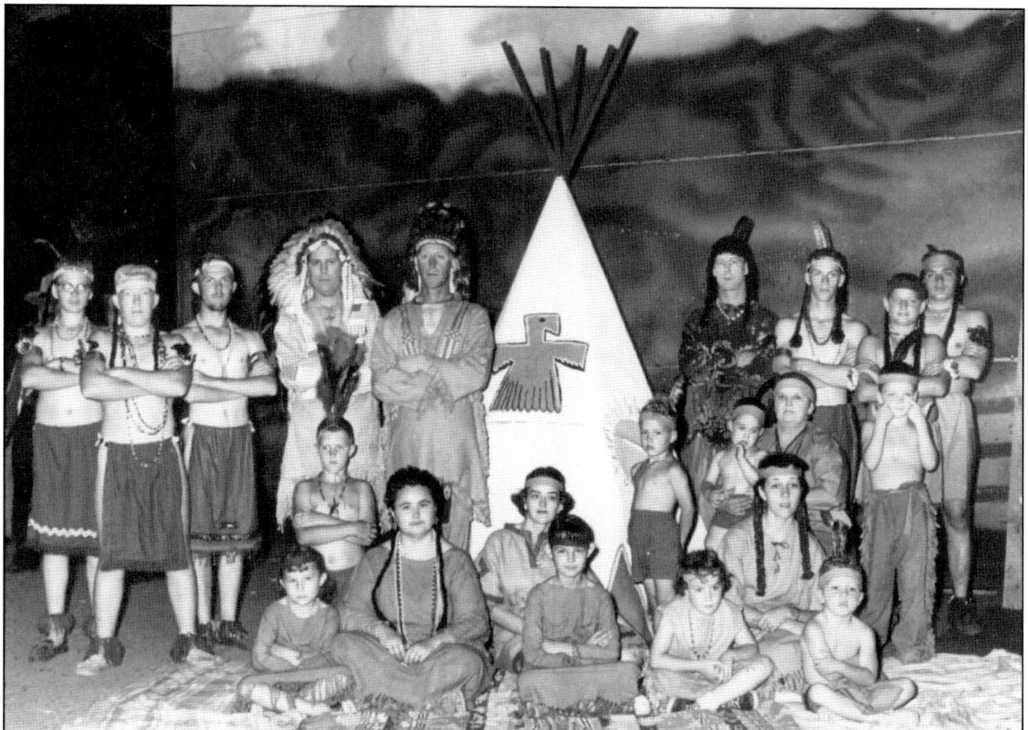

A pageant played an active role in Webster County's centennial celebration. Pictured is the production's first scene; according to the script, it was set in an "Indian village where usual life of the village is going on, with squaws cooking, grinding corn, working leather, etc. Medicine man is sitting before his teepee." The scene depicted the push of Native Americans westward by white men. (Courtesy of the Webster County Historical Museum.)

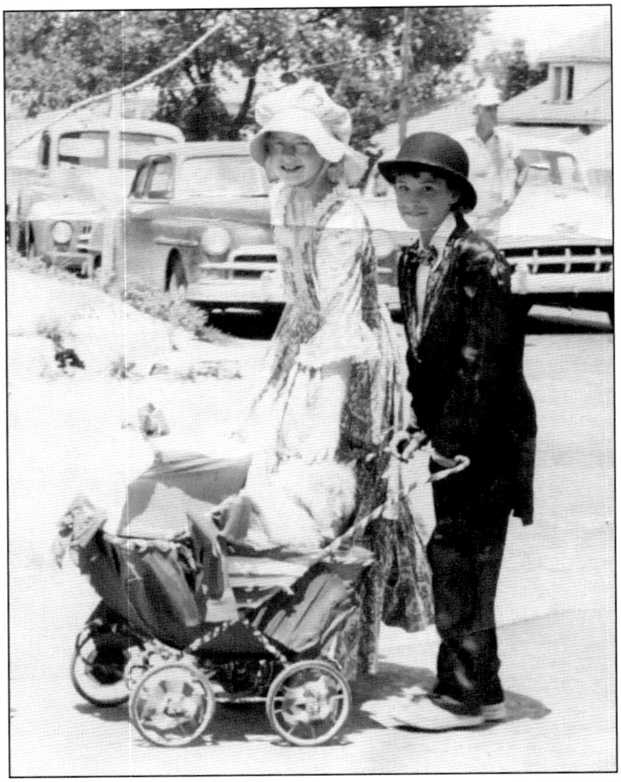

A part of the Webster County centennial activities was a children's parade held during the four-day event. Pictured are 11-year-old Lib Haymes Sims (left) and Patsy Brown, who pushed baby carriages in the youngsters' event—but they did not push actual babies; instead, there was at least one dog in the carriages. (Courtesy of the Webster County Historical Museum.)

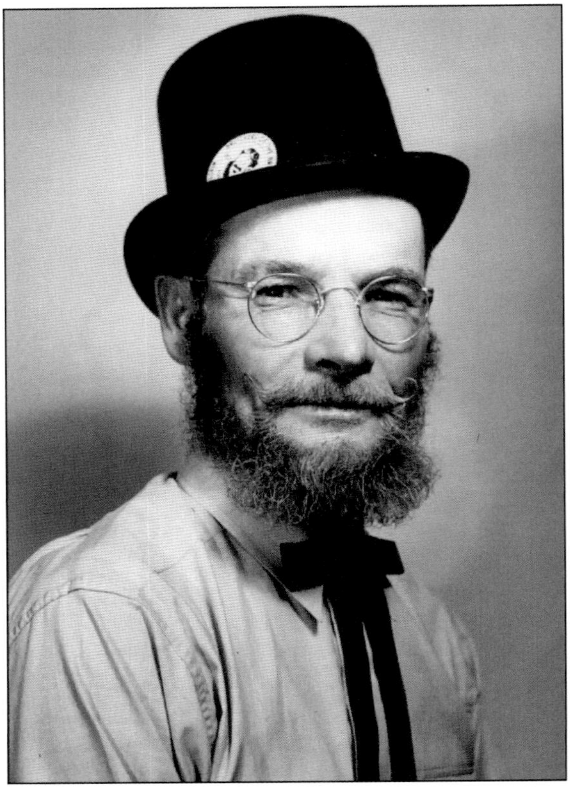

Leonard Hagan is all spiffed up in centennial dress for his portrait in 1955. Despite his beard, Hagan is also wearing a shaving permit issued by the centennial committee. During the celebration, all male attendees were required to either grow a beard or purchase a shaving permit. The permits allowed clean-shaven men to walk the streets without fear of being thrown in "jail." (Courtesy of the Webster County Historical Museum.)

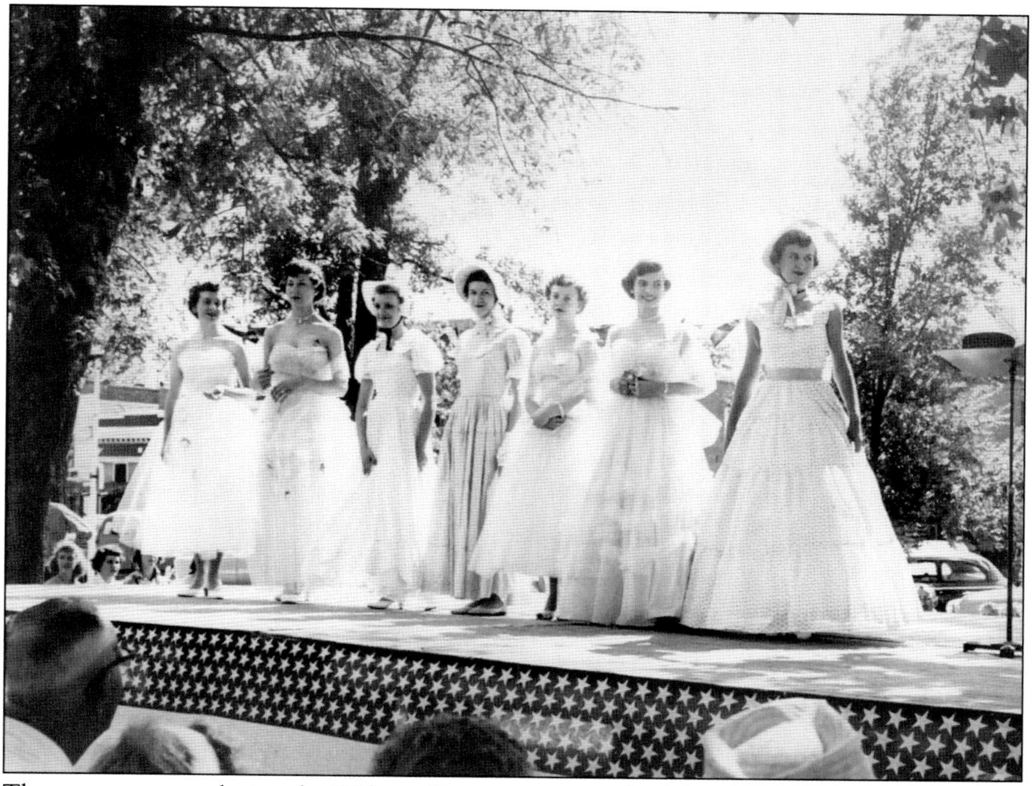

The queen contest during the Webster County centennial celebration is pictured in 1955. The queen held her title until 2005, when Webster County celebrated its sesquicentennial celebration and two new queens were crowned, one for each age division. Lesley Kays and Kaitlyn McConnell will reign until 2055, when they will crown Webster County's bicentennial queens. (Courtesy of the Webster County Historical Museum.)

"Brothers of the Brush" gather during the centennial celebration. Men were required to grow a beard or buy a shaving permit. There were also contests for various prizes in conjunction with the contest; the longest beard and overall beard were among the categories judged. (Courtesy of the Webster County Historical Museum.)

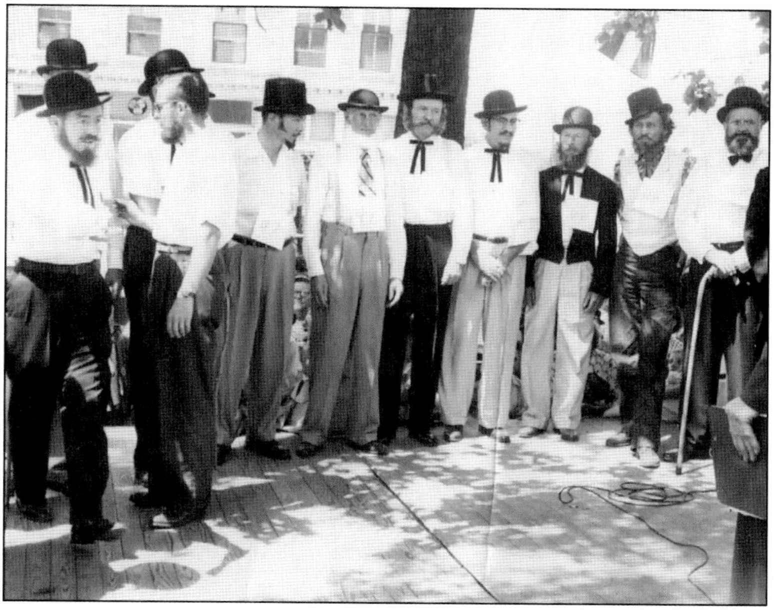

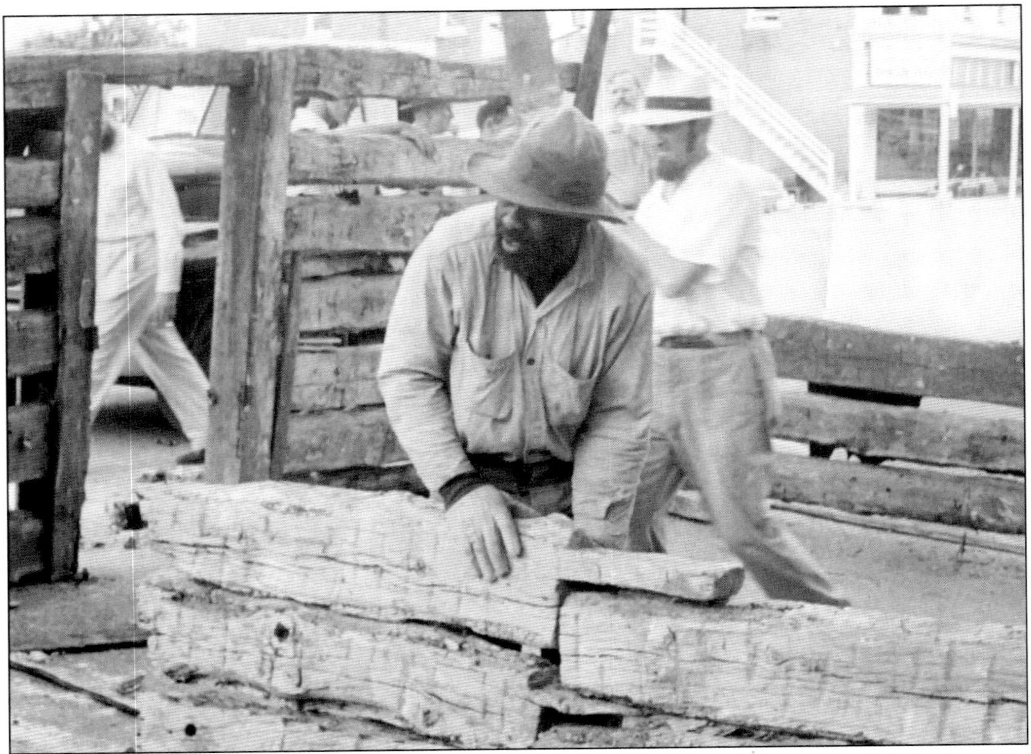

Delmar "Del" Massey is pictured while helping rebuild a historic log cabin on the town square during Webster County's centennial. Del and his mother, Rosie Mosby, are heralded as being Marshfield's last African American citizens through much of the early 20th century. However, Del is best remembered as the namesake of Massey Park and for his unique connection with Marshfield's children. (Courtesy of the Webster County Historical Museum.)

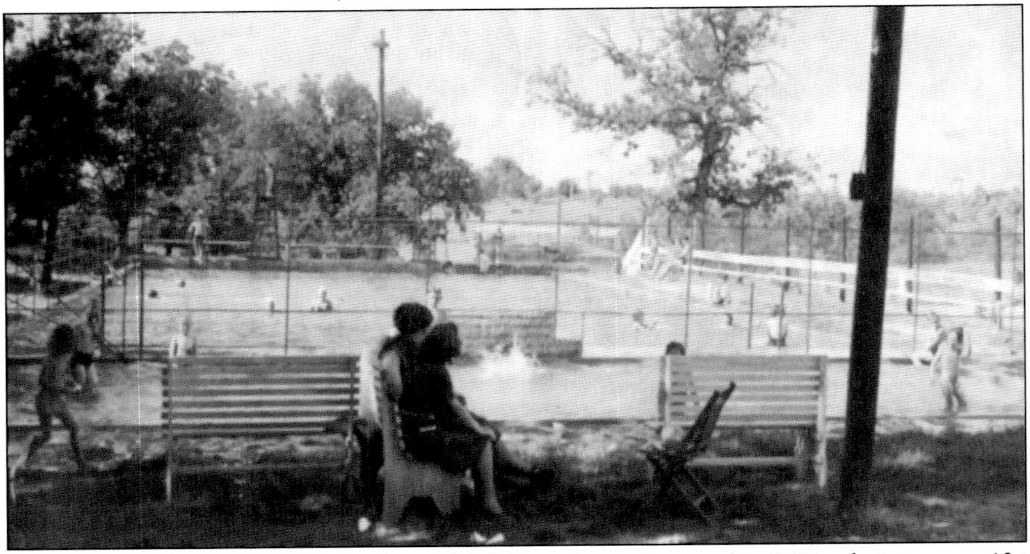

Marshfield's old city pool is pictured in 1956. When the pool opened in 1938, admission was 10¢ and 15¢. The money was used for improvements and to pay a lifeguard during the pool's operating hours from 2:00 p.m. to 9:00 p.m. At the time, the pool was emptied weekly to keep the water fresh and stood empty once a week for the sun to sterilize it. (Courtesy of Randy Clair.)

Ella Dickey and Donna Nichols are pictured at a celebration in Marshfield's Carnegie Library. In 1961, Dickey celebrated her own golden anniversary as Marshfield's librarian, a position that only she had filled to that point. Nearly 200 people attended a program and reception at the Marshfield Christian Church for the occasion. (Courtesy of the Webster County Historical Museum.)

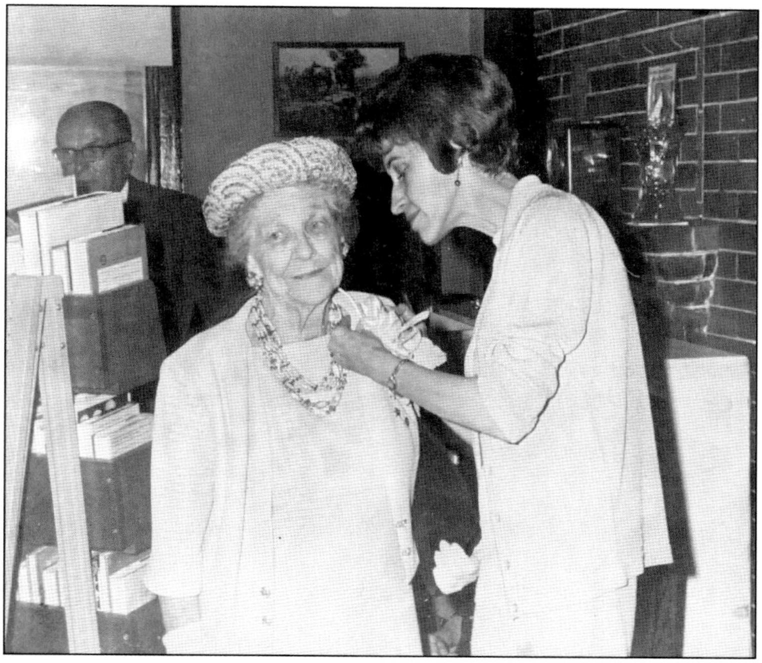

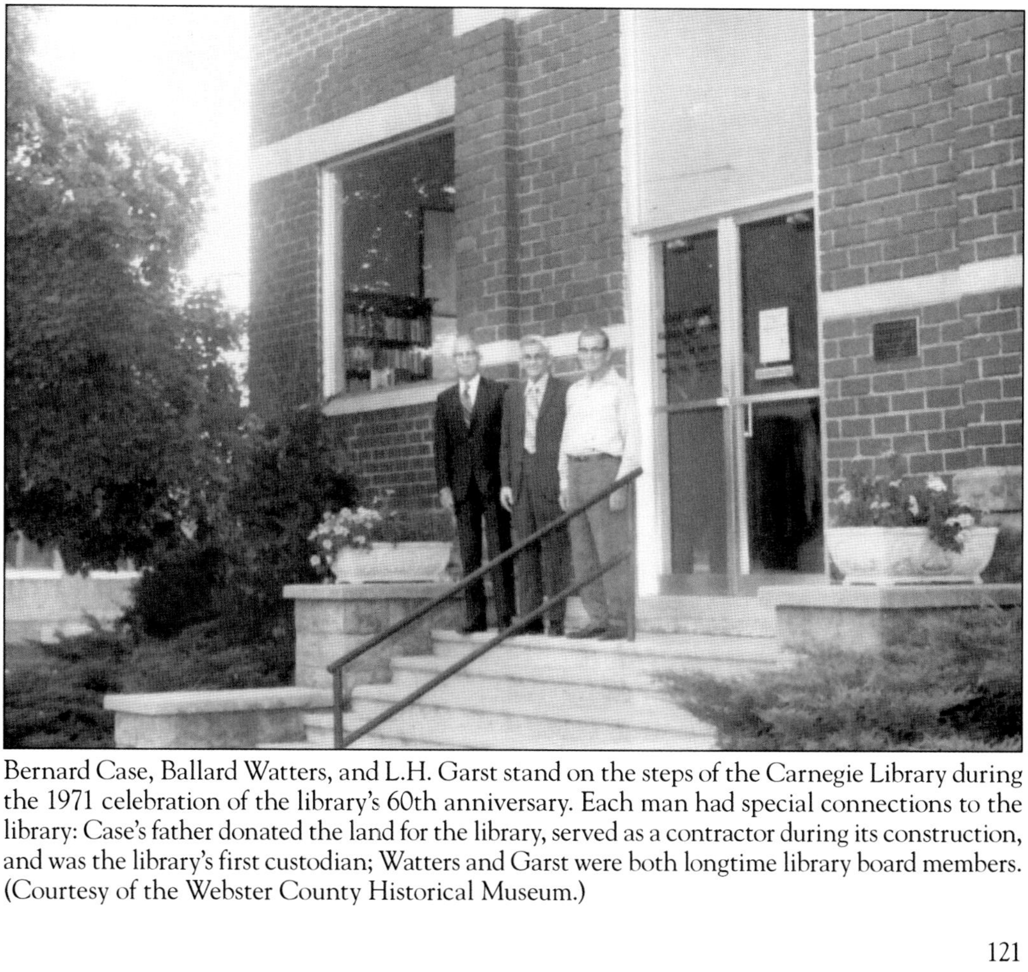

Bernard Case, Ballard Watters, and L.H. Garst stand on the steps of the Carnegie Library during the 1971 celebration of the library's 60th anniversary. Each man had special connections to the library: Case's father donated the land for the library, served as a contractor during its construction, and was the library's first custodian; Watters and Garst were both longtime library board members. (Courtesy of the Webster County Historical Museum.)

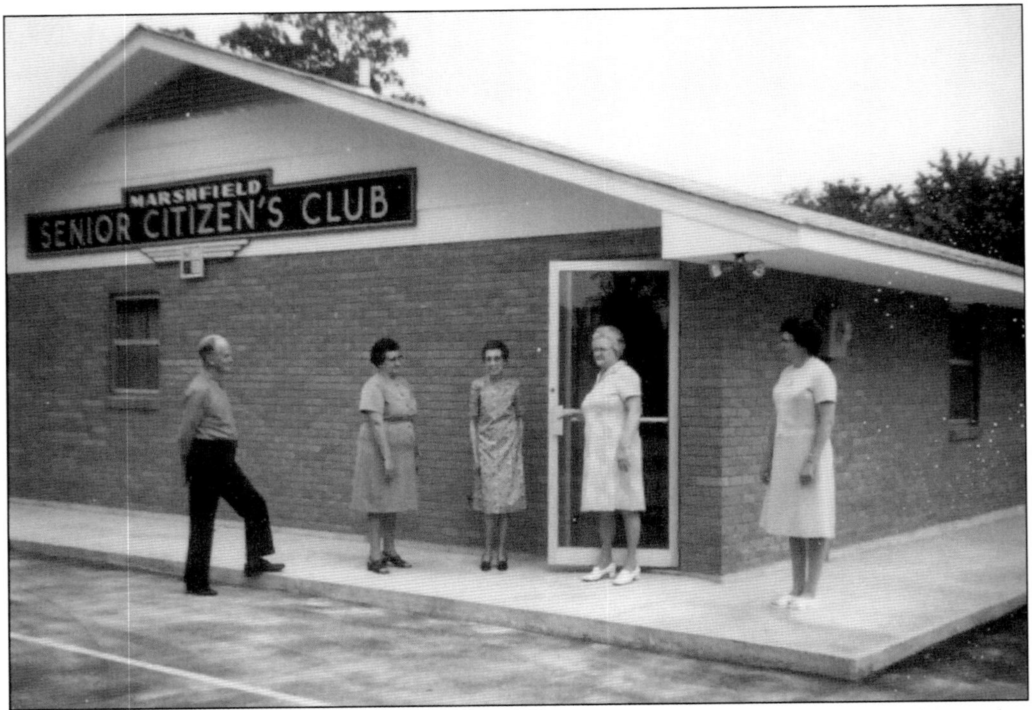

Several members of Marshfield Senior Citizen's Club stand outside the club's new building after its completion in 1976. Founded in 1964 as part of the Community Betterment Program, the club actively hosted meetings, trips, and service projects. In 1965, the club was also responsible for the organization of the Marshfield Housing Association, resulting in the construction of 20 apartments for seniors. (Courtesy of the Webster County Historical Museum.)

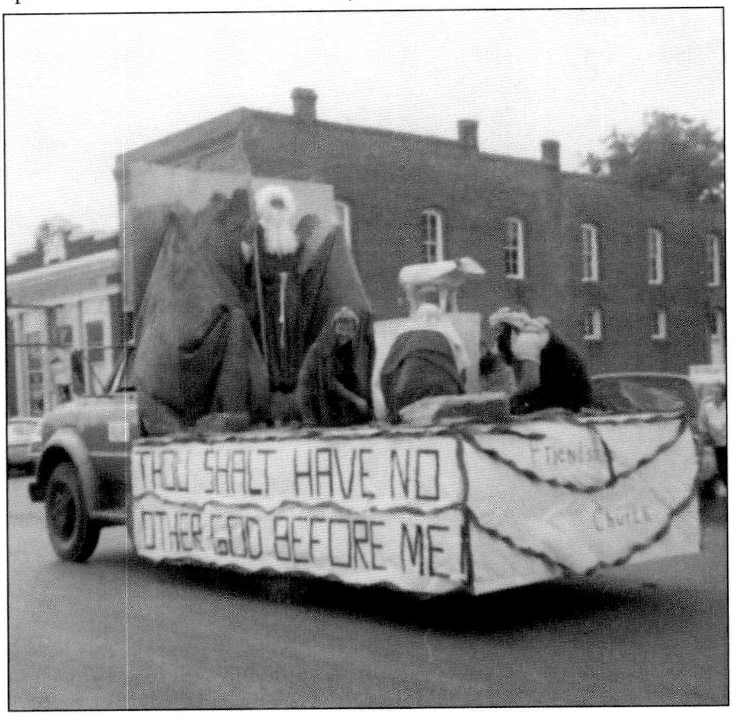

Friendship Baptist Church's members appear with their float in the Bible Echoes Parade in the 1970s. With over 30 entries in its first year, the parade became an annual tradition for several years in Marshfield. Each year, floats were based upon a particular biblical theme or verse, and the day finished with a program of music and addresses by various individuals. (Courtesy of the Webster County Historical Museum.)

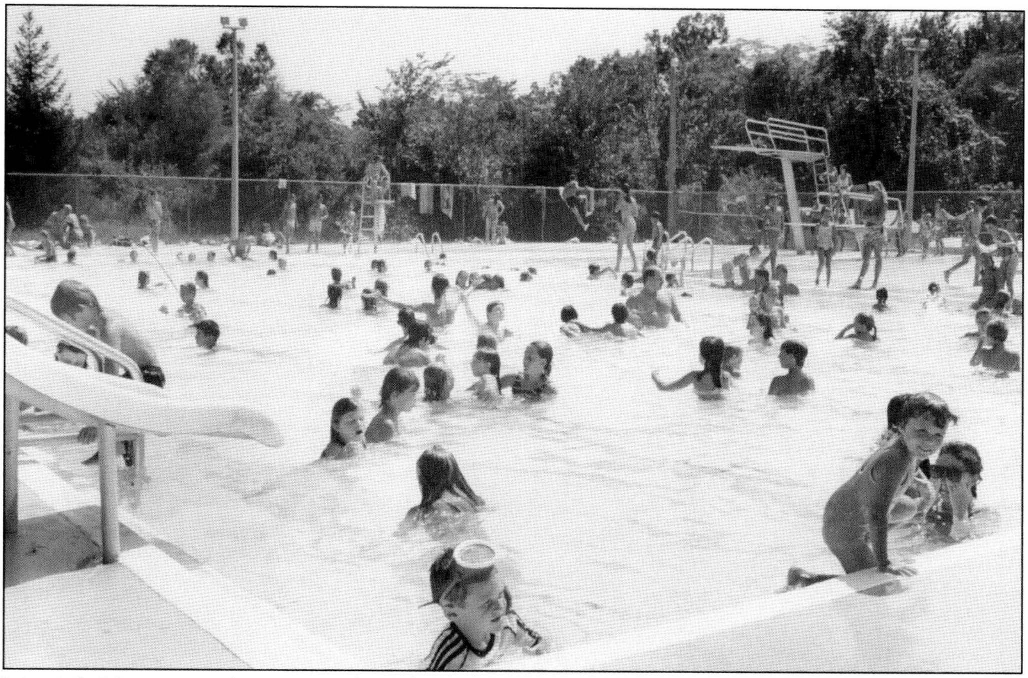

Marshfield's city pool is pictured in the 1990s. The new pool opened in the early 1970s after the state health board deemed the old one inadequate for Marshfield's needs. When it opened, it cost 35¢ for those under age 18, and 50¢ for adults. In 2008, the pool underwent renovations to comply with new federal regulations regarding potential drowning hazards. (Courtesy of the Webster County Historical Museum.)

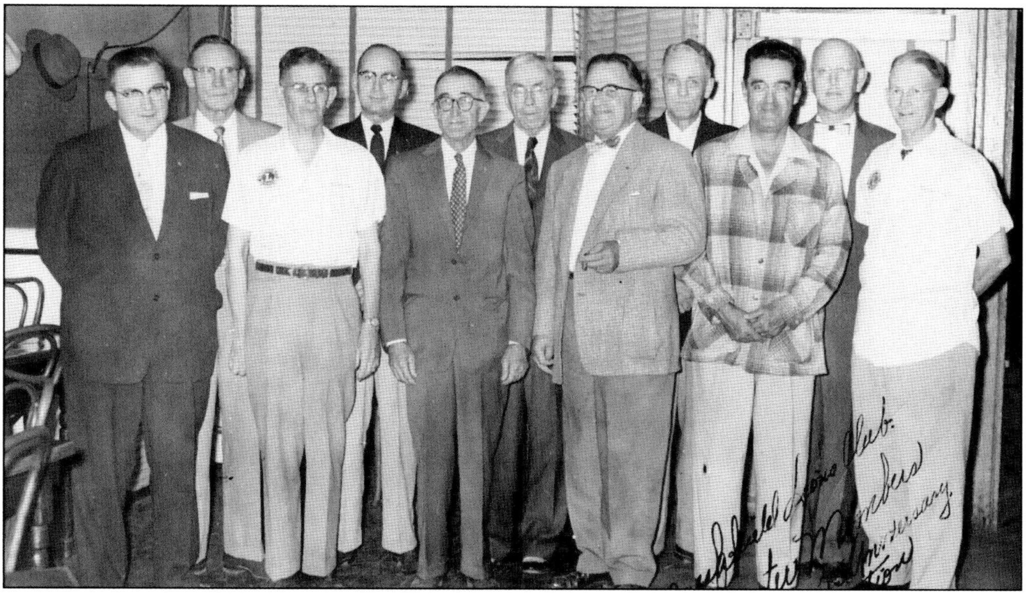

The members of Marshfield's Lions Club celebrated the club's 50th anniversary in 1981. The club was established in 1931, and over the years it has played a variety of roles in the community, such as sponsoring the first county health council and county nurse, numerous agricultural projects, and youth initiatives, including a school milk program. (Courtesy of the Webster County Historical Museum.)

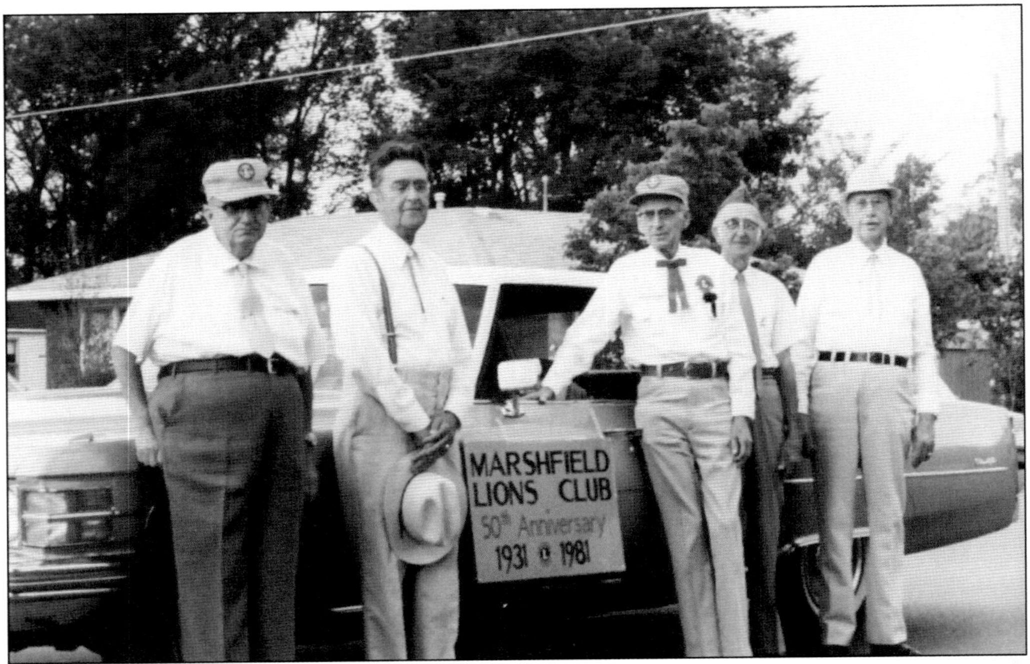

The five living charter members of the Marshfield Lions Club prepare to ride in the 1981 Fourth of July parade. From left to right are John Andrews, Roy Tindle, Earl Shields, Perry Shook, and Dr. Orin Cardwell. Dr. Dean Cansler, a fellow Lions Club member, was responsible for the photograph and its presentation. (Courtesy of the Webster County Historical Museum.)

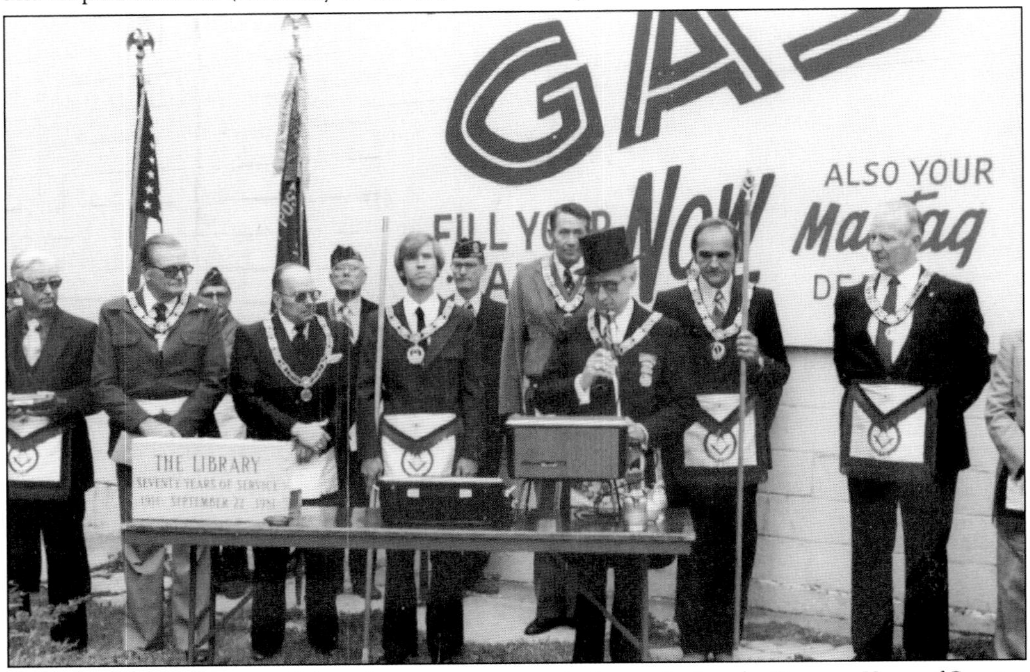

The laying of the Carnegie Library's new cornerstone is shown during the Seventy Years of Service celebration in 1881. In addition to the cornerstone, a plaque was dedicated to Miss Ella Dickey, who served as the town librarian for over 50 years; the new set of doors was also dedicated in her memory. (Courtesy of the Webster County Historical Museum.)

Home to the longest-running Independence Day celebration west of the Mississippi, Marshfield has seen its share of Fourth of Julys. However, 1991 takes the prize as most notable when Pres. George H. Bush and his wife, Barbara, came to town. The couple wanted to visit a town full of small-town American spirit and chose Marshfield based on the advice of Missouri governor John Ashcroft. (Courtesy of the Webster County Historical Museum.)

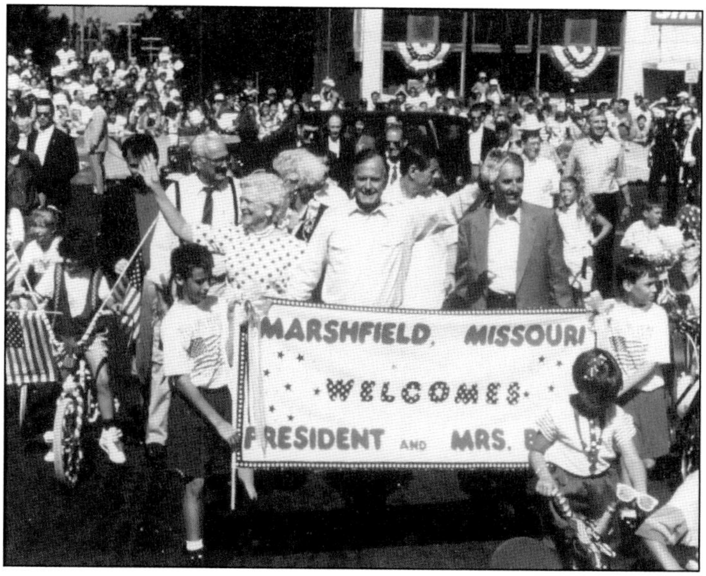

The Webster County Fair was in full swing when this photograph was taken sometime during the late 1990s. The fair has been an annual Webster County tradition since 1937; in all those years, one of the only cancellations that was seriously considered was during World War II, when gas was rationed. Its numerous features include competitions for livestock, home arts, poultry, and other interests. (Courtesy of the Webster County Historical Museum.)

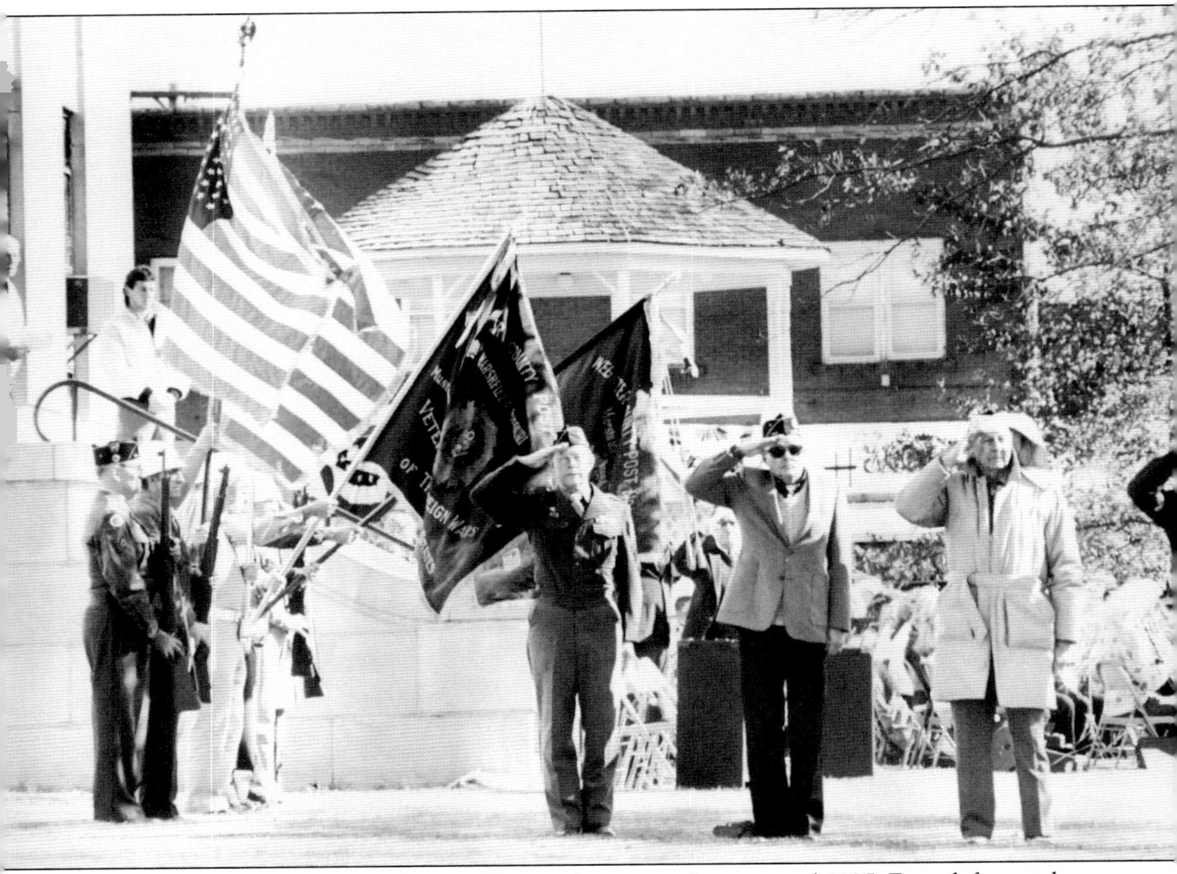

Marshfield commemorates Veterans Day in this image from around 1995. From left to right are Virgil Hunt (World War II veteran), Dr. Tommy Macdonnell (World War II veteran), Frank W. Welch (Korean War veteran), and Cecil Davis (World War II veteran); Davis also served in Pearl Harbor. A very patriotic community, Marshfield has had many ceremonies in recognition of Veterans Day, even dating back to when it was Armistice Day. (Courtesy of the Webster County Historical Museum.)

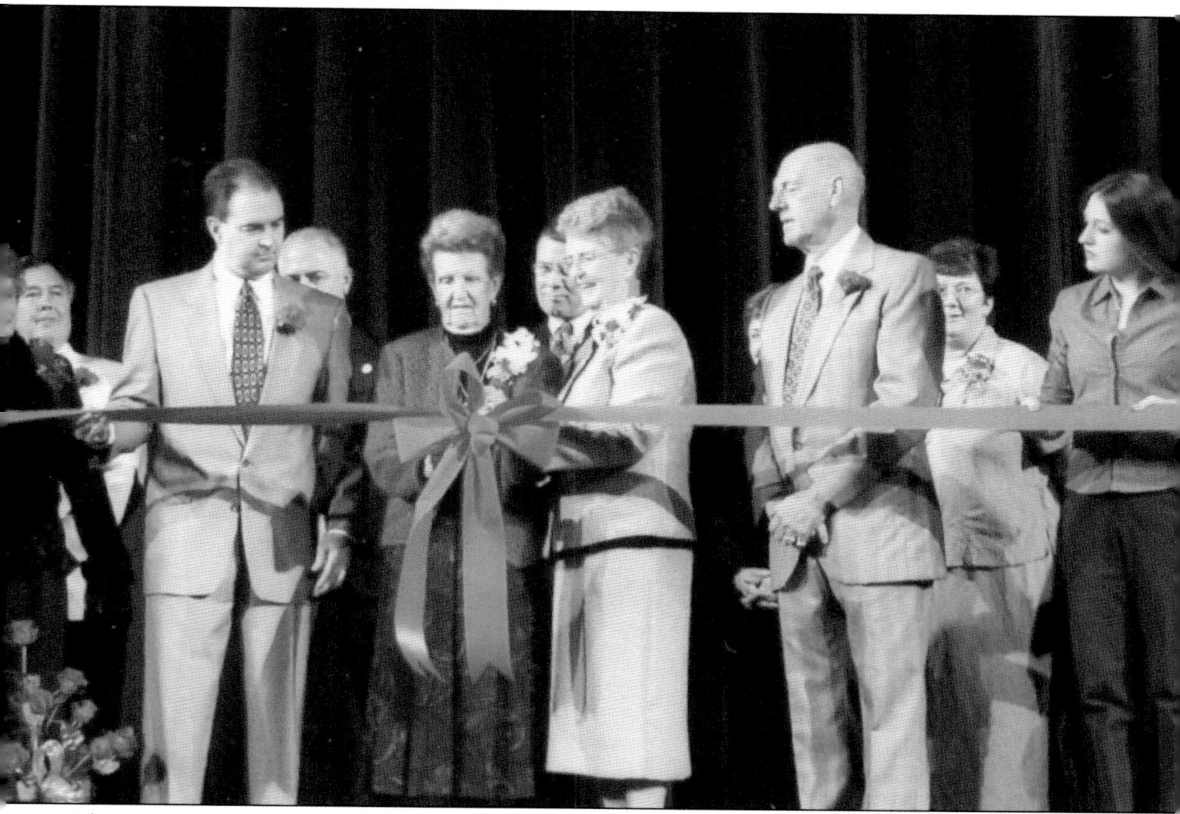

Glessie Young (fifth from the left) and her daughter Carlene are pictured during the dedication of the Carl and Glessie Young Auditorium in 2002. In 2000, the Youngs donated 15,000 shares of Wal-Mart stock, worth $1.1 million at the time, to the school system. The money aided in the construction of the community auditorium, built adjacent to Marshfield's high school. Carl passed away shortly before the auditorium was dedicated. (Courtesy of the Carl Young collection.)